WOOD
TECHNOLOGY

Michael Cross

THE EDUCATIONAL COMPANY OF IRELAND

First published 2019

The Educational Company of Ireland
Lower Ballymount Road
Walkinstown
Dublin 12
www.edco.ie

A member of the Smurfit Kappa Group plc

The
paper used in
this book comes
from Managed
Forests in
Northern
Europe
For
every
tree
felled, at
least one new
tree is planted

ISBN: 978-1-84536-840-1

Editorial Assistants: Alison Bryan, Diarmuid O'Hegarty, and Victoire Lemaire
Book and Cover Design: Linda Kavanagh
Book Layout: Carole Lynch
Photography: Michael Cross
Proofreader: Jeffrey Gormly
Illustrator: Keith Barrett
Indexer: Jane Rogers

Acknowledgements and thanks for images to Alamy, Bogwood Sculptures, Boxford,
C. Clarke, Forest Stewardship Council, Inpho Photography, iStock, Mark Ripley, Matt
Jones, Original Marquetry, Record Power, Robert Sorby, Ronseal, Rustins, Science
Photo Library, and Shutterstock. Please see page 338 for a full list of image credits.

05M23

Preface

Written for the new Junior Cycle, *Wood Technology* aims to foster students' interest and abilities in wood technology. It is based on the **statements of learning** from the NCCA specification and develops students' knowledge through the three strands: **Wood Science and Materials, Principles and Practices, and Design Thinking.**

Features of *Wood Technology*

- **Learning intentions** are stated at the start of each chapter in student-friendly language.

- **Keywords** are listed at the start of each chapter to allow students to become familiar with important terms.

- **Diagrams** and **illustrations** are labelled and drawn in a clear and simple style to allow students to understand and recreate them easily.

- **Safety rules are** emphasised throughout the text where appropriate and necessary.

- **Questions** are included within the text and at the end of chapters. These offer the opportunity for different teacher strategies to be used. In particular, there are chances for group work and pair work to enhance communication and cooperation.

Digital Resources

The *Wood Technology* digital resources will enhance classroom learning by encouraging student participation and engagement. They support the New Junior Cycle Specification's emphasis on the use of modern technology in the classroom and are designed to cater for different learning styles.

To provide guidance for the integration of digital resources in the classroom and to aid lesson planning, they are **referenced throughout the textbook** using the following icons:

Useful **Weblinks** documents provide links to additional material.

A series of unique **videos** to support classroom learning.

Easy-to-use, editable **PowerPoint presentations** highlight key topics and enhance classroom learning.

Informative **worksheets** and **posters** complement textbook exercises.

Teachers can access the *Wood Technology* digital resources and interactive e-book at **www.edcolearning.ie**.

Contents

Section 3: Design Thinking

Section 4: Projects

Learning Outcomes

	Planning and managing	Communicating	Creating	Environment and sustainability
Wood Science and Materials	3.1 identify common species of wood 3.2 evaluate the characteristics and properties of common species of wood 3.3 understand the properties associated with a range of materials applicable to Wood Technology 3.4 evaluate the use of wood in comparison to alternative materials	3.5 explain the properties associated with the classification of wood 3.6 discuss the use of wood in comparison to alternative materials 3.7 justify the use of materials based on characteristics and properties within a context	3.8 utilise the natural aesthetics and properties of wood to enhance the appearance and function of an artefact 3.9 create an artefact that demonstrates an understanding of the properties associated with a range of materials applicable to Wood Technology	3.10 appreciate the role of forestation and wood in terms of local/ global ecology and sustainability 3.11 investigate the use of wood from forest to end use 3.12 consider the impact on the natural environment when sourcing materials
Principles and Practices	1.1 explore key elements required for the completion of tasks 1.2 justify the selection of plans, processes and materials for the completion of tasks 1.3 collaborate effectively in a workshop learning environment 1.4 manage themselves and their resources	1.5 represent key information graphically 1.6 create sketches and working drawings to recognised standards using a variety of media 1.7 explain the function and application of a range of tools, equipment, fixtures and fittings	1.8 apply knowledge of and skills in a range of appropriate existing and emerging principles, processes and techniques 1.9 demonstrate principles of craft excellence through the design and realisation of tasks and artefacts 1.10 apply recognised health and safety practices in the use of tools, equipment and materials	1.11 investigate the environmental impacts of using wood as a natural and renewable resource 1.12 appreciate sustainable practice throughout their learning
Design Thinking	2.1 explore design problems 2.2 manage information and thinking to support an iterative design process 2.3 evaluate their own progress to inform future learning 2.4 understand key principles of design and ergonomics	2.5 communicate relevant information 2.6 produce sketches, drawings and models/ prototypes to explore design ideas 2.7 communicate a suitable approach to solving a problem 2.8 compile a folio through appropriate media	2.9 evolve their solutions based on critical reflection 2.10 devise templates and models using various media 2.11 produce purposeful, functional, appealing artefacts 2.12 create an artefact having considered factors such as materials, cost, time resources and skills	2.13 recognise the environmental and social impacts of design decisions 2.14 investigate how to minimise material use and manage waste

1 Introduction

For the student

Welcome to secondary school and your new Wood Technology textbook, *Wood Technology*. As you develop your understanding and skills, this book will help you appreciate ecological and environmental factors as well as the use of natural resources. This textbook comes with a **Student Activity Book** which has a wide range of activities for you to work on at home and at school.

Wood Technology is a new subject to students. This textbook will support you in learning practical and design skills and explore ways of using wood and other materials to create useful artefacts. This book will be a reliable resource as you learn from your teacher and work with other students in your practical classes.

Examples of project work

Wood Science and Materials

Wood is a natural material that comes from trees, a fantastic **renewable** resource that humans have used for many centuries. The wood we get from trees is used for many things, including construction, furniture making, and transport. You will use it to make beautiful and useful artefacts in the Wood Technology room. In *Wood Technology*, you will learn about the unique characteristics of trees, wood in its various forms, and other commonly used materials.

Principles and Practices

In *Wood Technology*, you will learn to create useful artefacts from different woods and other materials using a variety of tools and power tools. You will develop skills which will help you to accomplish your tasks effectively. You will work independently and with others to plan and complete the tasks safely and efficiently.

Design Thinking

You will also learn sketching techniques to communicate your ideas effectively. You will develop drawing skills to allow you create working drawings of task work. Over the three years, you will learn to design and create attractive artefacts using wood and other materials that you can take home to use and enjoy.

The Wood Technology room

The Wood Technology room is different to other classrooms. It is a workshop with tools and specialised equipment that will be used by you and your teacher in designing and producing high quality artefacts. The tools and machines in the room can be dangerous, so you must always be very careful when in the room.

The Wood Technology room

You will work at a bench that has a vice to hold your work securely while you work on it. A **bench hook** at each workstation is used when sawing pieces of wood. The bench hook is made from **beech.** You will have basic tools for marking and processing that are stored in a locker at the end of the bench or in organised units around the room. It is important to use all tools only as you have been taught and only with the teacher's permission.

Woodwork bench showing the vice, bench hook, and locker

There are basic rules that must be followed in the room to keep everyone safe and to keep the room neat, tidy and well organised.

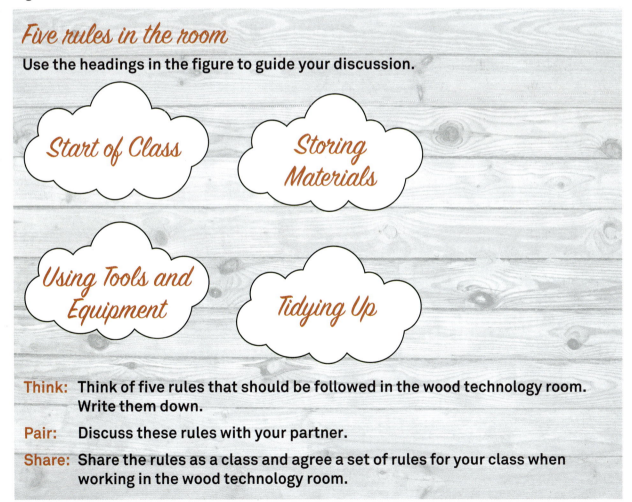

Five rules in the room

Use the headings in the figure to guide your discussion.

Start of Class

Storing Materials

Using Tools and Equipment

Tidying Up

Think: Think of five rules that should be followed in the wood technology room. Write them down.

Pair: Discuss these rules with your partner.

Share: Share the rules as a class and agree a set of rules for your class when working in the wood technology room.

3

2 Health and Safety

KEYWORDS

- accidents
- face shield
- flammable
- hazardous
- precaution
- safety feature
- safety glasses

LEARNING OUTCOMES

- 1.1, 1.2, 1.3, 1.4, 1.10
- 2.11

Learning intentions

At the end of this chapter students will:

- Be able to identify key safety features in the wood technology room.
- Know and follow key safety rules when using tools, equipment and materials.
- Work with others to maintain a safe working environment.

The workshop can be a **hazardous** place. Safety must always come first. You must always think of yourself and others' safety when working.

Safety rules

With a partner, write down three safety rules that you should follow when in the workshop. Share these with the class. How do they compare to the rules on this page?

General Workshop Safety Rules

⚠ Always walk in the workshop. Never run!

⚠ Keep your work area tidy. Store bags and coats out of the way.

⚠ Follow teacher's instructions.

⚠ Report all **accidents**, breakages, or damaged equipment immediately.

⚠ Read and follow safety signs and warning labels.

⚠ Always use safety equipment provided.

⚠ Tie back loose hair. Secure loose clothing and remove jewellery.

⚠ Always keep hands and fingers behind the cutting edge of tools.

It is easier and safer to work in an organised, tidy area. Replace tools after use and clean the room at the end of class. Keep your hands clean to avoid getting dirt on your work piece.

Consider why keeping your bench and the room tidy helps safety

Long hair should be tied back and clothing secured

Tools and Equipment

The tools and equipment you will use can cause harm. Be responsible: use all tools as you are shown. Report all damaged tools immediately to the teacher. Always carry tools by your side. When working, keep your hands behind and away from the cutting edge of tools.

Keep hands behind cutting edge

Safety in the workshop

Practice carrying a chisel by your side and handing it safely to someone else. What could happen if you did handled a chisel incorrectly?

Materials and Processes

The processes and materials we use in the workshop can cause harm, so extra precautions must be taken.
- Dust from sanding can get into your eyes and lungs, irritating them.
- Machinery noise can damage hearing.
- Adhesives and finishes may contain harmful chemicals.

Passing a chisel safely to someone

5

Signs

Safety signs inform us about health and safety. They tell us about procedures and equipment that should be used. Warning signs on containers also warn of dangerous contents.

Caution signs

Prohibition signs

Positive action signs

Mandatory signs

Always read and follow instructions

Sign safety

Divide into small groups. Each group is tasked with finding and explaining as many examples of a specific type of safety sign as possible (mandatory, positive action, prohibition, etc.). Using the template provided in your workbook, the small groups will work together to compile a comprehensive class safety sign handout.

Equipment and Safety

There are a number of **safety features** that make the equipment and the room safer to use. Personal protective equipment (PPE), such as safety glasses, give added protection where hazards cannot be avoided. Protective equipment should always be worn when using power tools and machines. Dust masks protect us from breathing in dust particularly when sanding. Ear defenders protect our hearing from excess noise.

Every room has fire extinguishers. You should know the emergency procedure for your room. There is dust extraction in the room to remove dust and fine particles from machines, keeping the air clean. Extractor collection bags should be emptied regularly.

Machines have safety features like guards and emergency stop buttons that protect the user. Guards should always be in place.

Electric power tools are dangerous because of sharp blades and cutters moving at high speed. There is also a risk of electric shock. Modern workshops use electric transformers to reduce the risk by cutting the voltage from 220 volts to 110 volts.

Personal protective equipment

Pillar drill. Machines have safety guards and an emergency stop.

Emergency stop button

Electric transformers reduce the voltage from 220V to 110V, reducing the risk of shock

Safety features

Divide into small groups. Each group examines one piece of equipment to learn its safety features and precautions. Choose a spokesperson in each group to share the points with the rest of the class.

CHAPTER QUESTIONS

1 List two key safety precautions that should be followed in the wood technology room.

2 Explain the term PPE.

3 Describe a situation or piece of equipment where you should wear ear defenders or ear plugs in the wood technology room.

4 Describe when it would be appropriate to wear a dust mask.

5 Design a poster that could be displayed in the wood technology room to encourage students to report accidents.

6 Explain the meaning of the following safety signs.

(a)   (b)   (c)   (d)

7 The items shown below all contribute to safety in the workshop. Name each one and describe how it helps to keep people safe.

(a)   (b)   (c)   (d)

8 List two safety precautions that should be observed when using portable electric power tools in the wood technology room.

9 Consider rules that apply to your wood technology room. Make a list and organise them in order of importance.

10 Why is it important to report a broken or damaged tool or piece of equipment to the teacher?

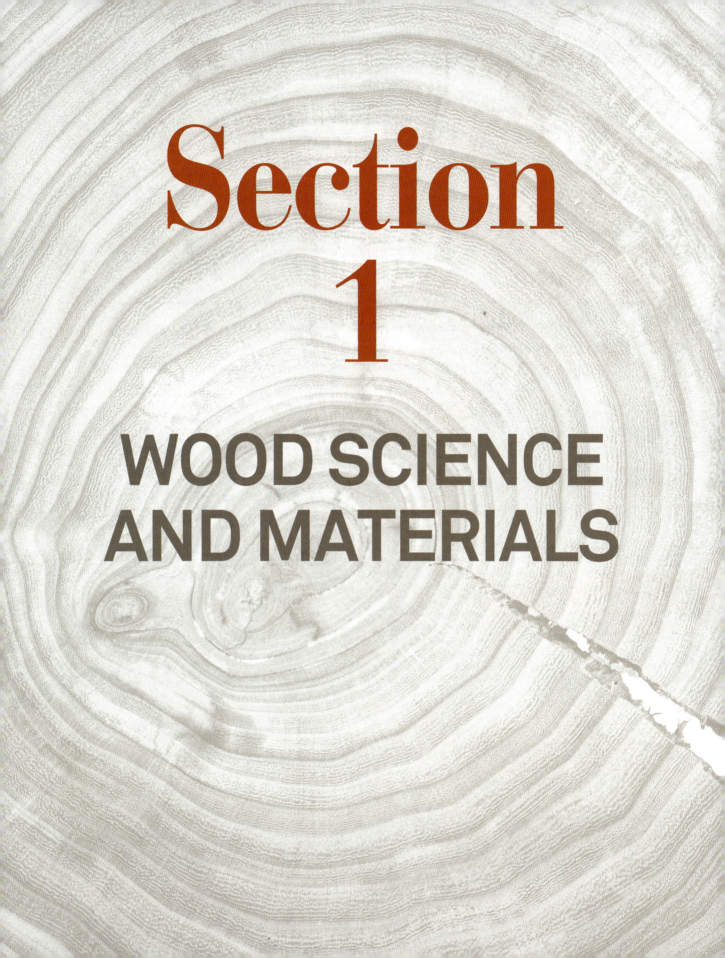

Section 1

WOOD SCIENCE AND MATERIALS

3 Wood: What is it? Where does it come from?

KEYWORDS

- afforestation
- carbon dioxide
- forestry
- managed forest
- natural forest
- oxygen
- rainforest
- renewable
- sustainable

LEARNING OUTCOMES
- 1.1, 1.2, 1.3, 1.10
- 2.11

Learning intentions

At the end of this chapter you will be able to:
- Describe a variety of common benefits of trees and wood.
- Explain the difference between natural and planted and tropical forests.
- Explore the role of forestation in terms of global and local ecology and sustainability.
- Understand the use of forestry and timber from tree to end use.

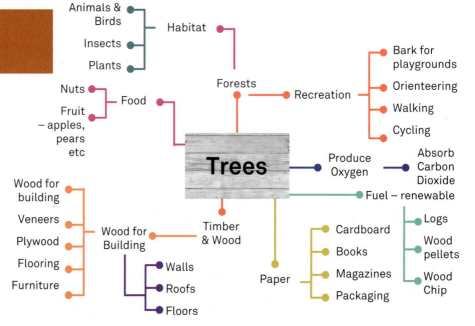

A mind map of the benefits of trees

Trees are vital to life in the world. Like all plants, they produce **oxygen** and absorb harmful **carbon dioxide**. Trees are **renewable** and **sustainable** because they can be replanted. Wood made from trees provides us with many familiar and useful products.

Perhaps the greatest advantage of wood is that it comes from a renewable resource. We have depended on trees and wood for centuries to create high quality buildings and furniture.

Modern timber building

High quality wood furniture

Much of the wood we use was grown in specially planted (**managed**) forests. **Forestry** is planted and managed and harvested like a crop. Forestry is generally planted with only one species of tree. Conifers are commonly planted this way because they can grow quickly on hilly forestry land with poorer quality soil.

Natural forest

Planted forestry

Natural forests, which have evolved naturally over many years, usually have a mix of tree species. Ireland was once covered in natural forests, mainly of oak. These forests were cut down to be used in construction, boatbuilding, and barrel making. Today, the largest areas of natural oak forest are

Renewable:

A renewable resource can be replaced naturally over and over again in a managed way. Trees are a renewable resource.

Benefits of trees

In small groups, create a poster highlighting the many products and benefits that come from trees. Use the mind map on page 12 to help you.

located in Cork, Kerry, and Wicklow. **Rainforests** are found in tropical regions of the world with hot and damp climates.

Rainforest

Comparing forests

Consider the rainforests, natural forests, and planted forestry, then compare them under the headings age, types of tree, habitat, management, and potential uses.

The story of a tree

Land is first drained and fenced before being planted with young trees raised in the nursery. The forests are maintained and thinned out periodically as the trees grow larger. Forests are thinned at about 15 years old to give more space to other trees. Thinnings can be used for fuel or chipped and pulped for manufactured boards.

Trees are harvested at 30 to 50 years old. It is usual for the entire forest to be clear-felled at the same time. The branches are stripped and the trees transported to the sawmill or processing plant. There, the logs are stripped of bark and cut into planks before being dried for use in making furniture or construction. Logs can also be processed into manufactured boards like plywood, chipboard, OSB (oriented strand board) or MDF (medium density fibreboard).

OSB. Oriented strand board is made from special wood chips.

Story of a tree

The Timber Industry

Ireland has planted more trees since 1990 through increases in **afforestation**. However, it remains one of the least forested countries in Europe, with over 10.5% forest cover. This compares with an average of 43% for the 28 countries currently in the EU.

> **Afforestation:**
>
> **The process of establishing a forest, especially on land not previously forested.**

The Department of Agriculture, Food and the Marine is the government department responsible for the development of forestry in Ireland. Coillte is the state body responsible for state forests. It plants, manages, and harvests trees. Grants are available for individual land owners to plant both coniferous and deciduous forest plantations.

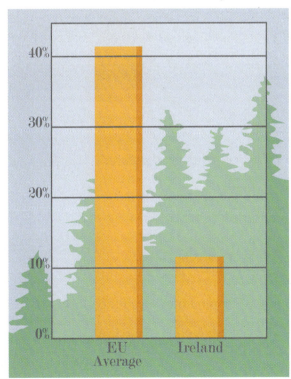

Country	% Woodland coverage
Netherlands	15
Denmark	20.4
Ireland	25.3
Belgium	26.3
France	33.8
Germany	34.9
Luxembourg	37.2
Italy	39.5
Spain	45.7
Austria	48.3
Portugal	52.8
Greece	56.7
Sweden	69.8
Finland	72.3
European average	**44.8%**

Comparison of woodland coverage within Europe (2017)

The forestry sector directly and indirectly contributes more than €2 billion to Ireland's economy every year. The government has invested heavily into research and development of forestry, thus creating employment in many areas. Overleaf are some examples of the many products in use that come from trees.

Wood pellets are used as a biofuel. Willow, poplar, and waste wood are used for wood pellets.

Bark mulch is used on flowerbeds

Garden fencing

Wood products in use

Prepare an investigation sheet with examples of where wood or wood products are used. From this, produce a presentation of your findings with images and basic facts.

CHAPTER QUESTIONS

1 What government Department is responsible for forestry in Ireland?

2 How much of Ireland (%) is currently under forest cover?

3 What is the average forest cover in the countries of the EU?

4 Explain the term 'natural forest'.

5 List five ways that trees benefit you.

6 Consider how trees, forestry and wood create employment in your county. Make some notes to share with your class group.

7 Describe how woodland is managed using the following headings to guide you:

(a) planting   (b) thinning   (c) harvesting

8 Investigate which EU country has the most % forest cover and which has the least.

9 Outline ways in which forest thinnings and bark might be sustainably used.

PowerPoint Summary   Weblinks

4 Trees

Learning intentions

At the end of this chapter you will:
- Sketch the parts of a tree and outline the function of each part.
- Explain the processes of transpiration and photosynthesis.
- Recognise the common species of wood and evaluate their properties.
- Explain the properties associated with the classification of wood.
- Discuss the choice of woods suitable for different projects.

Trees begin life as a seed that germinates and they go through a life cycle like all plants. Different tree species grow at different rates and to different heights and sizes. Some giant redwood trees in the United States have archways large enough to drive a car through. Each species has its own characteristics which are evident in the woods they produce.

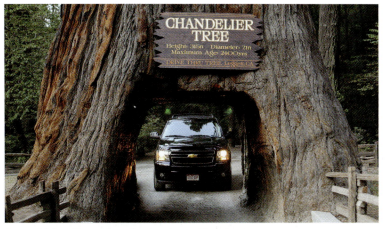

A car driving through a giant redwood trunk.

15

The life cycle of a tree

In nature, seeds of trees are spread in many ways. They drop to the ground or the wind, birds, and animals spread the rest. In the nursery, seeds are raised in pots until they are ready to be planted. Seeds **germinate** and the root (radicle) grows into the ground. The shoot (plumule) grows towards the heat of the soil surface.

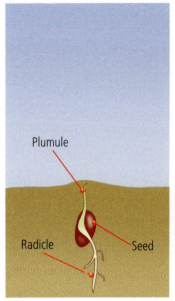
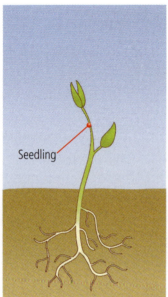
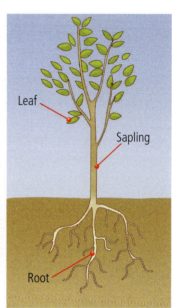

Growth stages of a tree

1 The seed germinates.
2 The **plumule** or shoot, grows to the surface.
3 The **radicle** or root grows into the soil.
4 The **seedling** develops roots and leaves.
5 The **sapling** develops into a young tree.

Parts of the tree

Crown

The branch system and leaves of the tree are spread wide to capture sunlight. The leaves in the crown allow transpiration and photosynthesis to occur.

Roots

The root system extends beyond the width of the crown, which anchors the tree in the ground. It also absorbs water and minerals from the soil.

Trunk

The branches and the leaves are supported by the trunk, keeping them off the ground. The trunk contains the majority of the wood. Both the trunk and branches are covered in bark. As moisture evaporates from the leaves, sap carrying water and nutrients from the soil is drawn up through the trunk.

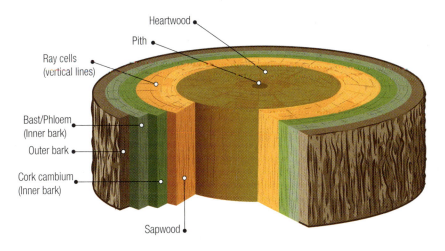

Parts of the tree trunk

Bark

The bark is the outer protective skin of the tree. It is tough and it protects the wood from damage by the weather, animals, insects and fungi. It helps to keep moisture in the tree.

Bast (phloem)

The **bast** is the layer of cells just inside the bark. This layer of cells channels food in the form of sap (sugar and nutrients dissolved in water) down from the leaves to the rest of the tree.

Cambium layer

This thin layer of cells between the bast and the sapwood is where the growth of the tree takes place. Cells are added to the outer layer to form the annual rings. These **xylem** cells then carry water and minerals up from the roots to the leaves.

Sapwood

This is the lighter-coloured wood. Each year layers of cells are added to the outside of the **sapwood**. Cells carry water and nutrients up and down the trunk nourishing the tree. The sapwood is lighter, softer and less durable.

Heartwood and sapwood of a softwood log

17

Heartwood

The **heartwood** is located in the centre of the tree and is usually darker in colour. It gives support and is the oldest inactive part of the tree. The heartwood is more durable and is resistant to insect and fungal attack.

Ray cells

Ray cells radiate out from the centre of the trunk. They move sap between the centre and outside of the trunk. These ray cells are clearly seen in oak as **silver grain**, when it is cut radially.

Ray cells in Australian silver oak

Pith

This soft spongy material is at the centre of the trunk. It is the remains of the young tree.

Annual rings

Trees in the temperate areas of the world grow with the seasons. Each year a ring of cells is added; during spring and summer the growth is rapid and cells are wider, during the autumn and winter the cells there is less growth so the cells are smaller and more compact. Counting the annual rings allows us to estimate the age of a tree.

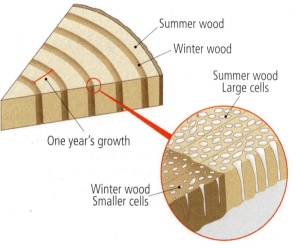

Summer wood
Winter wood
Summer wood
Large cells
One year's growth
Winter wood
Smaller cells

Annual rings

Cross section of an oak tree

Transpiration

Trees absorb water through their roots which evaporates through tiny holes in the leaves. As the water evaporates, more water is drawn up from the roots. This cycle is called **transpiration**.

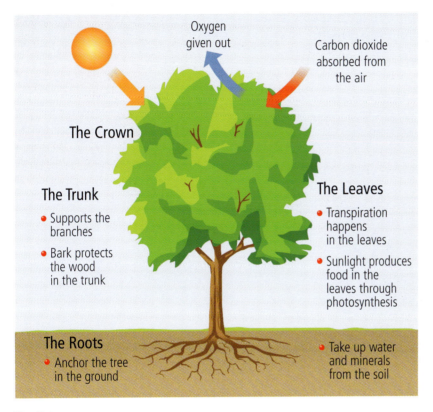

Oxygen given out

Carbon dioxide absorbed from the air

The Crown

The Trunk
- Supports the branches
- Bark protects the wood in the trunk

The Leaves
- Transpiration happens in the leaves
- Sunlight produces food in the leaves through photosynthesis

The Roots
- Anchor the tree in the ground
- Take up water and minerals from the soil

The living tree

Chlorophyll:

Green substance in the leaves

Photosynthesis

The tree grows by making food using sunlight. It does this using a green substance in the leaves called **chlorophyll**. The light is used to convert carbon dioxide and water into glucose (a simple sugar the cells use as energy). This process is called **photosynthesis**.

Photosynthesis:

The process by which plants make food in their leaves using sunlight.

$$6\ CO_{2(g)} + 6\ H_2O + photons \rightarrow C_6H_{12}O_{6(aq)} + 6\ O_{2(g)}$$

carbon dioxide + water + light energy ➜ glucose + oxygen

Wood Structure

All wood is made from cell-like tubes arranged vertically with ray cells radiating from the centre horizontally. Hardwoods and softwoods have slightly different structures. Hardwoods are divided into ring-porous and diffuse-porous types. Ring-porous hardwoods have their vessel and pore cells grouped into distinct rings, while diffuse-porous hardwoods have pores and vessels spread throughout the growth.

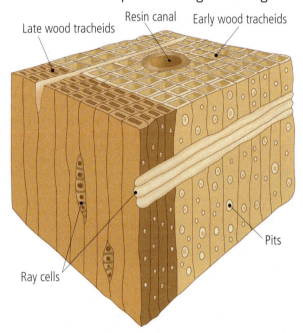

Late wood tracheids   Resin canal   Early wood tracheids

Pits

Ray cells

Softwood cell structure

Ring-porous oak wood

Diffuse-porous pine wood

Deciduous and coniferous trees

Trees are grouped into two main categories: **deciduous** and **coniferous** trees. Both types grow in Ireland and each has different characteristics. In general deciduous trees give us **hardwood** timber while coniferous trees provide **softwood** timber. Some trees are **native** to Ireland (they have always grown here) while other species were introduced from abroad.

Coniferous trees have needle-leaves and softwood

Deciduous trees have broad leaves and hardwood

Deciduous	Coniferous
• hardwood timber (more durable and valuable) • leaves lost in autumn (except holly) • broad leaves • seeds are borne in nuts/berries • slow growing • large, irregular branches	• softwood timber (less durable and cheaper) • evergreen (except larch) • needle-like leaves • seeds borne in pine cones • grows more quickly • symmetrical shape of small, regular branches • wood is lighter in colour

21

Wood portraits

Discuss what we know about trees already, what we want to find out about different trees. At the end of the chapter, list the new things you have learned. Create sketches to show the different characteristics of hardwoods and softwoods. These will help you to find out about the different trees.

Irish Hardwood Trees

Oak

There are about 600 varieties of oak found around the world. A native tree to Ireland, it was once the main woodland tree found here. Although many of the oak forests were cut down and used in shipbuilding and barrel-making, natural oak forests can still be found in Killarney, Glengarriff, and County Wicklow.

Oak tree

The tree has a broad crown and large central trunk. Its wood is durable and hard with a light to medium brown colour that finishes well. When it is cut radially, oak reveals an attractive pattern known as silver grain. Always use brass fittings with oak, as chemicals in the wood corrodes (rusts) steel.

Oak barrels

Oak leaves and acorns

Silver grain in oak

USES

- furniture
- windows and doors
- flooring
- barrels
- boatbuilding

Ash

Ash is a common Irish tree with a distinct leaf. It grows quickly in most soils and is planted in forestry plantations. In winter the buds on the tree are black in colour.

The wood is light in colour with attractive grain. It is a hard and dense wood, yet also has good elastic properties.

 USES

- used for Hurleys
- furniture
- tool handles
- wood laminating

Ash tree

Table made of ash wood

Ash leaves and seeds

Beech

Beech is a common tree in Ireland and it grows in good soil. It was introduced in the 17th century. It is slow growing with a smooth grey bark and the leaves turn a lovely bronze colour in autumn. The seeds of the mature tree are contained in a triangular shell called **mast**.

 USES

- flooring
- mallets, marking gauges, and bench hooks
- kitchen utensils

Beech tree

23

The wood is a light to medium brown colour. It is a close-grained wood, which makes the wood dense. Beech has a plain figure that is not very distinct. The wood is durable and hard-wearing, which makes it suitable for making mallets and marking gauges.

Beech leaves and seed

Birch

Birch is a commonly found native hardwood. It is a small, decorative tree that often has white bark.

The wood is light in colour with a straight grain. It has a close grain with a plain figure.

USES

- making plywood
- furniture
- flooring

Birch tree

Birch bark

Birch leaves and seeds

Elm

Our tallest native tree with a large crown, most of our mature elm trees have been killed by a fungal disease (Dutch elm disease) that is spread by a beetle. A disease-resistant strain of this hardwood has been developed in recent years.

The wood features an attractive, coarse grain and a medium to dark brown colour. The wood is strong, durable, and resistant to water, but it warps easily.

Elm leaves and seeds

Elm tree

USES

- woodturning
- project work
- garden furniture
- furniture

Elm table top

Horse chestnut

The horse chestnut is a familiar tree because of its distinct leaves and seeds, known as 'conkers'. It was introduced to Ireland from south-east Europe and western Asia. It prefers good soils. The large leaves are arranged like fingers and the seeds are contained in a spike-protected shell. It has white flowers in the spring time.

The wood is light in colour but not very durable and is therefore of little value.

USES

- woodturning
- rustic furniture
- packing cases
- pallets
- wood pulp

25

Horse chestnut leaves, flowers, conkers, and seeds

Horse Chestnut tree

Spanish chestnut

The Spanish or sweet chestnut is a large hardwood tree with a broad crown. The leaves are slightly different to the horse chestnut. Its seeds are contained in a shell similar to the conker, but they have a more spiny exterior.

The wood is light brown to cream in colour and has an attractive grain pattern similar to oak.

Chestnut tree

Spanish chestnut leaves and seeds

USES

- flooring
- kitchen units
- furniture

Lime

Lime (also called Linden) is a tall, fast-growing hardwood tree, not to be confused with a tree that produces lime fruit. It absorbs pollution, so limes are planted in cities and built-up areas. The flowers are yellow-white and have an attractive smell. The leaves are heart-shaped.

Lime leaves and seeds

Lime tree

USES

- woodcarving
- musical instruments
- pencils

The wood is light cream in colour. It is soft to work with, but is quite durable. Lime wood finishes well, but is prone to shrinkage.

Cherry

The cherry is a small decorative tree that is grown in gardens throughout the country. It has lovely pink or white flowers in spring.

Cherry leaves and blossoms

Cherry tree

Cherry wood is rich orange to brown in colour with a beautiful grain pattern. It is an expensive wood due to its popularity and rich appearance. It is easily finished to a high standard.

USES

- high-quality furniture
- cabinet making
- hardwood floors and veneers

27

Sycamore

A member of the maple family, the sycamore tree grows widely all over the country. It is fast growing and has distinct, five-pointed leaves and winged seeds.

Sycamore is very light in colour with an indistinct grain.

Sycamore leaf and seeds

Sycamore tree

USES

- wood carving
- violin making
- veneers
- woodturning

Maple

Maple is a hardwood. It is a medium sized tree. You might notice that it is related to the sycamore. As the national tree of Canada, much of the maple used in Ireland is imported.

Maple leaves and seeds

Maple tree

Maple is an expensive wood, but is hard and durable. Its light cream colour creates an attractive grain.

USES

- kitchen unit doors
- maple flooring
- furniture-making
- veneers

Canadian flag

Irish Softwood Trees

Scots pine

Scots pine is widespread throughout Europe. It is grown as forestry in many countries, including Scotland. Its shape is unlike other conifer trees; it is not conical and it stands tall with few large branches. The bark is reddish brown in colour and the needles of the tree grow in pairs.

The wood of the Scots pine is a light brown-cream colour and is the wood we use most commonly for tasks in the wood technology room. It is a strong wood known as **red deal**. The wood is easy to work with and finishes well.

Scots Pine needles, pine cones, and seeds

USES

- school project work
- pine furniture
- construction timber
- doors

Scots pine tree

Douglas fir

The Douglas fir (also called Oregon pine) is a native tree of North America. This tall tree grows quickly. It prefers well-drained soils and sheltered areas away from high winds. The needles grow all around the twig, which has reddish-brown buds that form into oval-shaped pine cones.

Douglas fir needles and cone

The wood is a reddish-brown colour with a decorative grain that has clearly visible annual rings. Its tough durable wood will withstand heavy wear. Although the wood is light, it is very strong and resistant to decay.

Douglas fir trees

- gates and outdoor furniture
- plywood manufacture
- railway sleepers
- structural timber

Table and benches made from Douglas fir wood

Norway spruce

A native of central Europe, this tree grows at high altitudes and in mountainous regions. Norway (common) spruce comprises about 4 per cent of Irish forestry. This type of tree is prone to being blown down because of its shallow root system.

The wood is known as **white deal**, which is easily worked, but softer and less durable than red deal. It has a light cream colour.

USES

- floorboards
- internal woodwork
- construction timber
- fibreboard and chipboard
- Christmas trees

Norway spruce branch with cones

Norway spruce

Which tree is it?

Gather examples of leaves and needles from different trees. Working in pairs or groups, identify the different types. Make sketches of the leaves you have found.

Sitka spruce

The Sitka spruce, named for a town in Alaska, is the most commonly planted tree in Irish forestry. It thrives on Ireland's wet soil. The tree's blue-green needles make it easily identifiable.

The light yellow wood of the Sitka spruce is strong and straight-grained.

Sitka branches with cones

Sitka forest

USES

- structural timber such as roofs and floors
- paper making
- floorboards
- fibreboard and chipboard manufacture

Larch

The larch is widely grown in Ireland. Unlike other conifers, it loses its needles in the autumn. Its light green needles are arranged in small groups on the branch. It is a fast-growing, attractive tree that requires good light and clean air.

Larch wood has a distinct red colour. The wood has elastic properties and is durable. Larch is resistant to water, but tends to warp.

Larch needles and cones

Larch tree

USES

- boat building
- light furniture
- exterior joinery
- fence posts

31

Lodgepole pine

The lodgepole pine is widely planted in Irish forests. A native of western America, it was introduced here as it grows well on wet soils and in poor conditions. The needles are grouped densely on the branches and are borne in pairs.

The lodgepole pine's attractive wood is reddish-brown. If not properly cared for, the tree develops many branches, giving the wood a lot of knots that make it unsuitable for use.

Lodgepole pine trees

USES

- internal woodwork
- chipboard and fibreboard manufacture

Lodgepole pine needles and cone

Yew

The yew tree is a slow-growing, evergreen tree that grows well in Ireland. It can be found in many graveyards (it can grow for hundreds of years), but it is not generally planted in the Irish countryside because it is poisonous to livestock if eaten.

Yew tree needles and arils, which contain the seeds

The yew's wood is unusual as the sapwood is a light creamy colour and the heartwood (of which there is a

USES

- turning
- carving
- fine cabinetmaking

Yew tree

large portion) is a beautiful orange-brown colour. The wood is very hard and is sought after for furniture-making.

Timber regions of the world

Softwood or hardwood?

Gather examples of a variety of woods from the classroom and wood store, then swap your examples with someone else. Sort them according to whether you think they are hardwood or softwood. Discuss the examples under the following headings: colour, hardness, durability, grain, and possible uses.

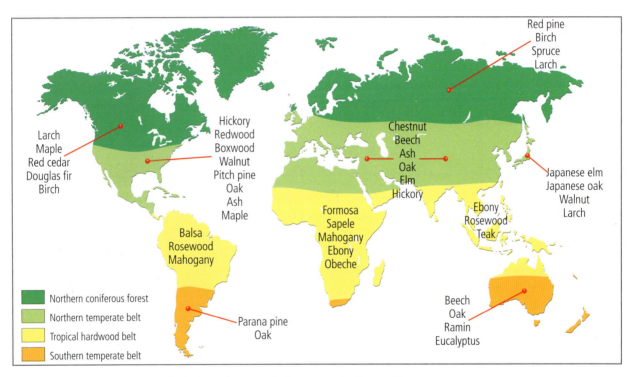

Map showing the different regions (belts) where timber grows in the world

Other timbers

We use many other woods from around the world when making projects. The map above shows the regions of the world where some of the most common woods come from. Some timber comes from tropical rainforests. These are being cut for logs and to make way for farming. To conserve these forests, we should only use woods sourced from properly managed forests (FSC labelled).

Cedar

Cedar is a tall, coniferous tree with a full crown imported from Canada. The wood is a rich red to brown colour. The oils in the wood have a strong scent that repels insects, so it is often used in drawers and wardrobes to keep away moths. Although it is lightweight, the wood is very durable and decay resistant. It is used outdoors and doesn't need to be painted.

Cedar

USES

- cladding on buildings
- pencils
- outdoor furniture

Ebony

Ebony is a very dark wood, almost black in colour. It grows in the tropical areas of Africa and south-east Asia. The wood is hard and dense, which makes it heavy. Its hardness makes it difficult to work. It is very rare, so it is expensive.

USES

- musical instruments
- carving
- inlaying

Sculpture made from Ebony

Mahogany

Widely used for furniture, mahogany is possibly the best-known tropical hardwood. Mahogany varies from light red to a deep chestnut brown. The grain can be very attractive. Although it is a hardwood, it is quite easy to work with. The wood is resistant to fungal and insect attack and it is a stable wood (it does not warp easily).

Mahogany jewellery box

USES

- furniture making
- veneering
- woodturning
- woodcarving

Iroko (teak substitute)

Iroko grows in tropical areas of Africa, India, and Asia. The timber is a dark golden colour. It is an oily wood. It is resistant to fungal and insect attack. The wood is hard and can be difficult to work, but it is durable. The dust from the cut timber is quite irritating and causes people to cough when working with it.

USES

- making hardwood windows and doors
- outdoor furniture
- gates
- flooring

Iroko floor

Walnut

The walnut tree grows widely in North America, but it is a native of south-east Asia. It grows in Ireland and Britain. The wood is usually imported from North America. Walnut is dark brown with a beautiful grain pattern. It is durable and finishes very well.

USES

- high quality furniture
- hardwood flooring
- marquetry and veneers
- woodcarving and woodturning

Walnut cabinet

Identifying woods

Gather examples of a variety of woods from the classroom and wood store. With your teacher, try to identify the names of each type.

CHAPTER QUESTIONS

1 Outline the stages in growth of a young tree.

2 Make a sketch of a cross section through the trunk of a tree. Label the following parts:

(a) pith
(b) annual rings
(c) heartwood
(d) sapwood
(e) bark
(f) bast

3 Describe what is meant by the following terms:

(a) chlorophyll
(b) transpiration
(c) photosynthesis

4 Explain the function of the roots of a tree.

5 Explain the function of the bark of a tree.

6 Explain the difference between the heartwood and sapwood of the tree.

7 Name three coniferous trees and three deciduous trees.

8 Outline five characteristics of deciduous trees and five characteristics of coniferous trees.

9 From the list below of common trees found in Ireland, state whether each is deciduous or coniferous.

(a) Scots pine
(b) Beech
(c) Ash
(d) Oak
(e) Douglas fir
(f) Sycamore

10 List two hardwoods that are light in colour.

11 The table shows images of common leaves. State from which tree each leaf comes from.

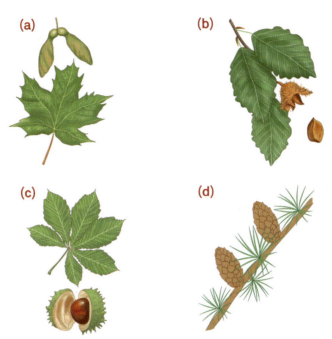

(a)

(b)

(c)

(d)

12 Select three examples of hardwood and softwood available in your wood technology room. Name each type and describe the wood under the following headings

(a) colour
(b) grain pattern
(c) annual rings

13 You are asked to make a small table lamp using contrasting woods. Select two contrasting woods for the project and give reasons for your choice.

14 You have been asked to make a bird table similar to the one pictured. Choose a suitable wood for the task and outline the characteristics that make it a suitable choice.

PowerPoint Summary   Weblinks   Worksheet

5 Timber, Environment, and Sustainability

Learning intentions

At the end of this chapter you will be able to:
- Describe the process of deforestation and explain how afforestation improves environmental sustainability.
- Outline the ways we can make better choices to improve the environment and work in a sustainable way.
- Make a more informed choice about the materials and woods that you use.
- Describe how the environment is affected by our use of woods and other materials.

How much do you know?

Discuss what you know about Trees and the Environment in small groups. Make a mind map or similar presentation about different aspects of our natural environment. Discuss how trees and wood can help our environment.

The environment is all around us and it is constantly under threat. We all have responsibility to make choices that ensure improvements to the environment. We have learned that trees play a key role in keeping our environment healthy. Trees have also been a source of fuel and raw materials for centuries.

Despite our knowledge about the negative effects of **deforestation** and climate change, the loss of tree cover has nearly doubled in the past 15 years. In 2017, an area of tropical forest equal to 1.5 times the area of Ireland was cut down for timber or farm land.

Nature and the environment are complex and interconnected. Deforestation is a major cause of climate change. It affects climate temperature and levels of oxygen and carbon dioxide. Decreased levels of oxygen and increased levels of carbon dioxide from deforestation are a major cause of the **greenhouse effect**.

These greenhouse gasses act like a blanket trapping heat radiation from the sun, which adds to global warming. Greenhouse gases are released by burning fossil fuels and from methane gas produced by cattle as well as other chemical pollutants produced by industry.

Deforestation:

The process of clearing forests for farmland or other uses.

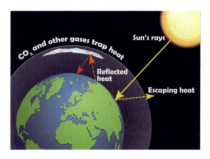

Deforestation – how might this type of felling affect the environment?

Greenhouse effect

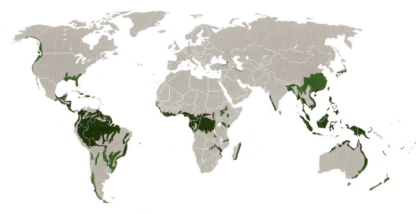

Tropical regions with rainforests

Rainforests

Vast areas of rainforests grow in tropical regions, as shown in the map above. These dense forests have a tall canopy of 40 metres high. The trees absorb huge amounts of carbon dioxide and release large quantities of oxygen. The forest regions are humid because the water released by the trees form clouds, which then produce rain, sustaining the forest. When areas of trees are removed, there is less evaporation and rainwater runs off to rivers, which in turn causes soil erosion.

Tropical rainforest

How do these tropical rainforests benefit the planet?

What causes deforestation?

There are many causes of deforestation.

- **Agriculture** – forests are cleared to provide land to graze cattle or to plant crops. Often just a few acres are cleared and burned to create small farms.
- **Logging** – trees are cut for commercial logging for wood and paper products. Commercial and illegal loggers cut trees and develop access roads deep into the forest, leading to further deforestation.
- **Population growth** – increased population from development of towns, cities and roads leads to forests being cleared to meet the increased demand for timber.
- **Fuel** – wood remains a major fuel source for native people in many parts of the world.
- **Natural causes** – storms and forest fires also destroy trees.

What are the effects of deforestation?

- Reduced levels of oxygen in the atmosphere.
- Increased levels of carbon dioxide in the atmosphere leading to increased global warming.
- Loss of natural habitat, threatening millions of species of plants, animals and insects.
- Trees also help drive the water cycle by returning water vapour to the atmosphere and by shading the soil, keeping it moist.
- Increased soil erosion in deforested areas.
- Increased likelihood of flooding.
- Possible medicinal plants found in rainforests have been lost.

Effects of deforestation

Investigate

Divide into base groups of five people. Each student is assigned a topic from the list below which they then research. Each person reports back on their research to the group with statements about their section from the following:

- **Rainforests**
- **Deforestation**
- **Causes of deforestation**
- **The effects of deforestation**
- **What we can do**

Groups will present their findings to the class.

Sustainability

In pairs, list other resources which should be managed sustainably. Describe how this might be achieved and the consequences of not managing these resources in a sustainable way. Prepare a slideshow or information sheet on your findings.

Sustainable Resources

Sustainability is about caring for our world, managing and **conservation** of all its **resources** so that people and animals can continue to enjoy them long into the future.

Trees are a renewable resource, but forests are being cut down faster than they can be replaced. To be sustainable, forests must be replanted and managed carefully so that a balance is maintained. Wood and other materials should not be wasted. This is everyone's responsibility. Reusing and recycling wood and other materials plays an important role in minimising waste of resources.

How do we help?

We must work to reduce our **carbon footprint**. A person's carbon footprint is the measure of the quantity of greenhouse gas an individual produces or uses (directly or indirectly) in daily living. It is given as kilograms of carbon dioxide (CO_2) per year. Everyone has a responsibility to reduce their carbon footprint and improve the environment.

Your carbon footprint

Outline two things you can do to reduce your carbon footprint.

Choosing Materials

- Use native hardwoods and softwoods instead of tropical woods.
- Always choose woods from sustainably managed sources showing the Forest Stewardship Council (FSC) label.
- Use manufactured boards rather than solid tropical woods.
- Choose veneered boards and veneers instead of solid woods.
- Avoid wasting wood particularly hardwoods and tropical hardwoods.
- Recycle woods if possible.
- Avoid wasting paper and try to recycle more.
- Plant more trees at home and in the community.

Consider your carbon footprint and how you can reduce it.

The Forest Stewardship Council logo reflects responsible forest management

Tropical rainforests are essential to the health of our environment and should be protected and conserved.

CHAPTER EXERCISES

1 Describe briefly what deforestation is.

2 Give two ways in which rainforests are being threatened.

3 Suggest two ways that we can reduce our use of hardwoods.

4 Copy the table below into your copy. List the woods used in the Wood Technology room. Highlight the tropical hardwoods.

Softwood	Hardwood	Manufactured board

5 Investigate tropical rainforests to find out more about where they grow and the people who depend on them.

6 Outline briefly how tropical rainforests contribute to a healthy environment.

7 List the factors that contribute to tropical deforestation.

8 Investigate how forests might be managed properly and develop a three-slide presentation to show this.

9 Design a brief slide presentation that examines two aspects of your carbon footprint. (Different groups could present different aspects.)

10 Outline two reasons why you believe that rainforests are essential to the environment.

11 Discuss two things that you do in school to reduce your carbon footprint.

12 Suggest two ways in which we can continue to use attractive hardwoods in an environmentally friendly manner.

13 State two ways that the use of manufactured boards can help reduce the current rate of global deforestation.

 PowerPoint Summary Weblinks

6 Conversion of Timber

Learning intentions

At the end of this chapter you will be able to:
- Identify different methods of conversion.
- Discuss characteristics of wood converted in different ways.
- Understand the properties and characteristics of wood.

Trees are felled (cut down) and the branches are stripped before the logs are transported to the sawmill to be cut into smaller sections. Mature forest plantations are often harvested by clear **felling** (cutting all the trees in a forest area).

Felling trees

Clear Felling Pros and Cons
Write down and discuss what the advantages and disadvantages of clear felling might be to the local environment.

Conversion:

The process of changing or converting logs into boards of usable timber size.

What is Conversion?

Conversion is when logs are cut into usable boards in a sawmill. However, not all logs are converted to boards. Logs and even small boards can be processed into chips or strands to be used to make manufactured boards. Bark is removed and processed into bark mulch for gardens.

43

Logs are converted into boards because:

* it allows the wood to dry faster
* it produces wood of even size and shape
* the wood is more usable
* the quality of the wood is easy to see and defects can be seen.

Logging

Old style saw pit

Modern horizontal bandsaw. How does it compare to the old style saw pit?

Modern sawmills have large machines which process sort and saw logs into various boards. However there are three main methods of converting logs: **tangential sawing**, **plain sawing** (also called through and through), and **radial sawing** (also called **quarter sawing**).

Log conversion
Consider why logs are converted into boards?

Conversion Methods

Plain sawing (Through & through)	Tangental sawing	Radial sawing (Quarter sawing)

Through and through sawing

Through and through sawing also called plain sawing or slash sawing is the most popular method of conversion. It is the fastest and the easiest to do. Parallel cuts are made through the logs and the boards are lifted off.

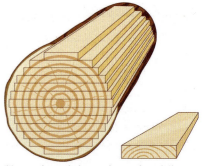
Through and through sawing. What might these boards be used for?

Advantages	Disadvantages
• A fast easy method: a log doesn't need to be turned • Can get wider boards • Low cost method • There is little waste	• Boards cut this way are prone to cupping • Boards show no particular grain pattern • There is a lot of sapwood in the boards and they are less durable • Prone to fungal and insect attack

Cupping

Cupping occurs naturally as wood dries. Wood on the outside (bark side) of the board shrinks more than the wood on the heart side of the board. This uneven shrinkage causes the wood to curl away from the heart.

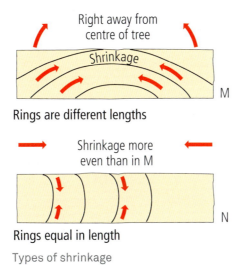

Types of shrinkage

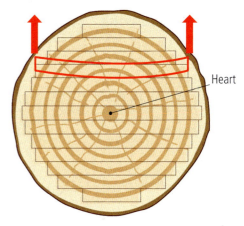

Cupping. Boards always tend to shrink away from the centre of the log. Why?

Quarter sawing

Here the logs are quartered before cutting the boards. This method displays an attractive grain pattern when the ray cells are cut and revealed. This silver grain is very distinct in oak. Cutting the log in this way involves turning the log for each cut, so is labour intensive.

Radial sawing also shows silver grain. It involves cutting the quartered log in cuts toward the centre of the log as shown.

 Through and Through and Quarter Sawn by WoodlandsTV

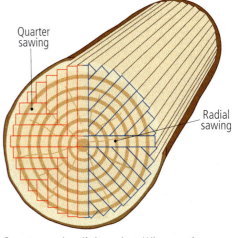

Quarter and radial sawing. Why are these methods more expensive?

Advantages	Disadvantages
• Produces attractive silver grain pattern • Boards cut this way are stable and shrink less • Boards wear more evenly (good for flooring) • Lengths of the rings are about even producing a stable board.	• Boards cut this way are smaller – not as wide • More waste produced • It requires more handling of the log so more labour • More expensive method

Tangential sawing

Cuts in tangential sawing are made at a tangent to the annual ring as seen in the diagram. Boards converted this way display an attractive **flame figure** that is seen particularly in woods with distinct annual rings such as ash, pitch pine and douglas fir.

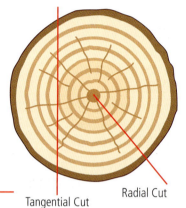

Tangent

Tangential Cut

Radial Cut

Sketch other examples of tangents

Flame figure

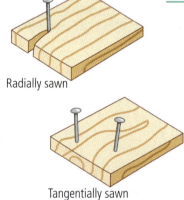

Radially sawn

Tangentially sawn

Can you explain why tangentially sawn boards are less likely to split when nailed?

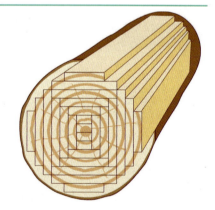

Tangential sawing. What properties might these boards have?

Advantages	Disadvantages
• A range of wide boards produced • Able to keep sapwood and heartwood separate • Reveals attractive grain ('flame figure') • Boards are strong and resist splitting	• Boards prone to cupping and shrinking • More handling of the log means high labour cost • More waste produced

CHAPTER QUESTIONS

1 What is clear felling? Write down two ways it affects the local community?

2 The process of sawing logs into usable sections is called _____?

3 List three reasons why logs are sawn into boards.

4 How does converting timber help timber conservation?

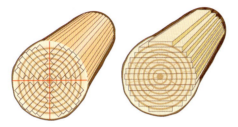

5 The diagram shows ends of boards C and D, cut using two methods of conversion. Describe the characteristics of the boards cut as shown.

Consider: Size
                 Annual rings
                 Cutting process – (the work
                 necessary to make the cuts).

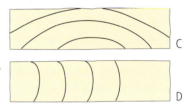

6 Which of the two boards (C or D) would you think is most stable?

7 One of these boards is more likely to shrink. Draw a neat sketch to show the result of this shrinkage.

8 Give the name for this type of shrinkage and explain briefly how it occurs.

 **PowerPoint Summary**    **Weblinks**

7 Timber Seasoning

KEYWORDS
- case hardening
- equilibrium
- hygroscopic
- kiln
- moisture content (MC)
- relative humidity
- stickers
- seasoning

LEARNING OUTCOMES
- 1.1, 1.2, 1.3, 1.8, 1.10
- 2.11
- 3.2, 3.3, 3.5, 3.11

Moisture content (MC):

The amount of moisture in timber.

Seasoning:

The controlled drying of timber.

Learning intentions

At the end of this chapter you will be able to:
- Identify and explain methods of seasoning.
- Understand and explain the need for seasoning.
- Understand how seasoning affects the properties of wood positively and negatively.

How does wood dry?

Consider how other items are dried and also what are the factors that influence how wood dries.

A newly felled tree contains about 50% water. This begins to dry out quickly in newly converted (green) boards. Carefully controlling the rate of drying prevents the boards from splitting and changing in shape. **Seasoning** aims to dry the wood so that the **moisture content** (MC) is below 20%.

Seasoning

Reasons for seasoning:
- Seasoning reduces the moisture content of the wood to below 20%.
- Dry wood is easier to work with.
- Seasoning allows the natural drying process to be controlled.
- Seasoning helps prevent wood from splitting.
- Fungi do not attack dry timber.
- Dry wood is lighter, harder and stronger.

- **20%** • The limit of good air seasoned wood & limit of fungal attack
- **16%** • Outdoor furniture
- **10 to 12%** • Indoor furniture & wood used in heated spaces

Moisture content. How would a project made from wood with higher moisture content be affected if positioned in a living room?

Air seasoning. Discuss why the wood will not dry properly in this stack

In controlled seasoning, water must be gradually removed by evaporation. As the surfaces dry, moisture moves from the centre of the board, and it too dries. If the surfaces dry too quickly, they prevent further evaporation, which leads to **case hardening**. This defect is caused by uneven drying and introduces distortion due to uneven forces in the wood.

Relative humidity

The **relative humidity** of the air affects the rate at which things dry, including wood. Relative humidity is the amount of moisture in the air at any time.

Wood is **hygroscopic**, meaning it is affected by moisture changes. It absorbs and releases moisture to reach a balance (**equilibrium**) with the surrounding air. An external wooden door will swell as it tries to reach this balance of moisture, which is called its equilibrium moisture content (EMC). This equilibrium will change with the relative humidity in the air.

Relative Humidity:

The amount of moisture in the air at a given temperature compared with the maximum amount it could hold at that same temperature. It is given as a percentage (%).

Methods of seasoning

There are two methods used to remove moisture from wood:
- Natural seasoning (Air seasoning)
- Kiln seasoning

49

Natural (air) seasoning

In natural or air seasoning, planks or boards of timber are stacked to allow air to pass over the boards. The stack is built on large battens raised off the ground to keep the timber clean and dry. The stack is about two metres wide and is made of timber layers separated by **stickers** placed one above the other to allow an air gap between each layer. A slight gap between each board allows air to flow evenly around the boards.

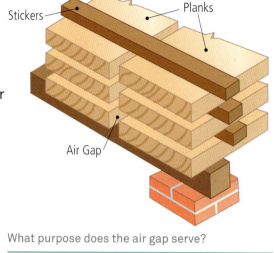

What purpose does the air gap serve?

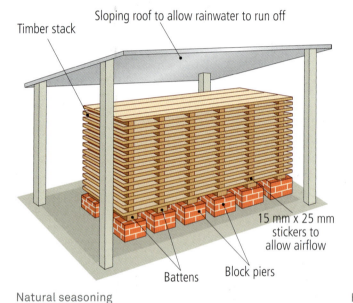

Natural seasoning

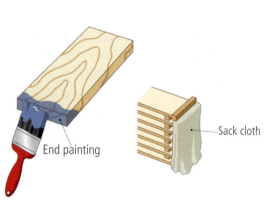

How does protecting the ends of boards help?

The stickers (also called skids) are small pieces of wood about 25mm thick. When they are positioned in line vertically and at regular intervals along the boards, they allow air to circulate through the stack. Using this method, the boards season evenly.

Important	
• The stack is raised off the ground to keep it clean and dry. • An overhanging roof keeps the rain away from the wood stack. • The stack is a maximum of two metres wide to allow an even flow of air through the boards so all the boards dry evenly.	• Timbers of the same species are stacked together • Boards of the same thickness are kept in the same stack to allow uniform drying. • The ends of boards should be protected from the sun. If they dry too quickly, the ends will split.

Natural seasoning can only reduce the moisture content of boards to between 18% and 22% just at the limit of protection from fungal attack. Air dried wood could be used for outdoor work but it must be dried further using a special oven called a **kiln** for any indoor construction or furniture.

Advantages of natural seasoning	Disadvantages of natural seasoning
• It is simple low tech, no specialised equipment needed • Once the stack is made no labour required • Low cost method • Low energy method	• Slow drying rate (3-6 months) • Weather dependent • No control on rate of drying • Only dries boards to 18 – 20% MC • Large areas of space for stacks

Kiln Seasoning

This method uses a large heated chamber like an oven to control the rate of drying of the wood. The stack is made on a trolley. The trolley is wheeled into the kiln where the drying takes place.

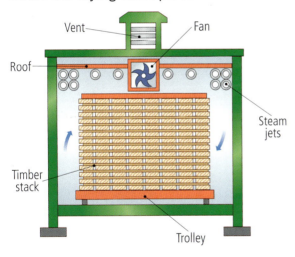

Kiln Seasoning – Consider how does drying occur? What is the steam for?

Timber being loaded into a kiln

The drying process
- Hot **steam** is forced into the kiln heating the boards through to the middle.
- The **steam** keeps the wood and kiln moist.
- **Fans** keep the air circulating evenly around the stack.
- **Vents** allow fresh air in and moist air out, helping to regulate the relative humidity.

51

- When the boards are fully heated, the moisture levels are reduced. This allows the air to absorb moisture drying from the boards.
- This process gradually continues as the boards dry to the desired level.

Trained operators ensure the correct rates of drying (drying schedules) for different types of wood and boards of different thicknesses. Timber is often partly air seasoned before finishing in the kiln. This is efficient and helps the drying process by speeding up the kiln stage while also helping reduce waste of energy and the final cost.

Advantages of kiln seasoning	Disadvantages of kiln seasoning
<ul><li>Boards dry more quickly</li><li>Lower moisture content is possible (10%)</li><li>Greater control over the drying process (drying schedules)</li><li>Different thickness of board and different types of wood are dried accurately.</li><li>Defects associated with seasoning can be minimised.</li></ul>	<ul><li>Costly to set up and expensive to run</li><li>Uses a lot of energy to heat the kiln for long periods</li><li>Requires supervision by trained operator</li></ul>

Moisture content

The amount of moisture in the wood is shown as a percentage (%) of the weight of the wood when dry. Boards are checked for moisture content periodically during the seasoning process. A moisture meter is used to measure the moisture content of boards.

Moisture meter

In school, you can find the moisture of a sample of wood by cutting a sample from a piece as shown.

Accurately measure the weight of the sample (wet weight). Then, completely dry out the sample. Measure and record this dry weight.

$$\% \text{ Moisture} = \frac{\text{Wet weight} - \text{Dry Weight}}{\text{Wet Weight}} \times 100$$

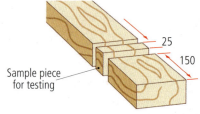

Take the sample from the end of the board

CHAPTER QUESTIONS

1 Green timber is timber _____?

2 Explain what the following letters stand for?

E _____ M _____ C _____

3 What is meant by the term 'seasoning'?

4 List three reasons why it is necessary to season timber.

5 What is the purpose of the gaps between the boards in the timber stack?

6 Timber seasoned to a moisture content below _____% is not affected by fungal attack.

7 Explain the term moisture content.

8 List three advantages and disadvantages of natural seasoning.

9 List three advantages or disadvantages of kiln seasoning.

10 Outline the function of each of the terms associated with kiln seasoning listed below.

(a) the fan   (d) heating coils
(b) steam jets   (e) stickers
(c) vents   (f) trolley

11 Why is the stack of wood raised above the ground in air seasoning?

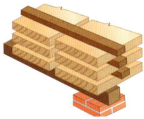

Stack of wood being air seasoned

12 Compare the two methods of seasoning under the following headings

(a) moisture content achieved
(b) environmental sustainability
(c) cost

 **PowerPoint Summary**   **Weblinks**

8 Preserving Timber

Preservative:

Chemicals used to treat wood to give it protection that will extend its useful life.

Learning intentions

At the end of this chapter you will be able to:
- Describe different methods of preserving timber.
- Consider the impact on the environment when choosing materials.

Timber needs to be protected from rotting, especially if it is outside or in contact with the ground. What should wood be protected from?
- Wear and tear
- Weather
- Attack by insects and fungi.

Because softwoods are less durable and less expensive than hardwoods, they are often treated with **preservatives**. Treated timber is used for construction timber, fence posts and fences, gates, and outdoor furniture.

At-risk items

Make a list of common outdoor wooden items that might need to be protected from weather and rot.

Wooden fencing

Picnic table

Preservative types

There are three main types of preservatives used to protect timber.

- Tar oil preservatives
- **Water-borne** preservatives
- **Solvent**-based preservatives

Preservatives protect the wood by creating a barrier that stops fungi and insects from attacking the wood. These chemicals make the wood poisonous to invaders.

Different types of preservatives. How do they protect wood?

Tar oil preservatives

Tar oils like **creosote** and creosote substitute are well known. They are poisonous chemicals that are used to treat telephone poles, fence posts and railway sleepers. They can be applied by pressure treatment, dipping or painted on using a brush. Tar oils are very **toxic** and are not used indoors.

Railway sleepers treated with tar oil preservative

Advantages of tar oils	Disadvantages of tar oils
• plentiful and cheap • very toxic to insects and fungi • soak (penetrate) well into the timber • permanent: not easily washed out of the wood	• strong smell • toxic to plants and wildlife • cannot be painted over until well weathered, as the tar oil bleeds out • not suitable for indoor use

Water-borne preservatives

Toxic salts are dissolved in water to make this type of preservative. When they are applied to wood, the water evaporates, leaving the chemicals behind.

Advantages	Disadvantages
• Timber is clean after treatment • No bleeding (tar oils bleed in hot weather) • Generally colourless • Generally odourless (has no smell) • Timber can be painted • Not a fire hazard	• Can often be washed out of wood • Timber must be dried out after treatment • The water can cause swelling or distortion • They don't protect against weathering

Solvent-based preservatives

These are toxic chemicals dissolved in solvents other than water, usually an oil based solvent that evaporates quickly (e.g. white spirit). When the solvent evaporates, the chemical is left in the wood. The solvents also give better penetration of the chemicals.

Advantages	Disadvantages
• Resistant to leaching • Can be used indoors and outdoors • Can be painted over • Usually do not stain • Not corrosive to metals • Allow good penetration	• Can be a fire hazard (solvents) • Can have a strong smell • Can be more expensive

Safety

Care must be taken with preservatives because they are harmful.

⚠ Always read and follow manufacturer's instructions.
⚠ Always wear gloves and protective clothing when using preservatives.
⚠ Protect your environment by disposing of chemicals and containers properly.

Application methods

A number of methods are used to apply preservatives. The method chosen will depend on:

• the quantity of timber to be treated
• the quality or depth of treatment
• the time and cost of treatment.

Brushing and spraying

Preservatives can be applied using a brush or spray gun. These methods are very suitable for general use and are not costly. The preservative will not soak into the

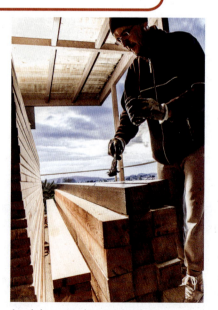
Applying wood preservative

Brushing and spraying

Immersion

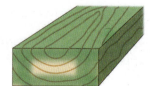
Pressure treatment

Penetration effect of different application methods

wood and regular applications are required to maintain protection. Creosote substitutes and solvent based products are applied this way.

Dipping/immersion
The wood is dipped into a container of preservative, which is left to soak into the wood. This process allows for deeper protection as the preservative soaks deeper into the wood.

Pressure treatment
This is the most effective method. The preservative is forced into the wood under pressure in a special pressure treatment tank. The wood is sealed inside the tank and the preservative is pumped in. Using pressure and vacuums, the preservative is forced deep into the wood fibres.

Pressure treatment cylinder

These fence posts have been pressure treated with preservative

 ## CHAPTER QUESTIONS

1 Explain the term 'decay'. Describe what causes wood to decay.

2 Name two different types of wood preservative.

3 Discuss in groups whether hardwoods or softwoods are more resistant to decay. List reasons for your conclusions.

4 Give two reasons why preservatives are used on external woodwork.

5 Outline two disadvantages and two advantages of each type of wood preservatives

6 Creosote substitutes are only used outdoors. Outline why this is so.

7 Describe three ways to apply preservatives to wood.

8 Describe three safety precautions you would take when applying preservatives to wood.

9 Explain why you agree or disagree with the statement, 'Preserving timber helps to conserve the earth's resources'.

10 List the advantages and disadvantages of a solvent-based preservative.

 PowerPoint Summary   Weblinks

9 Manufactured Boards

Learning intentions

At the end of this chapter you will be able to:
- Understand properties and characteristics of man-made boards.
- Compare common manufactured boards.
- Justify the use of materials based on characteristics and properties.

Manufactured boards

Solid boards have a limited width. Boards can be joined together to create a wide board. Man-made boards are made by processing timber or timber products into sheet form. These large sheets have become an important substitute for solid woods with many advantages. In using timber products that would otherwise be wasted, such as timber **particles**, wood chips, and smaller wood sections, boards made of **veneers** help to conserve trees and tropical forests. Man-made woods provide large, flat pieces of stable wood with uniform thickness. They are mainly used for worktops and bedroom and kitchen units.

Man-made boards in the classroom

Working in small groups, list different types of man-made boards in your classroom or that you are familiar with. Create an investigation sheet to describe the following characteristics of these materials:
- content • size • appearance • grain • strength • edges.

Share differences between the boards with the class.

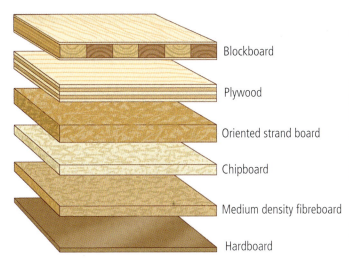

Blockboard

Plywood

Oriented strand board

Chipboard

Medium density fibreboard

Hardboard

Types of manufactured board. Find examples of these materials at home.

Production of manufactured boards

> Search online for a 6:43 minute video called 'Manufacturing plywood boards: then and now' by the Victoria and Albert Museum.

Plywood

Thin sections of solid wood break easily across the grain. Therefore, wide sheets are weak. **Plywood** is made by layering and gluing thin plies of wood together. The grain of each layer is at 90 degrees to the next. This makes the sheet stronger while maintaining an even surface with few knots or uneven grain. It doesn't warp or twist and does not split even when nailed near the edge.

Thin **veneers** (thin sheets of wood called **plies**) are glued together like a sandwich to form the thickness of the board required. Veneers are sheets of wood cut from the surface of a plank, or cut from a log by rotary cutting.

A cabinet made of plywood

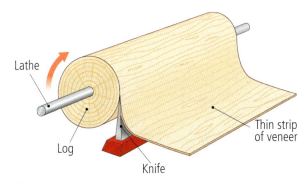

Lathe

Log

Knife

Thin strip of veneer

Rotary cutting of veneer

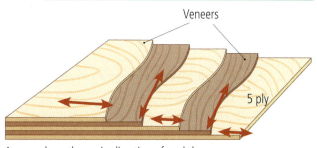

Veneers

5 ply

Arrows show the grain direction of each layer. Each layer is at 90° to the next

Makeup of plywood

The grain of each layer is positioned at a right angle (90°) to the layer below it, as shown in the illustration on page 59. There are always an uneven number of plies in plywood, e.g. 3, 5, 7, so the grain of the two facing (outside) veneers point in the same direction.

Boards made this way are both strong and thin. Different types and quality of plywood are available. They can be grouped into two main categories: interior and exterior quality.

Interior quality plywood

Plywood for internal use is made from woods less resistant to decay and uses adhesives which are generally not water resistant. They are not suitable for outdoor use.

Exterior quality plywood

Plywood for outside use are made with more durable veneers and use water-resistant adhesives. **Water and boil proof (WBP)** is a term used to describe a general exterior grade plywood that resists water, heat, chemical, fungal and insect attack. Marine plywood is very durable plywood that contains high-quality veneers of naturally durable timbers bonded together with WBP glue. Marine ply is used when it will be exposed to water for long periods of time (such as in boat building).

Flexible plywood (Flexiply)

This flexible form of plywood can be formed into a variety of curved shapes. Made from several layers of thin plies, flexiply is useful where a curved shape is required.

Blockboard

Blockboard is a 'strip core board', which means it is comprised of thick strips or battens of solid wood (usually softwood) glued together and covered with veneers on both sides, just like plywood. It is usually a thicker sheet (18mm – 25 mm).

Examples of plywood

Flexiply

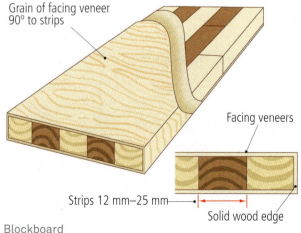
Grain of facing veneer 90° to strips

Facing veneers

Strips 12 mm–25 mm

Solid wood edge

Blockboard

Advantages and disadvantages of plywood and blockboard

Advantages	Disadvantages
• very strong • large sheets with uniform thickness • do not warp or shrink • flat surfaces with uniform quality and finish • available in a variety of thickness (4, 6, 9, 12, 15, 18mm) • complex shapes are easily cut from ply • thin sheets can be bent easily • they do not split easily when nailed into the face	• edges are unsightly and must be covered with a decorative strip • the surface veneers (plies) are usually plain • cannot easily screw or nail into the edge of plywood as it would split

Plywood at play

Refer to the playground item, pictured right. Suggest reasons why plywood is suitable for this example.

Plywood climbing wall

Pineboard/Lamwood

Pineboard, or lamwood, is a manufactured board made of strips of solid pine glued together into a wider board. When the glue is bonded, the sheets are sanded to a smooth, uniform thickness. Special hardwood examples are also made for use in worktops. The sheets can be obtained in thicknesses of 12mm – 25 mm.

Pineboard is generally used where larger pieces of wood are required in a solid form such as table tops, shelving units, and worktops. Decorative shapes can be easily cut from pineboard. It is sustainable because it uses strips of wood that might be unsuitable or too small as solid pieces. However, it does have numerous knots and is prone to cupping.

Pineboard/lamwood

Orientated stand board (OSB)

Orientated strand board is made in Waterford by Louisiana Pacific. It looks similar to chipboard, but has many of the characteristics of plywood. Wooden strands, or flakes, are processed from the tree log. These are sorted and bonded together under heat and pressure using a synthetic adhesive and resins. The strands are arranged so the grain directions overlap at right angles, giving the board its strength. Then, the strands are aligned in two outer layers with an inner core. The finished boards are sanded and cut to size.

Debarking of logs **1**

Stranding the logs **2**

Strands are soaked and dried **3**

Strands are blended **4**

The strands are laid into layers and pressed into sheets **5**

The sheets are finished to standard sizes **6**

Making OSB

Boards come in standard sizes (8ft by 4ft) and are suitable for a variety of uses, including packing cases, flooring, furniture manufacture, and timber framed buildings. It has moderate moisture resistance and resistance to fungal attack.

 Search online for a 03:06 minute video called 'How It's Made – OSB Wood Panels in Inverness, Scotland' by Norbord Europe Ltd.

Chipboard

Chipboard is made by taking small graded wood particles (chips) and mixing them with synthetic resin glue. The mixture is pressed to form rigid sheets of regular thickness. They are sanded down to give the finished product.

The surfaces of chipboard are often laminated with plastic laminates or decorative wood veneers such as oak, mahogany and ash for cabinet construction, worktops and for bedroom or kitchen units. A flooring grade is also available for the building industry.

Wood strands

Close-up view of oriented strand board (OSB)

Chipboard

Particle boards (chipboard and OSB) are very popular because:

- they help in tree conservation, improving the environment
- the waste from timber felling (forest thinning) and conversion are included in their manufacture
- they can use up to 70% recycled material.

The edges of chipboard and OSB are rough and unattractive and need to be covered. Below are some ways of finishing the edges of manufactured boards.

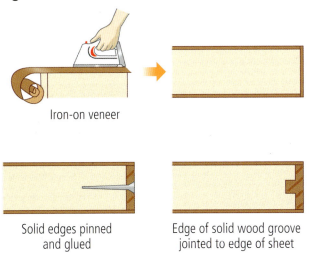

Iron-on veneer

Solid edges pinned and glued

Edge of solid wood groove jointed to edge of sheet

Edges of chipboard should be covered

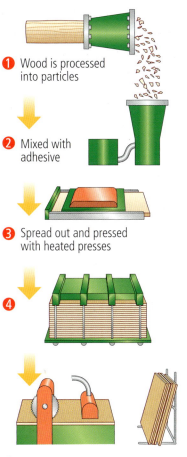

❶ Wood is processed into particles

❷ Mixed with adhesive

❸ Spread out and pressed with heated presses

❹

❺ Finished boards are finely cut and sanded

Chipboard manufacture. List the stages of manufacture of this board.

Medium Density Fibreboard (MDF)

Medium density fibreboard (MDF) is another common particle board. Fine wood particles and dust are bonded together with adhesive and resins and compressed into flat sheets. The sheets are trimmed to standard sizes. MDF is a dense material with very smooth, flat surfaces on both sides that do not need to be sanded before finishing. The edges of MDF are solid enough to be moulded with a router. Like chipboard, MDF can feature decorative veneers or laminated surfaces. It also comes in standard sheet sizes and thicknesses.

Other types of **fibreboard** include high density fibreboard (HDF) and low density fibreboard (LDF).

Medium density fibreboard (MDF)

Search online for a 04:19 minute video called 'How It's Made – MDF & Chipboard Flooring' by Norbord Europe Ltd.

Advantages and disadvantages of Particle Boards (MDF & chipboard)

Advantages	Disadvantages
• large sheets of uniform thickness • low cost • can be covered with decorative veneers and laminates • MDF edges can be moulded • no knots or blemishes • uses timber that might otherwise be wasted • environmentally friendly by using up to 70% recycled material	• edges normally covered with veneer or solid wood strip • chipboards are weak, break easily • edges are easily split by nails or screws • not water resistant, only used indoors/ not suitable for outdoor work • absorbs moisture and swells when wet

Hardboard

Hardboard is made of fine wood particles and wood waste. The wood is pulped with steam and heat, producing fluffy brown fibres. These fibres are bonded using glues and pressed between heated plates to produce finished sheets. The sheets have one smooth side and a textured side.

Hardboard is a uniform material with high density and like MDF it has no knots or grain. The sheets are thin, usually 3-4mm thick. Hardboard is inexpensive and can be given a laminated surface such as a coloured effect or wood veneer. It is used in the bottom of drawers, the back of cupboards and as a hard-wearing underlay to floor coverings. However, hardboard is not water-resistant, so is not used outdoors.

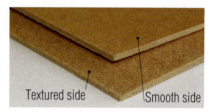

The smooth and textured sides of hardboard

Sheet Materials

Manufactured boards are made in large sheets of standard sizes: 2,438 mm (8ft) long and 1,219 mm (4ft) wide. However, smaller sizes can also be obtained in most shops.

Laminated chipboard panels in different colours are available in a variety of widths with the edges already laminated, ready to use. Most sheet materials are made in standard thicknesses from 6 mm to 25mm.

Because of their size, sheet material must be stored correctly. Incorrect stacking can result in sheets being damaged or bending out of shape. Sheets should be stored in dry conditions to protect them from the weather or dampness. Sheets are best stored lying flat with suitable support from timber battens as shown.

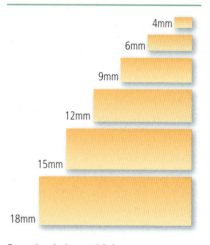

Standard sheet thicknesses. Investigate the standard sheet materials available in your school workshop.

Timber battens

Why should sheets be stored flat?

Environmental factors

Using manufactured boards assists the environment in a number of ways.

Why are manufactured boards sustainable?
- They are an alternative to solid wood.
- They are made mostly from softwoods, reducing impact on tropical forests.
- They are made using wood from managed forests.
- Particle boards like chipboard and MDF can use recycled timber, timber waste and forest thinnings.
- Sheet materials are suitable for veneering with quality hardwood veneers, reducing impact on tropical and slow growing hardwood forests.

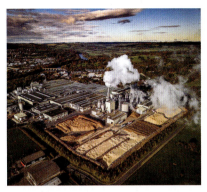
A wood processing factory in the UK

 CHAPTER QUESTIONS

1 Explain the term **manufactured board** in your own words.

2 List and describe **three** manufactured boards you have used in the workshop.

3 Suggest a manufactured board that could be used in the base of a drawer. Give reasons why it is suitable for this situation.

4 Explain the following terms:
   (a) MDF   **(b)** WBP.

5 Discuss the advantages of manufactured boards over solid woods.

6 Evaluate how manufactured boards are different from solid hardwoods and softwoods.

7 Using sketches, explain how veneers are cut to make plywood.

8 Describe four stages in making each of the following:
   (a) pineboard   **(b)** plywood
   (c) MDF   **(d)** chipboard.

9 Compare the suitability of the following two materials in making a top for a small hall table:
   (a) pineboard   **(b)** plywood.

 PowerPoint Summary   Weblinks

10 Diseases and Defects

KEYWORDS

🔍 **KEYWORDS**
- bowing
- burr
- knot
- larva
- pupa
- shake
- spalting
- waney edge

LEARNING OUTCOMES
- 1.3, 1.5, 1.8, 1.10
- 2.3, 2.5, 2.11
- 3.2, 3.3

Spalted wood logs

How would you describe spalted timber and burr wood and where would you use them?

Learning intentions

At the end of this chapter you will be able to:
- Identify and describe various wood defects and diseases.
- Explain how different wood defects affect the choice of materials.
- Utilise some of the defects in wood to enhance projects.

Every day drying

Consider how other items are dried (clothes, hair, hay). Also discuss what factors influence how wood dries.

Trees and cut timber can suffer from diseases and defects. Damage can occur naturally or can be the result of felling or improper seasoning. Diseases and defects affect the quality and strength of the wood. Often, defects can make wood look well or improve its value. **Burrs** or spalted wood are an example of this, but usually defects reduce the value and strength of the wood.

Natural defects

Natural defects occur in trees as they grow. Some can be attractive when incorporated into projects while others can be removed before processing.

Knots

A **knot** forms where a branch meets the trunk of a tree. Knots are either part of the wood (live knots) or are loose (dead knots). All knots reduce the strength of the timber and can affect the appearance.

Resin pocket

The grain in softwoods often contains open chambers that contain resin. When these chambers are cut into, the exposed resin leaks out. This weakens the wood and spoils the appearance of the wood, even if the hole is filled.

Shakes

These splits in the end grain of the wood take different forms. **Shakes** are caused by tension forces that build up in the tree while it grows or as the wood dries out after it is felled. These forces pull the fibres apart along weakness in the wood, causing the split to develop. Radial shakes radiate out from the centre of the tree. Tangential shakes occur along the annual ring lines. In general, splits must be removed, but doing so reduces the value of the timber.

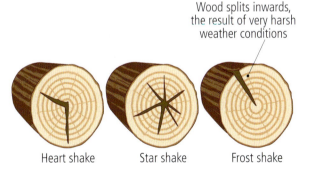

Wood splits inwards, the result of very harsh weather conditions

Heart shake   Star shake   Frost shake

Types of radial shakes

Winter wood separates from summer wood

Cup shake   Ring shake

Types of tangential shakes

Describe the difference between live and dead knots.

Resin pocket

Illustrate shakes

Make neat shaded sketches of the different types of shakes in your notes copy.

Waney Edge

During the conversion process where part of the bark is left exposed this is known as a **waney edge**. It can be cut out or is often used in projects to give a rustic natural edge to a piece.

Waney edge

How does the edge affect the appearance of these pieces?

Artificial Defects

Defects resulting from poor stacking or poor seasoning are known as artificial defects. They include staining and discoloration of wood as well as defects like cupping, twisting, and warping of boards.

Cupping

Cupping is caused by shrinkage that makes the board curve away from the heart of the tree. It forms a 'U' shape as you view it from the end.

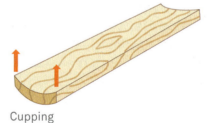

Cupping

Bowing

When a board is bent along its length, it is bowed. Like cupping, **bowing** is associated with poor seasoning.

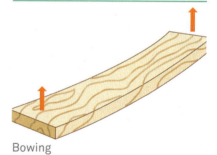

Bowing

Twisting/warping

A warp or twist might occur during seasoning or if boards are exposed to high temperature.

Twisting or warping

End splitting

Ends of boards dry more quickly. If they are exposed to the sun or seasoned too rapidly, splits can occur. Splits are common in naturally seasoned wood. Painting or covering the ends of the stack helps to prevent this happening.

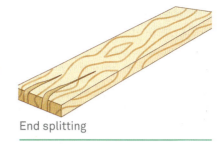
End splitting

Honeycomb checks

Wood that dries too fast may develop small splits or checks on the surface of the wood that go deeper as the drying continues, causing internal splitting. Unlike end splitting, honeycomb checks are often not spotted until the wood is cut or planed.

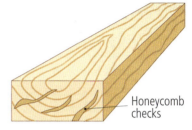
Honeycomb checks

Case hardening

If boards season too quickly, the outer surfaces dry, leaving the centre less dry. The resulting stress forces that remain in the wood are released when the boards are cut, distorting the wood.

Moisture is trapped in the centre of the board if surfaces dry too quickly

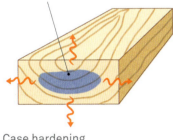
Case hardening

Case hardening. Boards bend when tension is released.

Finding defects

Collect examples of defects in wood found in your classroom and make an attractive display.

Stains & discoloration

Wood can be stained by chemicals, weathering, and fungi. The black colour of bog oak is the result of chemicals in the bog. Nearly all timbers react to acids or alkalis they come in contact with (soaps, detergents, etc.).

Bog oak

69

Fungal Attack

Fungi spores (seeds) are present in the air. A fungus needs certain conditions before it will grow on wood. Where conditions are suitable, the spores feed on wood cells. They soften and discolour the wood, resulting in damage and decay.

Conditions for fungal growth	
Moisture	Wood moisture content above 20%
Food source	Wood
Oxygen	Warm, still air

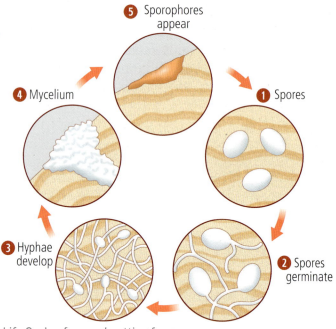

Life Cycle of a wood-rotting fungus

Spalting or dozing

When fungi infect wood, it feeds on the wood's carbohydrates, resulting in stains. The mould or fungus grows into the timber, weakening it and altering the wood's appearance. These moulds can cause coloured stains, often blue, black, or white patterns in the wood. This stained effect, known as **spalting** or dozing, can be attractive if the rot has not done too much damage.

Consider if these simple objects are improved by the staining effect (spalting) of the fungi?

Spalting

Spalted beech wood

Spalted maple wood

Wet rot (white rot)

Wet rot affects timber that is exposed to the elements or is wet. This often happens in exterior windows, doors, or fence posts. The affected wood becomes moist and slimy as it rots while a white residue often forms. Wet rot is confined only to the sections of timber that are wet or exposed and does not travel through the rest of the piece.

Wet rot

Dry rot (brown rot)

Dry or brown rot usually occurs indoors, for example, underneath wooden floors. The fungus attacks the wood, eating the cellulose in the wood. Affected wood appears dry and cracked with cube-like cracks on the surface as if it had been burned by fire. There is usually a musty smell present.

Dry rot

Dry rot
- Occurs in damp areas with poor ventilation.
- Spreads and can penetrate brick and block walls.
- Can seriously damage wood beyond the affected area.

Treating dry rot
- Remove all infected wood and uninfected timber 500mm beyond the area of infection. It is cut away and burned.
- All remaining wood and blockwork must be treated with a fungicide to kill any remaining infection.
- Identify and correct the causes of the infection (improve ventilation or address dampness).
- Replace infected timber with new pressure treated timber.

71

Insect attack

There are insects that attack timber. Eggs laid in the wood hatch and the **larva** eats through the wood, causing the damage. These insects have a common life cycle.

Life cycle of a wood-boring insect

1 Eggs are laid by the adult in a hole or crack in the timber.
2 The eggs hatch and a larva or grub then feeds on the starch or moulds in the wood. As it feeds it tunnels under the surface of the wood.
3 When fully developed, the larva makes a cocoon-like shell around itself. During this **pupa** stage it changes into an adult beetle.
4 The adult emerges from the shell, burrows to the surface to fly away and continue the cycle. It leaves behind an exit hole and fine dust (waste) called **fras**.

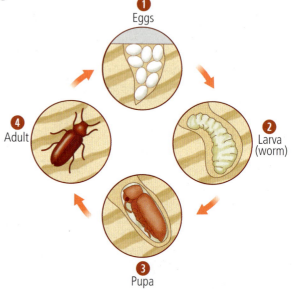

The life cycle of wood-boring insects

Draw the life cycle

Sketch the above figure into your copy, illustrating and outlining the descriptions with each life cycle stage.

Furniture beetle (woodworm)

The furniture beetle, or woodworm as it is often called, is a common insect causing damage to wood in Ireland. It attacks hardwoods and softwoods such as mahogany, oak, and pine. It usually only attacks the sapwood of the timber. Adult beetles emerge in June and July. Some tropical hardwoods are immune to attack as well as many types of plywood and chipboard because adhesives used in making them are harmful to the beetle. Timber preservatives can be used to treat and protect wood from attack.

Larva

Furniture beetle

Common furniture beetle (woodworm)

Wood infested with furniture beetles

Pictures of a furniture beetle larva and an adult magnified many times

Treatment

Timber infected with furniture beetle can be treated:

- Apply coats of insecticide to the wood according to the manufacturer's instructions.
- Ensure all surfaces and cracks are fully coated with the chemical.
- An applicator is used to inject chemical into the exit holes.

Other insects infect wood but are not commonly found in Ireland. The deathwatch beetle is found in England and is larger than the furniture beetle. It attacks damp wood – usually the ends of decaying beams. Filling all cracks in the wood and fully painting the timber greatly reduces the risk of attack.

The powder post beetle is reddish brown in colour and is approximately 4mm long. It attacks the sapwood of new hardwoods, especially during seasoning.

Deathwatch beetle

Powder post beetle

CHAPTER QUESTIONS

1   Name two defects that occur naturally in a piece of wood.

2   A cavity in a piece of pine filled with sap is known as a _____. Why would this be a defect?

3   Sketch and name two common radial shakes found in a log.

4   What is the term for wood coloured by fungal attack?

5   Cupping is when wood _____

6   A warped piece of wood is difficult to use in making a table top because _____

7   Outline the main difference between wet rot and dry rot.

8   Describe the stages of growth of wood-rotting fungi.

9   Outline the steps you would take to treat and replace a section of wooden floor that had been infected by dry rot.

10   Outline the furniture beetle's stages of development and state at which stage most of the damage is done by such an insect.

 PowerPoint Summary   Weblinks

11 Properties of Materials

KEYWORDS
- conduction
- density
- ductility
- durability
- elasticity / elastic limit
- insulation
- malleability
- property / properties

LEARNING OUTCOMES
- 1.3, 1.8, 1.10
- 2.11
- 3.3, 3.4, 3.5, 3.6, 3.7

Property:

An attribute, feature, or quality (e.g. steel is a hard material that will rust).

Learning intentions

At the end of this chapter you will be able to:
- Identify and describe properties of materials.
- Give examples of materials with particular properties.
- Consider properties of materials when designing artefacts.

Wood is a natural material with many great **properties**. Other materials are available, each with properties that make them stand out as being useful.

Having a better understanding of the properties of various woods and materials will allow us to choose the most suitable material for any task or artefact we wish to make.

Name some properties of the different materials pictured above

Necessary properties

Analyse (consider) what properties are needed for the following items. You can do this individually or in groups. Compare your thoughts to learn more.

Ruler	Copy	Workbench	Vice

Colour

Different woods have different shades or natural colours. Colour is an obvious property that affects the appearance of any artefact. Some materials such as acrylic (also known as plexiglass or Perspex®) are available in a range of different colours. The transparency of glass and acrylic is useful in cabinet doors, windows, and other items.

Coloured acrylic

Why is the use of contrasting woods effective?

Contrasting colours of light and dark shades can be very effective in project work. Paints and stains can also be used to add or change the colour where required.

Strength

Strong materials can withstand force or pressure without breaking or bending. Since there are different types of force, there are different types of strength.

Strong materials withstand forces without breaking or being changed in shape (deformed). Many materials have strength. It is important that you choose the correct material and size of piece to make sure it can take the load.

> **Strength:**
>
> **the ability of a material to withstand force or pressure**

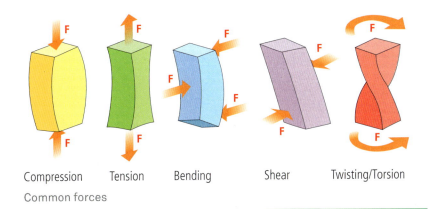

Compression   Tension   Bending   Shear   Twisting/Torsion

Common forces

Hardness

Hard materials resist damage or change by strong force. They resist wear and tear well and will not scratch or dent easily. **Durability** is needed for work surfaces, floors, and tools. Chisels, plane blades, and drill bits must be hard in order to keep their edge and shape. Blades are made from hardened steel; if they were made from softer metal their edges would blunt more easily.

Density

Why do two pieces of material with the same size or dimensions have different weights (mass)?

Hardwood vs Softwood. Which damages more easily and why?

Density is the mass of material per unit of volume, or the amount of material packed into the space. Each material has a different density.

Mass	=	Weight of an object (Kg)
Volume	=	The space an item takes up (m^3)

$$\text{Density} = \frac{\text{Mass}}{\text{Volume}} \quad \left(\frac{kg}{m^3}\right)$$

Hardwood   Aeroboard   Metal

Explain why three materials of the same size have different weights.

Water has a density of approximately 1,000 (kg/m^3). Can you explain why most woods float on water?

Toughness
A tough material can absorb energy well. Ash is an example of a wood that will not crack under load. Brittleness is the opposite of toughness. A material can be hard, but not tough. Glass, for example, is a hard material, but it is brittle. Tough materials resist impact forces well.

Elasticity
An elastic material can return to its normal shape after being stretched or bent. Ash has good elastic properties, which make it suitable for hurleys.

Hurley

Wood with elasticity can be bent into shape

Most materials have some elasticity, but if stretched beyond their **elastic limit,** they will not return to their original shape. Woods with good elastic properties are used when laminating or bending wood.

Durability
Durability measures how well a material lasts. It is also how it resists weathering, corrosion or decay. Hardwoods like oak and teak are more durable than softwoods like pine. Durable materials are chosen for outdoor artefacts.

Insulation

Insulation is a property that protects. Rubber is used to insulate electric wires to stop the electric current passing through. Other materials are good insulators of heat (aeroboard), sound (foam), or light (dark curtains). **Conduction** is the opposite of insulation.

Ductility & Malleability

Ductility and **malleability** are similar. Ductility is a measure of how well materials can be stretched without breaking while a material's malleability dictates how much it will change shape under pressure. Ductile materials can change shape easily; malleable materials can be formed and shaped by hammering or compressing. Copper and steel are ductile metals and lead, by comparison, is very malleable.

Water resistance

When designing artefacts to be used in damp or wet conditions we need to consider how a material will be affected by water. Some materials, e.g. glues and finishes, are water proof or resistant to water while others are damaged by water. Water resistant materials might be used in bathrooms, kitchens or outdoor areas.

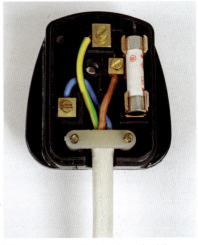
Wiring in plugs is insulated with rubber

Absorbency:

An absorbent material soaks up liquid.

Some woods, like cedar, are durable in damp conditions

Chopping board. Which factors will influence the materials for this chopping board?

79

CHAPTER QUESTIONS

1. List two properties of the following materials:
   - foam rubber
   - pine
   - oak
   - ash
   - glass
   - aluminium.

2. A brittle material will _____ if it is dropped on a hard surface.

3. Describe the relevant properties of the materials used in making the chisel pictured.

4. Name three materials that have good elastic properties.

5. Describe a hard material and give two examples.

6. Give an example of a good electrical insulating material.

7. Suggest two woods that resist decay well. What is this property called?

8. Suggest the properties of materials necessary for making the following items:
   - **(a)** fruit bowl or container
   - **(b)** child's toy
   - **(c)** chopping board
   - **(d)** writing surface.

 # CHAPTER EXERCISES

1. Test three thin strips of different woods and compare them under a bending force using weights.

2. Test and compare three samples of wood to evaluate their resistance to scratching.

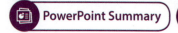 PowerPoint Summary   Weblinks

12 Metals

Properties of metals

Work in pairs to compile a list of important properties of metals that you know. Share and discuss these among the class.

Learning intentions

At the end of this chapter you will:
- Understand about different types of metal.
- Be able to identify different metals and their properties.
- Appreciate how different metals can be used in projects.

Metals like gold and silver have been used for thousands of years. Early civilisations discovered that metals could be heated and hammered to form jewellery, tools, and weapons.

Properties of metals

- Most metals are solids.
- They are dense.
- They are durable.
- They are good conductors of heat.
- They are good conductors of electricity.
- They are ductile and malleable, so they can be bent, formed, and shaped.
- Most have good strength properties.

Ardagh chalice, made in the 8th century AD

Types of metal

Metals are used in many ways

Metals

Ferrous	Non-Ferrous	Alloy
steel	aluminium	brass
iron	copper	bronze
	zinc	
	lead	

Metals can be divided into three main groups

Molten iron being poured into a mould

Ferrous Metals

Ferrous metals contain iron. They are magnetic. Iron is produced as a molten liquid in a furnace, then cast into raw form, called **pig iron**.

Ferrous metals:

Metals that contain iron.

Iron

Pig iron is melted down and poured (cast) into moulds to produce railings or gates and is known as **cast iron**.

Steel

Steel is a mixture of iron and carbon. It is produced in a furnace. Scrap steel can be mixed and melted in with molten iron, but only a maximum of 30% scrap can be added. Carbon gives steel its strength. Graphite, found in pencils, is a common form of carbon. Adding carbon to steel makes it harder and stronger.

Mild Steel

Mild steel, or carbon steel, is the most common form and is used for nuts, bolts, and nails.

High Carbon Steel

A carbon content of 0.6% to 1% makes this type of steel harder. It is used for tools like chisels and plane blades.

High Speed Steel

This is an alloy of steel with tungsten (18%) which makes the steel very hard and wear resistant.

Stainless Steel

Stainless steel is an alloy (mixture) of steel with chrome and nickel. It is used for cutlery and kitchen sinks because it is corrosion resistant.

Why is cast iron suitable for this decorative work?

Stainless steel

List items in the workshop that are made from different steels

Investigate how tool steel is made

83

Non-ferrous metals

Non-ferrous metals contain no iron. There are four main non-ferrous metals: aluminium, copper, zinc, and lead. These and their many alloys account for much of the metal in use today.

Aluminium

Aluminium is plentiful. The natural material, Bauxite, is processed into alumina, from which aluminium is made.

Pure aluminium and its alloys are used in a wide range of products: electric wire, foil, kitchenware, drink cans, windows, boats, and aircraft.

Products made from aluminium

Copper

Copper is a pure metal. It is reddish brown in colour and it can be highly polished. It is a good conductor of heat and electricity so it is used in electric cables. It resists corrosion so it is popular in water pipes and in roofing. It is not as hard as steel and is easily worked and filed.

Products made from copper

Zinc

Zinc is a dull metal that is silver in colour and resists corrosion. It is used with copper to make brass. It is principally used as a coating to prevent steel rusting. The process is known as **galvanising**. Galvanising involves dipping the object into a bath of molten zinc or tin, which coats the surfaces.

Lead

Lead is a dull grey metal which is very dense. It is soft and malleable which makes it easy to form into shape. It is toxic and was used to make paints in the past. It is used in car batteries and in gutters and around chimneys because it does not corrode.

Why is lead suitable for use for roofing?

Investigate other examples of where galvanising is used to protect against rusting

Alloys

Alloys, such as brass and bronze, are metals made by mixing two or more other metals. They usually have improved strength or resistance to corrosion.

Alloy:

A metal made by mixing two or more other metals.

Brass

Brass is an alloy of copper and zinc. It is a hard durable metal, light silvery yellow in colour. Since it polishes well, brass is often used as a decorative metal. It is a good conductor. As a metal

Objects made from brass

85

that resists corrosion, it is used for pipes and plumbing connections as well as screws, hinges and decorative fittings.

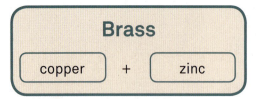

Brass

| copper | + | zinc |

Bronze

Bronze is an alloy of copper and tin. It has been in use since the Bronze Age (2000 – 500 bc). Bronze is a strong, hard and durable metal that resists corrosion. It is dark reddish brown in colour. Bronze is used in casting statues, bells, machine parts and ship fittings.

Bronze

| copper | + | tin |

Bronze is used for statues

Working with metals

Because of their hard surfaces, metals are marked out using a scriber instead of a pencil. The marking process is similar to timber. These are some of the common tools:

Scriber
Used like a pencil to scratch a line on the surface of metal.

Centre Punch (dot punch)
Used to set a small hole in the metal surface where a hole is to be drilled. This mark stops the drill bit from slipping out of position and ensures an accurate hole is drilled.

Scriber

Centre punch (dot punch)

Hacksaws

The hacksaw and junior hacksaw is used to cut small sections of metal.

Hacksaw

Junior hacksaw

Hacksaws

Cutting with a hacksaw

Files

Files are used to smooth and shape the edges of metal. Files are also used for filing plastics. They are obtained in a variety of shapes and grades.

Files

Using a file

Drilling Metal

When drilling a hole in metal, the centre of the hole is first marked with a centre (dot) punch. This centres the point of the drill bit and stops the bit skidding on the smooth surface. Ensure the chuck key is removed from the chuck. Secure the piece on the drill and drill slowly, pulling down the lever of the drill. Drill small sections at a time and allow the waste (burr) to clear the hole.

Safety

⚠ Always wear eye protection.

⚠ Avoid touching the drill or metal after drilling. It will be hot!

⚠ To avoid metal splinters, do not handle the waste.

⚠ Brush up the waste using a dustpan and brush.

Metal Finishes

Many metals – particularly ferrous metals – decay over time. They get scratched and dirtied and are corroded by rain and other chemicals. They are corroded or rust through oxidation.

When exposed to water and moisture in the air, rust is formed on the metal's surface, causing a chemical reaction. The rust gradually eats away at the material. Ferrous metals such as iron and steel are very prone to rust. Copper, aluminium, lead, and brass will tarnish, creating a protective coating that prevents further rust. Copper's tarnish shows as a green **patina**.

Metals can be finished to add protection and to improve their appearance. The finish depends on the type of metal and where it is to be used.

A copper roof's green patina

Polishing
Metals, like brass and copper, can be polished to improve their appearance.

Painting
Iron and steel are often painted for appearance and protection. Metals can be painted similarly to wood.

Surfaces are first prepared and grease removed. A special primer coat is applied. Then undercoats are put on and left to dry. Finally a top finishing coat of gloss paint is put on.

Paints must be maintained by regular repainting. One advantage of paint is that colours can be changed to suit taste each time you repaint.

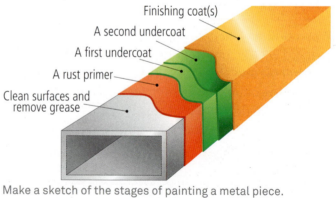

Finishing coat(s)

A second undercoat

A first undercoat

A rust primer

Clean surfaces and remove grease

Make a sketch of the stages of painting a metal piece.

Plastic Coating
Metals are often covered in plastic coating to protect the metal. Coating with plastic allows bright colours to be used to improve appearance. The method uses a thermoplastic powder such as polystyrene. The metal is heated in an oven and dipped into the plastic powder or the plastic is sprayed

onto the heated metal. The plastic melts onto the metal before being cooled.

Metal coating

Metals are often protected or finished by coating them with another metal. This is done by either dipping the piece into a bath of molten metal galvanising or by electroplating. It is done for protection and/or appearance. For example, in silver or gold plating, a piece is covered with a thin layer of expensive gold or silver by electroplating.

Galvanised corrugated sheets

	Stages in galvanisation process
1	Caustic cleaning
2	Rinsing
3	Pickling
4	Rinsing
5	Flux solution
6	Zinc bath
7	Cooling and inspection

Acid baths for the galvanising process

Metal in a zinc bath

Dipping, or galvanising, is used to coat a metal such as steel, that corrodes easily, with a metal that will protect it from corrosion, such as zinc or tin. This galvanising process is used to coat steel with zinc and is used on nails, gates and corrugated roofing.

 # CHAPTER QUESTIONS

1. List four properties common to most metals.

2. Metals can be grouped into three categories. Name these categories.

3. Name two metals that rust and four metals which do not rust.

4. Explain the term **ferrous metal**.

5. Name two alloys that you are familiar with and state where they might be used.

6. Describe the steps necessary for the preparation and finishing of a metal hand rail with a painted finish.

7. This simple elegant box is enhanced by a decorative metal catch. What type of metal is used for this type of catch? Outline two reasons why you would choose this type of catch.

 PowerPoint Summary   Weblinks

13 Plastics and Other Materials

🔍 **KEYWORDS**
- acrylic
- biodegradable
- ceramic
- perspex
- strip heater
- thermoplastic
- thermosetting plastics

LEARNING OUTCOMES
- 1.3, 1.4, 1.8, 1.10
- 2.3, 2.11
- 3.3, 3.4, 3.5, 3.6, 3.7

Learning intentions

At the end of this chapter you will be able to:
- Understand more about different plastics and other materials.
- Be able to identify different plastics and discuss how they are used.
- Be able to use plastic effectively in an artefact.
- Appreciate a wide range of different materials and include some into your practical tasks.
- Understand more fully the environmental impact of your choices of materials.

Plastics and us

Every day, we depend on plastics for a wide range of uses. The world would be very different without them. Although they are versatile and durable, plastic waste has been highlighted as a major cause of pollution for sea and land because of its long life. Most plastics do not break down easily (i.e. they are not **biodegradable**). Many can be recycled or burned (incinerated), but often they are dumped in landfill or in the environment where they don't decay for hundreds of years.

Consider and discuss the many uses of plastics

Plastic damages the environment. How can you make a difference?

How do you use plastics?

Consider how plastics are used in your daily life. Make a list and share with the class. Then, investigate more about the effects of your plastic consumption on the environment.

Properties

Plastics come in many forms that have various properties with advantages and disadvantages. Some are hard and some soft, some are brittle while others are flexible. Some plastics are resistant to high temperatures and to chemicals.

Advantages of plastics	Disadvantages of plastics
• Very durable • Can be formed into complex shapes • Resist corrosion • Poor conductors of heat and electricity • Water resistant • Resistant to chemicals • Many types – some with different colours	• Expensive • Difficult to dispose of/not biodegradable • Hazardous to the environment/not environmentally friendly • Use lots of energy to produce • Can be a fire hazard

Types of plastic

There are many forms of plastic but we can easily classify them into two groups.

Thermoplastics can be re-heated and re-shaped many times.

Thermosetting plastics cannot be reshaped once formed.

```
                    Plastics
                   /        \
   Thermosetting plastics    Thermoplastics
   Heated & formed once      Reheated & formed many
        only                      times
```

Thermoplastics

Thermoplastics can be softened and reshaped by re-heating again and again. Each type of plastic is softened at a different temperature. Some thermoplastics can withstand temperatures over 100°C, although most will soften at temperatures below 100°C.

Acrylic (also known as Perspex®, Plexiglas® and other trade names) is the most common form of thermoplastic used in the Wood Technology room. It is a hard sheet material available in many colours.

Types of thermoplastics
• acrylic
• nylon
• polyvinyl chloride (PVC)
• polythene
• polystyrene
• polycarbonate

USES

- flooring
- hose pipes
- plastic bags
- drinking cups
- clothing
- insulation
- signs
- windows, fencing, and greenhouses

Thermoplastics in daily use

Thermosetting Plastics

When formed, thermosetting plastic is rigid. It can be heated and shaped only once. Although it cannot be re-softened and shaped again, thermosetting plastic is perfect for items that must withstand high temperatures, such as in a handle of a saucepan. Polyurethane and polyester are thermosetting plastics.

Thermosetting plastics
• epoxy resins
• polyester
• polyurethane
• bakelite
• melamine resin

 USES

- bottles
- fabrics
- handles
- worktops
- kitchenware
- boats

Examples of thermosetting plastic in use

Working with plastic

Acrylic (**Perspex**®) sheet is widely used in the wood technology room and is suitable for many tasks. It is obtained in a range of colours and thicknesses (3-6mm). It is easily cut, filed, and finished with simple tools. Acrylic can be beautiful, especially when the edges are properly finished.

Marking out

Acrylic sheet is supplied with a removable protective layer to prevent surface scratches. Lines and other marking can be carried out as you would on a piece of wood using a fine marker or biro for clarity.

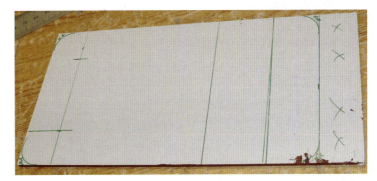

Marking out on a piece of acrylic. Why are the protective sheets left on?

Cutting

Thin plastic can be cut with a knife or scissors. Plastic sheet can be cut by the teacher using a circular saw, tenon saw, hacksaw, or scroll saw. It is important that the piece is held firmly in the vice or on the scroll saw table while cutting.

Polystyrene can be cut using a hot wire cutter. However, this must be done in a well-ventilated room and protective masks should be worn to protect from the resulting fumes.

Cutting acrylic

Filing and smoothing

After being cut, the rough edges of acrylic must be filed and polished to be as smooth as the surface. The plastic is held firmly in a vice while finishing the edges. Since its surfaces are easily scratched, leave the protective paper on for as long as possible.

Hot wire cutter. Why are protective masks required when using this?

Stages in smoothing and polishing the edges of acrylic

1. Once the piece has been cut to shape and drilled, the edges are filed smooth with a metal file.
2. Next, the edges are smoothed again using fine sandpaper (320 grit) to remove any marks.
3. Finally, the edges are polished with a clean cloth and metal polishing compound.
4. The finished edge will have a high gloss shine.

A finished acrylic piece

Drilling

Holes can be drilled in plastics for decoration, screws, nuts and bolts, and other fittings. An ordinary high speed steel (HSS) drill bit can be used. It is the same type as used to drill metal and wood. When drilling the plastic, the piece is held firmly to prevent it moving using a vice or clamp. A piece of wood underneath supports the piece so it doesn't splinter as it is bored.

Drilling acrylic

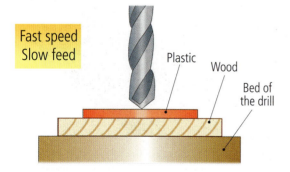

Fast speed
Slow feed

Plastic
Wood
Bed of the drill

What are the steps in drilling plastic safely?

To prevent chipping the plastic, the drill bit is pressed or fed slowly down through the piece (slow drill feed) and the bit is spinning quickly (fast drill speed).

Larger diameter holes may be cut using a hole saw and drilling from one side, then the other.

 Search online for a 4:40 minute video called 'Drill acrylic | Drill Perspex | Drill Plexiglas' by the Ultimate Handyman.

Hole saw drill bits

Bending

Thermoplastics, particularly acrylic, are used widely in wood technology projects. Acrylic can be heated and reheated to create shapes and simple objects easily. Heat is applied precisely using an electric **strip heater**. The heat softens the acrylic, which can then be formed to a particular shape. Once it cools, the acrylic hardens into the desired shape or position.

Electric strip heater

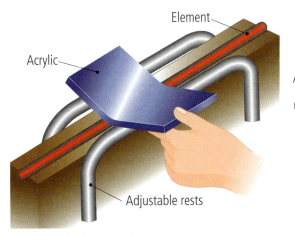

Using an electric strip heater

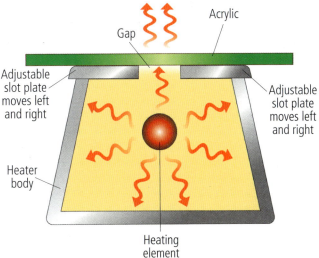

Section through a strip heater showing heat distribution as the plastic passes through the gap.

For each bend, add the thickness of the sheet to the length of the piece. This allows for the bend in the length of the piece.

Formers

A **former** is a simple mould that assists the accurate bending of the acrylic. It helps ensure the correct angle is obtained and that lines or spacing is accurately achieved.

Wood is a suitable material for making formers because it does not cool the plastic too quickly before it achieves its final shape. A wooden former can also be easily made into the necessary shape. Formers also ensure that the same shape can be accurately replicated many times.

When the acrylic is soft enough, the piece is clamped firmly to the shape former in the vice or to the bench. Using gentle and even pressure, bend the plastic to the required angle. As the hot acrylic cools, it tends to spring back to its original shape slightly. As you bend the piece, you should allow for this by bending it slightly further than needed.

The softened acrylic is bent around a wood former

Planning your project

In small groups, discuss the steps you would follow in marking out, drilling, cutting, and bending a simple piece of acrylic to form the pencil stand pictured here.

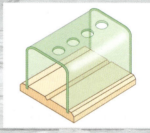

Artefacts made with acrylic need careful planning so each task is done in the correct order. The assignment above will help you with this. It is important that a development is first drawn of the piece, unfolded (flat), so the shape and positions of cuts, holes, and bend lines can be planned.

A **development** of the shape with the bend lines is drawn onto the protective sheet. When the shape is prepared, the piece can be heated along the bend lines to soften the acrylic. Care must be taken not to overheat the acrylic, as this damages the finished piece.

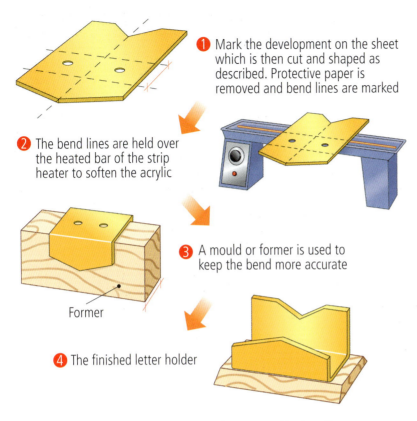

❶ Mark the development on the sheet which is then cut and shaped as described. Protective paper is removed and bend lines are marked

❷ The bend lines are held over the heated bar of the strip heater to soften the acrylic

Former

❸ A mould or former is used to keep the bend more accurate

❹ The finished letter holder

- When handling acrylic, care must be taken not to put too much pressure on the plastic, as it might crack.
- Remember to **wear protective gloves and eye protection** when handling hot materials like acrylic.

The basic stages of building an acrylic letter stand by bending.

Glass-reinforced plastic (GRP)

Boats and canoes are often made from glass fibre strengthened with polyester resins. This material can be formed into laminates and moulded to shapes. Glass fibre and carbon fibre are used to produce stronger materials. GRP is strong, tough, and durable enough to be used in boats, cars and bus body shells.

Glass-reinforced plastic (GRP) in use

Textiles

Textiles or cloths are widely used and will therefore suit many tasks and projects in the wood technology room. Cloth is used to add colour and texture. It makes chairs and stools comfortable. It is used to line the inside of jewellery boxes and other items. A layer of felt under lamps or ornaments protects surfaces from being scratched.

Protective felt layer under desk clock

There are a variety of textiles available for covering stools or chairs. Some, such as leather and leatherette, can be wiped clean, which is useful.

Foam

A variety of foam is available: thickness and densities vary. They are used for padding seats of stools and chairs. Foam can be easily cut with a knife. When buying foam, be sure that it meets fire safety regulations.

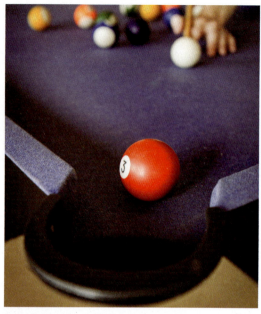

Snooker table. What are the materials used and why?

Applying cloth upholstery to a stool

Evaluate how this child's toy is enhanced by the choice of materials.

Glass & ceramics

Ceramic materials such as tile and glass are hard wearing and corrosion resistant. They are easily cleaned. Very resistant to heat, they are poor conductors of electricity. However, they are brittle and are difficult to cut and shape. Glass or mirror glass is used for picture frames or mirrors. Tiles can be used in projects for protection or to improve decoration or add colour.

Evaluate how these pot stands are improved by the materials chosen.

Glass can be obtained in different thicknesses and forms. It can be coloured or mirrored. Toughened glass should be used in projects where glass may break. Toughened glass has not only been treated to make it stronger, but additionally, toughened glass will break into small pea-sized pieces, which are much less dangerous. It is used in doors or table tops.

 CHAPTER QUESTIONS

1 List four properties common to plastics.

2 Explain the terms thermoplastic and thermosetting plastic.

3 A list of common plastics is given below. In each case state whether it is a thermoplastic or thermosetting plastic.

Plastic Type	Thermoplastic	Thermosetting
PVC		
Polyester		
Acrylic		
Melamine		
Nylon		

4 List three advantages of acrylic that make it useful in wood technology projects.

5 List two safety precautions you would take when drilling acrylic at the pillar drill.

6 Outline with notes and sketches the steps you would take to finish the edges of a piece of acrylic before you would bend it into shape.

7. List two precautions that should be taken when handling hot acrylic.

8. Analyse and list the factors that must be considered when planning the tasks needed to complete an acrylic piece like the small photograph holder pictured here?

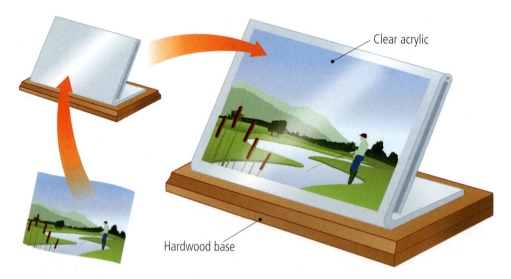

Clear acrylic

Hardwood base

9. Outline the steps you would follow in drilling the holes needed to take the screws which would attach the acrylic photo holder to the hardwood base in question 8 above.

10. Give two advantages of ceramic that make them useful in project work.

11. Describe the purpose of a former or jig when bending acrylic into shape.

12. Create a poster or instruction sheet to teach first year students how to drill acrylic in a safe and correct manner.

13. Create an instruction leaflet to inform first year students how to safely heat and bend a piece of acrylic using a former.

 PowerPoint Summary  Weblinks

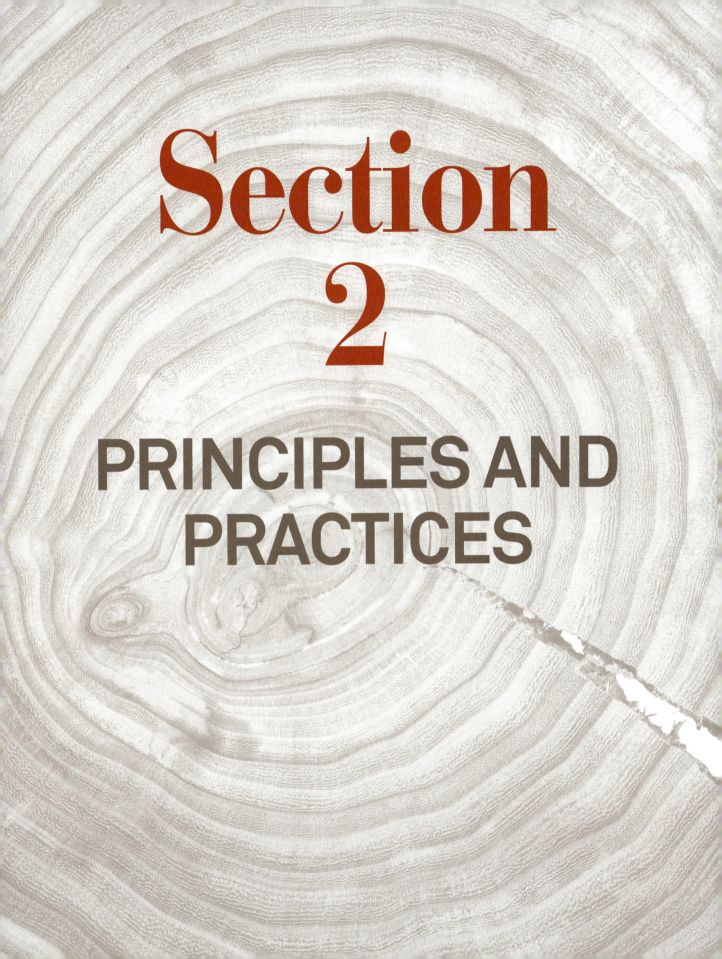

Section
2

PRINCIPLES AND PRACTICES

14 Hand Tools

Learning intentions

At the end of this chapter you will be able to:
- Be able to identify basic hand tools, their name, parts and function.
- Use basic hand tools safely and appropriately.

⚠ All of the many hand tools in the Wood Technology room should be used as instructed to keep you safe.

Marking out

Accuracy is the key to successful work. Steel rulers and measuring tapes are used to measure accurately. Distances are measured in millimetres (mm).

⚠ Measure twice. Cut once.

Steel rulers

Marking knife

A sharp 2H pencil is used to draw lines on wood and other materials. The **marking** knife is used to mark lines to be cut with a saw. The knife cuts the wood fibres which leave a clean finish when the wood is cut. It is also used to cut card, veneer, and light material. You must be careful when using any knife, so as not to cut your fingers. Also, any line scored in the wood is very difficult to remove.

Pencil and marking knife

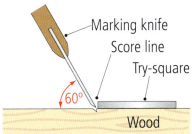

Why is the marking knife tilted at an angle when being used?

Try square

The **try square** is used to draw lines across the faces of material at right angles to the face side and edge. It is also used to check if surfaces are square to each other.

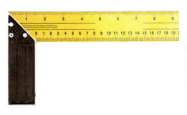

Try square

Squaring lines across timber

Try the try square

On a scrap piece of wood, test the try square in your bench to check if it is perfectly square.

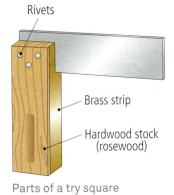

Parts of a try square

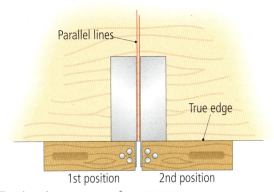

Testing the try square for accuracy

The blade of the try square is at 90° to the stock. Different sizes of blade can be obtained between 100–300mm. The square must be protected from damage and regularly tested for square.

Marking gauge

Marking gauges are made from beech. They have a plastic locking screw. Brass strips in the stock help to reduce wear.

The **gauge** is used by holding the stock firmly against the edge while dragging the spur so it scores the wood.

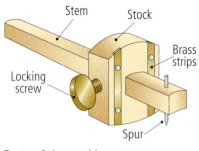

Parts of the marking gauge

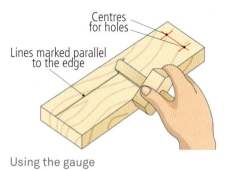

Using the gauge

USES

- To mark lines in the wood parallel to an edge or surface
- To mark centre points for holes to be drilled

Mortise gauge

Similar to the marking gauge, the mortise gauge has two spurs and is made from a hardwood – usually rosewood or mahogany. It has one fixed spur while the second spur is adjusted by a thumbscrew on the stem.

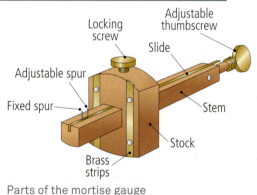

Parts of the mortise gauge

Mortise and tenon joint

USES

- To mark two parallel lines at once
- For marking a mortise and tenon joint

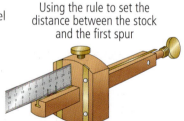

Using a mortise chisel to set the distance between the spurs

Using the rule to set the distance between the stock and the first spur

Setting the mortise gauge

Cutting gauge

The cutting gauge uses a small blade in place of a spur. The small blade is held in place using a wedge or screw.

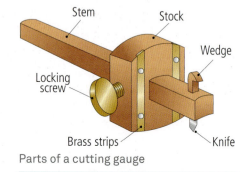

Parts of a cutting gauge

Thumb gauge

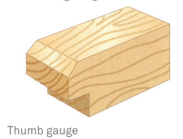

Thumb gauge

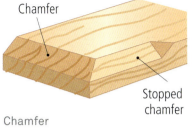

Chamfer

Chamfer

Stopped chamfer

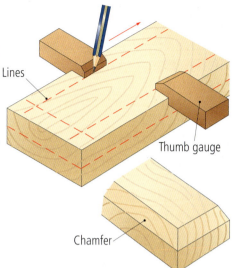

Lines

Thumb gauge

Chamfer

Using the thumb gauge to mark out chamfers

A thumb gauge is easily made from wood. It is used to mark out chamfers. A chamfer is where an edge is bevelled at an angle (usually of 45 degrees) using a plane or router as shown in the sketch.

Compass / dividers

Your compass or dividers can be used to mark circles or curves onto wood or other materials. The dividers can also be used to check measurements.

Problem solving

Investigate how you might draw a circle with a larger diameter than a compass can create.

Compass and dividers

Sliding bevel

The sliding **bevel** is used to mark lines of various angles on the wood. Similar to the try square, the blade can be adjusted easily to set the required angle.

Sliding bevel being set to a setsquare

Sliding bevel in use

107

Callipers

The Vernier **callipers** are the most popular callipers and are very useful for taking and transferring measurements. They are very accurate because the external jaws are used to measure the outside diameter of a cylinder (pipe/woodturning).

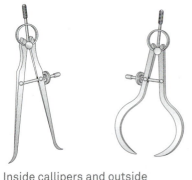

Inside callipers and outside callipers

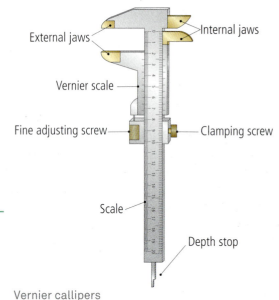

External jaws
Internal jaws
Vernier scale
Fine adjusting screw
Clamping screw
Scale
Depth stop

Vernier callipers

Cutting Tools

Saws

Saws come in many varieties, each designed for a particular use. Machines and power tools are becoming popular, but handsaws are still used for their safety, accuracy, and portability.

Handsaws can be divided into three groups according to use:
• Cutting larger sections and sheets
• Cutting smaller sections and finer cuts
• Curved work.

Selection of saws

Teeth

The difference between the saws is in the size number and shape of the teeth and the way they cut the wood. The number of teeth per 25mm (inch) of a blade is labelled on the blade. The teeth must be regularly sharpened and protected from damage. Take care to avoid cutting nails hidden in wood.

Kerf and Set

• Always cut on the waste side of the line
• The **kerf** is the cut made by the saw teeth. The kerf is wider than the thickness of the blade.
• The teeth of the saw are **set** wider than the blade. This allows the teeth to move freely in the kerf without getting stuck.

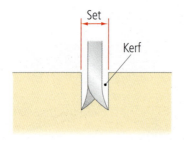

Set
Kerf

The saw kerf (groove) is slightly wider than the blade

Large handsaws

USES

● Cutting larger boards and sheet materials.

Ripsaw

There are three larger handsaws: the ripsaw, the cross cut saw, and the universal saw. The ripsaw cuts with a chiselling action and is used when cutting with the grain direction. The cross cut saw has teeth shaped like two knives to slice across the grain. The universal saw is the most common and it has teeth which that will cut both across and along the grain of the wood.

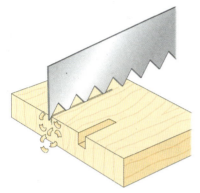

Ripsaw teeth leave a flat-bottomed cut

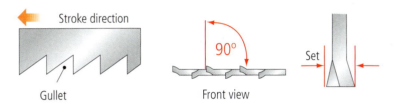

Ripsaw teeth are shaped with 4–8 teeth per 25mm

Modern handsaws with very sharp, hardened teeth are inexpensive and therefore tend to be disposed of after prolonged use.

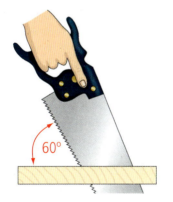

The angle of the blade to the face of the work is 60° for rip sawing

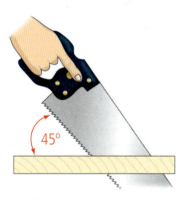

The angle of the cross cut saw is 45° to the work surface when cross-cutting

 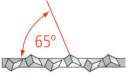 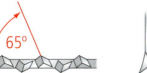

6–8 teeth per 25mm

Front view

Cross cut teeth are shaped with 6–8 teeth per 25mm

Tenon saw

USES

- General light bench work
- Cutting straight lines
- Cutting tenons (as its name suggests)

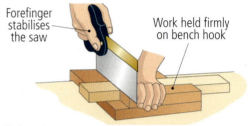

Cutting a tenon

Cut a tenon with your tenon saw and write out the step-by-step process of how it was done.

The tenon saw is the most commonly used saw in the wood technology room. It has a high carbon steel blade, hardwood handle, and a brass strip on the back of the blade to keep it stiff. A tenon saw usually has 10-15 teeth per 25mm.

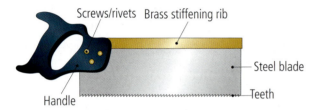

Screws/rivets Brass stiffening rib
Steel blade
Handle
Teeth

Parts of the tenon saw

Forefinger stabilises the saw
Work held firmly on bench hook

Using the tenon saw

Procedure for cutting a tenon

Correct
Saw cut on waste side of line

Incorrect
Saw cut on line

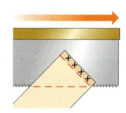

1 Firstly, place the piece vertically in the vice and make a vertical cut down of 5 mm–6 mm.

2 Make the saw cut on the waste side of the line that is marked on the timber.

3 Tilt the piece forward and fix it in the vice again. Continue the cut down along the gauge line, keeping the edge of the saw in the full kerf (groove) as the sawing continues.

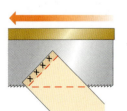

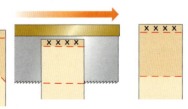

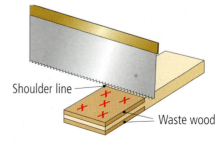

4 Reverse the piece and repeat the saw cut on the other side. This leaves a small triangular piece unsawn inside the tenon.

5 Fix the piece in a vertical position once more and cut down to the line, sawing through the triangular piece.

Shoulder line
Waste wood

6 Finally, remove the shoulders.

Dovetail saw

● Cutting dovetails and other light and fine work

The dovetail saw is smaller than the tenon saw, with finer teeth, usually 18–20 teeth per 25mm.

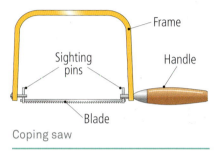

Dovetail saw

Coping saw

● The coping saw is used for cutting curves.

The coping saw has a fine metal blade stretched between two slotted pins in a frame. The blade is tensioned by twisting the handle. The blade can be adjusted or removed by loosening the handle. The blades break easily, but are cheap to replace. Coping saws cut on the pull stroke, so the teeth always point back towards the handle.

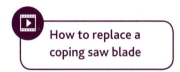

Coping saw

Replacing a broken blade
1 Remove the old blade or parts.
2 Twist the handle to loosen it.
3 Slot the new blade into the pins.
4 Make sure the teeth point backwards towards the handle.
5 Retighten the handle.
6 Align the sight pins.

How to replace a coping saw blade

Fret saw
This is similar to a coping saw, but with a larger frame and a very fine blade. It is used in very fine curved cuts in thin sheets of metal plastic and wood.

Compass saw and pad saw
Both the compass saw and the pad saw are used for cutting small holes in light sheets and in difficult to reach areas. The blades are easily bent, so care is taken when using them.

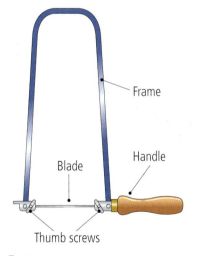

Fret saw parts

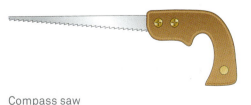

Compass saw   Pad saw

Chisels

Chisels are widely used in wood technology for paring and shaping wood. Their blades are made from high carbon steel. There are two main types, pictured: a square-edged chisel and bevelled-edged chisel. The bevelled-edge chisel is suited to pare into tight corners.

The ferrule is a brass collar that prevents the handle from splitting. Modern chisels have handles of timber or moulded plastic. The edge of the chisel is kept sharp with regular sharpening.

Chisels in your locker are mainly used for paring trenches and paring curves. There are chisels for mortising and specialist chisels for carving and wood turning.

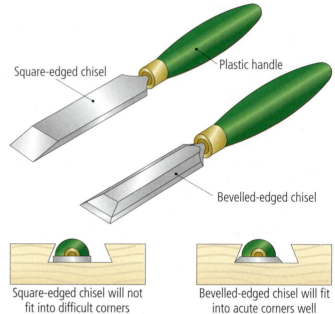

Square-edged chisel

Plastic handle

Bevelled-edged chisel

Square-edged chisel will not fit into difficult corners

Bevelled-edged chisel will fit into acute corners well

Square-edged chisel and bevelled-edged firmer chisels

Edge
Blade
Tang
Handle
Ferrule
Shoulder

Parts of a chisel

The cutting edge is made of two distinct angles (bevels). The grinding angle (20°–25°) is made by grinding the edge on a grinding stone. The second bevel (30°) is made by sharpening the edge using an oilstone. Sharpening is also known as honing.

Bevelled-edge chisel

Firmer Chisels

- Paring trenches
- Vertical paring to a line
- Paring curves
- Chamfers

Firmer chisels are available in a variety of widths from 3mm to 50mm.

Always keep both hands behind the cutting edge of the chisel and work away from the body.

Vertical paring

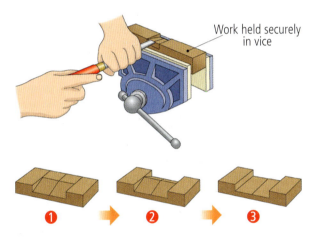

Work held securely in vice

❶ ➡ ❷ ➡ ❸

Paring a trench

Mortise chisel

The mortise chisel has a thicker blade and a stronger handle. It is designed to withstand repeated blows from the mallet while mortising. The handle is made from moulded plastic or durable hardwood strengthened with a metal ferrule to prevent splitting.

Mortise chisel

Using a Mortise chisel

Hammers and Mallets

Hammers and mallets are impact tools, so they must be strong and durable.

There are a variety of hammers available. They also vary in size according to their weight. The head of a hammer is held on with a wedge. If the head of a hammer is loose, it should be reported to the teacher.

The head of a hammer is held on with wedges

A claw hammer is a heavier hammer used for general work and carpentry (floors, roofs & carpentry). The claw is used to take nails and pins out of wood.

Fair blow – nail struck squarely; hand at bottom of shaft

Driving a nail

To upright

Pack and pull to upright

A claw hammer is used to pull out nails. Why is a waste piece used?

A Warrington hammer is for lighter work, furniture and cabinetmaking, while a pin hammer is for very light work and upholstery.

Which hammer for the job?

For each of the hammers pictured, outline its features and when it is the most appropriate choice.

Claw hammer

Warrington hammer

Pin hammer

114

Nail Punch

The nail punch is used in the Wood Technology room to drive panel pins and small nails below the surface of the wood. The resulting holes are filled with wood filler and then sanded. The punch has a slightly hollow point to stop it slipping off the head of the pin. Different sizes are available.

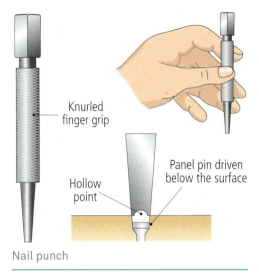

Knurled finger grip

Hollow point

Panel pin driven below the surface

Nail punch

Mallets

Mallets are usually made from beech. The faces are shaped so that they strike the top of the chisel squarely. The handle is tapered, so to hold the head firmly on. The carver's mallet is round so that it fits comfortably in the hand and will give good control as the carver strikes the chisel.

Carver's mallet in use

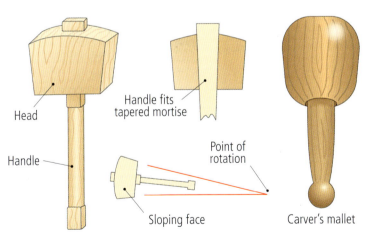

Head

Handle

Handle fits tapered mortise

Point of rotation

Sloping face

Carver's mallet

Mallet and carver's mallet. Why are they made from beech?

115

Pincers and pliers

Pincers are used to pull nails and panel pins out of wood. They have two handles pivoted in the centre that allow the nails to be tightly gripped.

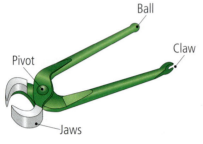

Use a block of waste wood under the jaws to give better leverage

Pincers. Consider carefully how this tool works. What forces are being used?

Using the pincers

Pliers are used for gripping items tightly, twisting, and for work on wires. There are different types suited for different tasks. Common types are pictured here.

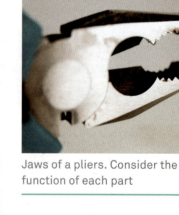

Jaws of a pliers. Consider the function of each part

Combination pliers, wire cutters, long nose pliers, vice grips, pincers (left to right)

Boring tools

A drill or other boring tool is used when holes need to be drilled. They come in different sizes and shapes. The drill bit is gripped firmly by jaws in a chuck. As the chuck turns, the drill cuts through the wood. Some boring tools are powered, while others are manual (hand driven).

Bradawl

The **bradawl** has a handle and a steel blade. It is used to mark small pilot holes for screws and nails. It may cause splitting if used too close to the end of a thin piece.

Bradawl used to make small pilot holes for nails and screws

Carpenter's Brace

The carpenter's **brace** has been used for many years. It uses a larger bit to bore holes between 6mm–25mm generally. Special auger bits are used with this drill.

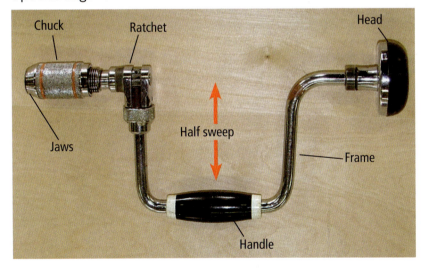

Carpenter's brace

Auger bits used in a brace or cordless drill

- The jaws hold the bit inside the chuck.
- The brace has a ratchet which allows the bit to turn in one direction only.

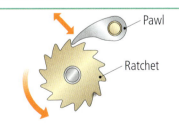

The ratchet mechanism allows movement in one direction only. Where would this be useful?

Using the brace

Care must be taken when boring a hole through a piece to avoid splintering as the bit breaks through. It is best to bore from both sides, one after the other. A scrap piece may be used to support the back when drilling from one side only.

When boring to a specific depth, a strip of tape can be wrapped around the bit to indicate when to stop. Alternatively, a special depth stop can be made as shown below.

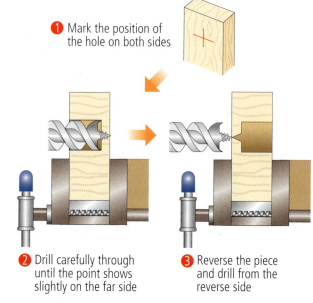

1 Mark the position of the hole on both sides

2 Drill carefully through until the point shows slightly on the far side

3 Reverse the piece and drill from the reverse side

Stages of boring a hole with a brace and a bit to avoid breakout

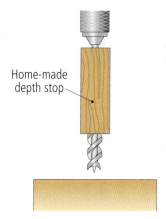

Home-made depth stop

Methods for drilling a hole to a specific depth

Hand drill

This simple hand drill or wheel brace is used to drill holes of small diameter (1mm–10mm), small pilot holes, or countersinking holes for screws.

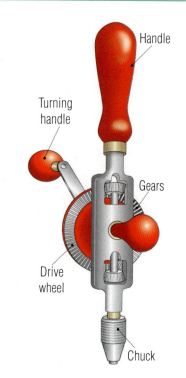

Handle

Turning handle

Gears

Drive wheel

Chuck

Features of a hand drill

Drill Bits

Drills or drill bits for drilling holes in wood, metal, and plastic come in a range of sizes. The centre of the hole is carefully marked in each case before drilling.

A range of drill bits. Name each type and state where they are used

Plug cutter drill bit

Forstner bit

Brad point bit

Twist bit

Countersink bit

119

Planes and Spokeshaves

Planes and spokeshaves are tools used to smooth and shape wood. In the past, planes were made from beech wood. Special moulding planes were made by individual craftspeople to suit particular tasks. A lot of smoothing tasks are now done by machine.

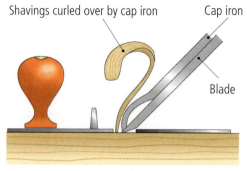

The cap iron is shaped to curl the shavings forward, keeping the mouth of the plane clear

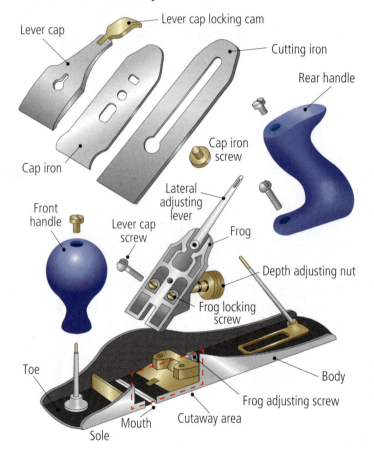

Parts of the plane

The jack plane

The name jack plane comes from the expression 'Jack of all trades'. It is a general purpose plane. Used to smooth surfaces and square the edges of boards, it is also used to plane material to width and thickness.

The plane should always be left resting on its side because its blade is easily damaged. The blade depth and position can be adjusted easily to take off the correct amount of wood shaving.

Jack plane and smoothing plane. Describe the differences between them.

The smoothing plane

The shorter smoothing plane is used for smoothing, removing minor blemishes, and preparing surfaces for sanding. It is also used to plane chamfers and basic shaping.

Try-plane

This is a long plane used to plane longer pieces to make them flat. It is used to smooth long boards and for preparing the edges of boards for jointing.

Try-plane

Block Plane

Small and versatile, the block plane is used for light work, small pieces, chamfers, and planing end grain. It fits easily into the hand, so it is easy to use. It's blade depth is easily adjustable, but it has no cap iron.

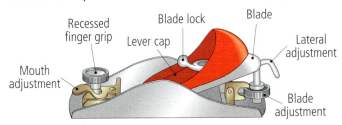
Parts of the block plane

Using the block plane

Rebate plane and plough plane

These specialist planes were used to remove rebates and plough grooves from wood. They are rarely used nowadays because these tasks are easily done using a router and specialist bits.

Rebate

Stopped rebate

Plough groove

Rebates and plough groove

Rebate plane

121

Planing end grain

It is important that end grain is finished smooth. When planing end grain, the fibres of the wood can splinter or tear at the edge. Care must be taken to avoid this. The diagrams below show ways that end grain can be successfully planed.

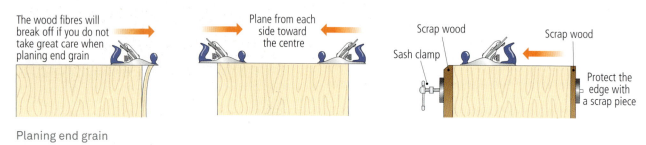

The wood fibres will break off if you do not take great care when planing end grain

Plane from each side toward the centre

Scrap wood
Scrap wood
Sash clamp
Protect the edge with a scrap piece

Planing end grain

Spokeshaves

Spokeshaves are designed for smoothing and shaping curved surfaces. They have a blade that is fixed in position with a locking cap and screw. There are two types.

Convex	Concave
• has a flat base • used for flat surface or convex curves	• has a curved base • used on concave curves

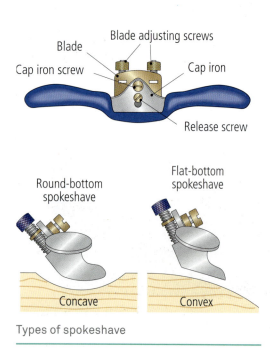

Blade adjusting screws
Blade
Cap iron screw
Cap iron
Release screw

Round-bottom spokeshave
Flat-bottom spokeshave

Concave
Convex

Types of spokeshave

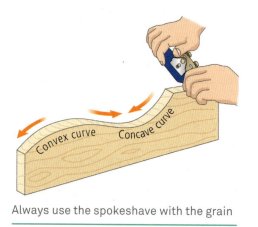

Convex curve
Concave curve

Always use the spokeshave with the grain

Shaping tools

Files and rasps

Files and **rasps** may look very similar to each other, but they are not used for the same purposes. Notice how rasps have larger teeth than files. Used for rough shaping and sculpting of wood, rasps leave a rough surface that must be cleaned and sanded. Files, on the other hand, have fine teeth that are used on plastics and metals. There are a variety of shapes available.

Files and rasps

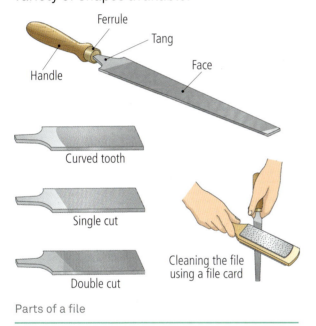

Parts of a file

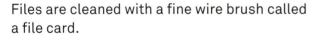

Files are cleaned with a fine wire brush called a file card.

Surform (shapers)

Surforms are rough shaping tools. They come with different shaped blades to suit particular tasks. The blades are simply replaced when blunt or damaged.

Surform tools

Screwdrivers

Screwdrivers come in a variety of shapes, sizes, and types to fit various screws. Common types are shown below.

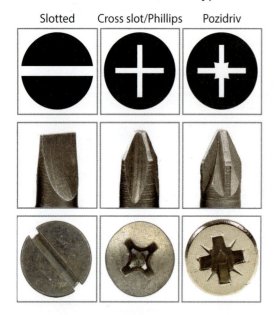

Slotted   Cross slot/Phillips   Pozidriv

Common types of screw found in the wood technology room

Screwdrivers. Why are they so different?

It is easy to damage the head of a screw if the correct type and size of screwdriver is not used. Over-tightening can also damage the head of the screw.

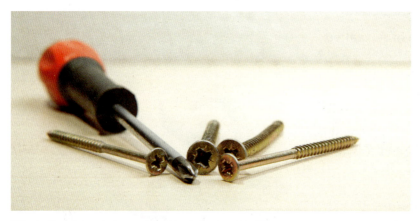

Why is the correct size screwdriver always used?

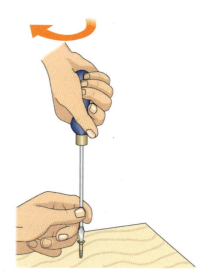

What type of force is being used here?

⚠ Always hold a screwdriver with both hands.

Using the force

Consider what type of force you are using when driving a screw.

Driving a screw

A pilot hole should always be prepared before driving a screw. A pilot hole makes it easier to fit the screw and prevents excessive force from being used and also prevents the wood from splitting. Pilot holes are especially important for hardwoods.

1 Bore a hole to take the shank of the screw

2 Bore a hole smaller than the thread of the screw

3 Countersink the hole with a countersink bit

4 Insert the screw

Steps in drilling a pilot hole for a screw

Cramps

In the Wood Technology room, there are a variety of **cramps**. Long sash cramps are for gluing wide boards and projects while smaller g-cramps and quick release cramps are used for securing material firmly on the bench and for holding pieces in place with pressure while glue sets.

Types of cramp

CHAPTER QUESTIONS

1 Give the name and function/use for each of the following tools pictured.

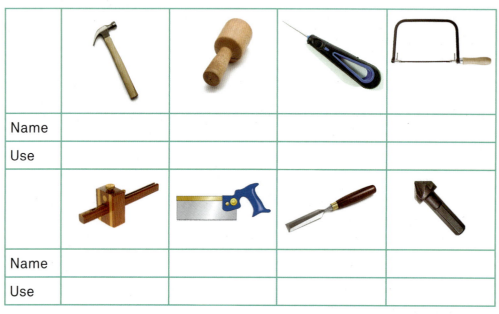

Name				
Use				
Name				
Use				

2 Describe what safety precautions you would follow when:

(a) pairing a trench with a chisel
(b) carrying a chisel across a room
(c) using a marking knife

3 Name the parts of the saw shown in the diagram.

4 Describe the function of the parts in the saw pictured right.

5 What is the groove made by the cutting action of the saw (right) known as?

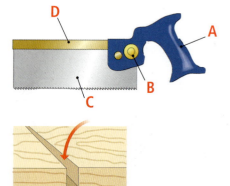

6 What causes the wood fibres to split away from the wood when planing end grain as shown in the photo?

7 Name the planes shown below and give a brief outline of where they are used.

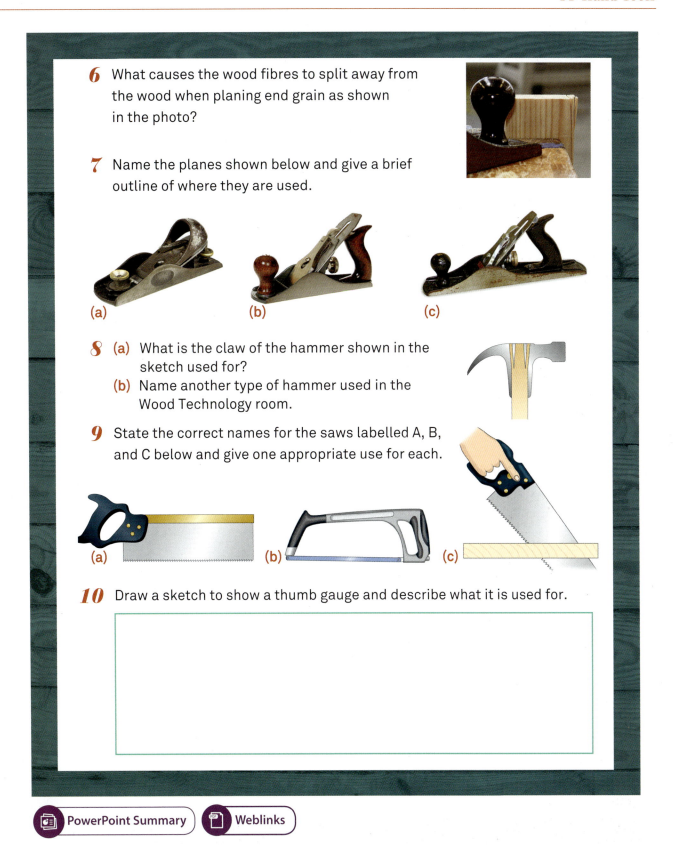

(a)   (b)   (c)

8 **(a)** What is the claw of the hammer shown in the sketch used for?
  (b) Name another type of hammer used in the Wood Technology room.

9 State the correct names for the saws labelled A, B, and C below and give one appropriate use for each.

(a)   (b)   (c)

10 Draw a sketch to show a thumb gauge and describe what it is used for.

PowerPoint Summary   Weblinks

15 Sharpening Tools

KEYWORDS
- grindstone
- burr
- oilstone
- saw set
- slipstone

LEARNING OUTCOMES
- 1.3, 1.8, 1.9, 1.10
- 2.11, 2.12

Learning intentions

At the end of this chapter you will be able to:
- Understand the importance of keeping tools in good condition.
- Be able to identify when a blade needs sharpening or grinding.
- Be able to outline procedure in grinding and sharpening blades.

Care of equipment

For safety and performance, all tools need to be maintained and cared for. They need to be kept in good condition, clean and sharp at all times. Since chisels, saws, and planes are the most regularly used tools, we will look at how they are kept sharp.

The sharp edges of blades on planes, chisels, and marking knives can be easily damaged or get worn over time. Chisel and plane blades are sharpened in two stages: grinding and sharpening. This produces the two bevels or angles at the edge.

Grinding chisels and plane blades
Grinding is done on an electric grinder or horizontal grindstone or sharpening system.

Electric grinder

Grinding is done periodically to reproduce a clean, ground edge on a blade of a chisel, marking knife, or plane to:

- fix a damaged edge
- bring back a clean bevel when the edge wears over time through repeated sharpening
- square the bevel and edge after they have become rounded through incorrect sharpening.

Sharpening system

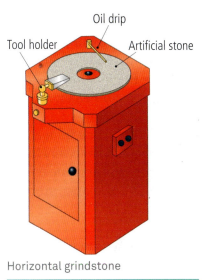

Horizontal grindstone

Grinding wears down the blade, so it is only done when needed.

The edge is damaged

The edge worn down through repeated sharpening

The edge is rounded by incorrect sharpening

When would you grind a blade?

Evaluate your chisels

Examine the chisels in your locker for evidence of damage. Do they need to be ground?

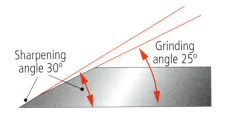

Sharpening and grinding angles

Grinding angle: 25°
Sharpening angle: 30°

Sharpening chisels and plane blades

Blades of planes and chisels are regularly sharpened on an **oilstone**. Regular sharpening keeps the edge very sharp so the blade cuts more easily.

Oilstones are made from abrasive stones or grits that vary between coarse and very fine. Combination stones with coarse grit on one side and fine on the other are very common. **Slipstones** are shaped stones that fit the shapes of other tools.

Oilstone

Slipstones

Sharpening stones. When you would you use the shaped slipstones?

Sharpening process

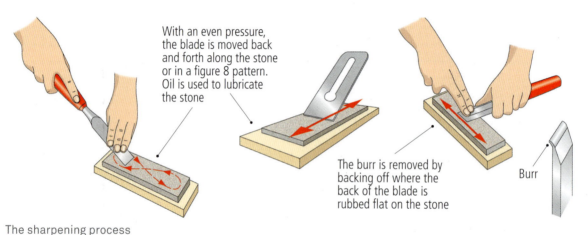

With an even pressure, the blade is moved back and forth along the stone or in a figure 8 pattern. Oil is used to lubricate the stone

The burr is removed by backing off where the back of the blade is rubbed flat on the stone

Burr

The sharpening process

Oil is used on the oilstone to:
• reduce wear and friction
• help the tool move on the stone
• prevent clogging of the stone.

Sharpening guides are often used to keep the blade at the correct angle.
1 Oil is spread on the stone.
2 The blade is moved with firm pressure in a forward and backward motion or figure of eight.
3 A **burr** builds up at the edge.
4 The blade is turned over with the back flat on the stone. It is moved back and forth to remove the burr.

Slipstones are used to sharpen gouges and carving chisels.

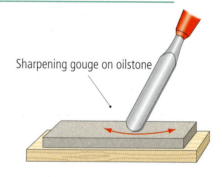
Sharpening gouge on oilstone

Removing the burr with a slipstone

Sharpening a gouge

Sharpening saws

Saws are sharpened by a specialist technician known as a saw doctor. Modern, inexpensive saws have teeth with specially hardened tips that stay sharp longer. They cannot be sharpened. The blade or saw is simply replaced when the blade becomes worn or blunt.

Steps to sharpen a saw

1 The blade is held firmly in the vice.
2 The tips of the teeth are levelled using a file.
3 A triangular file is used to file and shape new teeth.
4 A **saw set** is used to bend (set) each point alternately to the left and to the right.

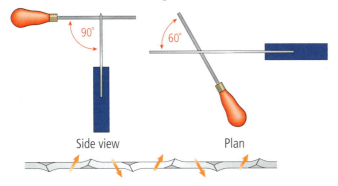

Filing the teeth of a tenon saw or cross cut saw

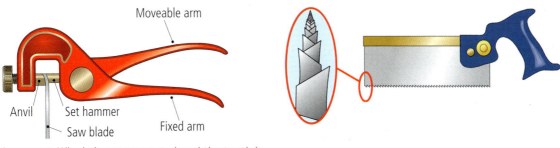

A saw set. Why is it necessary to bend the teeth in this way?

Teeth set on a saw blade

Chisel maintenance

Design a one page instruction card or leaflet detailing the process of keeping a chisel sharp.

CHAPTER QUESTIONS

1 Name one tool that is sharpened using a slipstone

2 What tools are sharpened using an oilstone?

3 What is the purpose of putting oil on the sharpening stone before sharpening a blade?

4 What steps would you take if a plane blade has been damaged like that shown in the illustration?

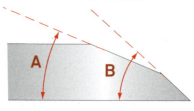

Damaged plane blade

5 What might cause the damage shown on the plane blade?

6 The diagram shows a close-up view of the cutting edge of a chisel. Draw a neat sketch showing the two angles and name each one.

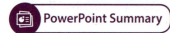

Cutting edge of a chisel

PowerPoint Summary   **Weblinks**

16 Power Tools

KEYWORDS
- cordless
- drill
- electricity
- fuse
- portable
- rechargeable
- extractor
- transformer
- biscuit joiner
- router
- sander

LEARNING OUTCOMES
- 1.3, 1.7, 1.10
- 2.11

Learning intentions

At the end of this chapter you will be able to:
- Name and describe the function of a selection of commonly used power tools.
- Outline the main safety precautions to be followed when using power tools.
- Demonstrate how certain power tools are used effectively in task work.

In the past few years, power tools of all kinds have become essential pieces of equipment for professionals and are common in most homes for DIY.

Since powered tools can be dangerous, care must be taken with them at all times. Only use tools with the permission of the teacher, as some equipment should not be used by students. Electrically powered tools also have increased risk because they are connected to mains electricity.

Selection of power tools

Advantages	Disadvantages
• Work processes can be carried out quickly. • Repetitive work can be carried out accurately. • Complex work can be done easily. • They are **portable**.	• They are expensive. • A power source is usually needed. • The **electricity** makes them more dangerous. • They take time to set up and use accurately.

Cordless tools

The variety of new power tools available has increased. **Cordless** power tools have also become very popular – they do not have electric cords, but are powered by a **rechargeable** battery.

Cordless tools

- use a rechargeable battery
- don't need a power supply nearby
- have a reduced risk of electric shock
- have a long battery life.

Cordless power tools

⚠ Power tools and machines are dangerous. Safety is vital. Always use power tools only with your teacher's permission. The teacher will show you how to use them safely. Any distraction can lead to very serious injury.

Follow these guidelines for your added safety:

⚠ Always use the tools as instructed.

⚠ Always wear the appropriate protective safety equipment.

⚠ Switch Off! Be sure the machine is off and unplugged before changing bits, belts, glass paper for sanders, or making adjustments to any power tool.

⚠ Always keep the cutters or moving part of the tool pointing away from yourself and others.

⚠ Keep the flex of the tool away from the cutter.

⚠ Guards must be kept in place.

⚠ Report any damage immediately.

⚠ Do not let others distract you while you are working and do not disturb others while they are operating equipment.

⚠ If in doubt, seek the assistance of your teacher.

⚠ Never leave a power tool running. Wait for it to stop before walking away.

⚠ Disconnect the power supply when the tool is not in use.

Power supply

Electricity drives power tools or charges the battery. Plugs on the power chords must be wired correctly to make sure they are safe to use.

Each electrical cable usually has three wires:

Colour	Wire
• Brown	• live
• Blue	• neutral
• Green & yellow	• earth

The earth wire is important for safety: in the event of an accident, the earth wire directs current safely to the ground through the electrical supply, preventing serious injury.

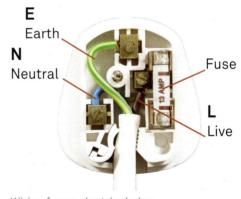

Wiring for an electrical plug

All plugs are fitted with a **fuse** to prevent too much current getting through to the appliance.

• Plugs should be sturdy to be able to resist occasional knocks.

• Wiring should be checked occasionally to ensure that wires are not loose, and that the tool is safe to use.

• Most plugs are supplied with a 13 amp fuse but this is generally unsuitable for most power tools.

Using Ohm's law

Calculate the correct fuse amps rating for a 600 watt power drill which will be connected to a 220 volt mains supply.

$$V = I \times R$$
$$I = W / V$$
$$I = 600 / 220$$
$$I = 2.73 \text{ amps}$$

According to Ohm's law, a 3 amp fuse will be sufficient for the drill. You should fit the correct fuse for the particular tool before it is used. The correct amps rating for the tool should be given in its instruction manual, but can be easily calculated. The calculation is based on Ohm's law:

Ohm's law

$$V = I \times R$$

Watts = Volts X Amps

Transformer

Mains electricity is supplied at 220 volts. This voltage is dangerous; a **transformer** reduces the voltage going to the power tool from 220 Volts to 110 Volts.

- A 110 volt tool must be used with a transformer.
- 110 volt tools have a special yellow plug.
- Power tools should be 110 volt or cordless for safety.

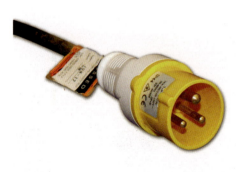

Transformer and plug

Extractors

Extractors are part of the health and safety equipment in the workshop. They act like heavy-duty hoovers. They remove dust and shavings from machines and power tools. The dust is sucked through the duct pipe to the machine, where it is filtered and collected.

Extractor

Sanders

The **sander** smooths down the surface of wood in preparation for a finish. Among the many types of sanders available, belt sanders, orbital finishing sanders, and random-orbit sanders are the most versatile. As long as you use the correct abrasive, one of these sanders should be able to smooth virtually any surface you encounter in the workshop.

Sanders. Can you name each type?

Belt sander

The abrasive belt on this large and robust sander is stretched over two rollers that drive forward, giving a constant cutting action. The sander has a dust collection bag or dust collection point that connects to an extractor.

Direction of the belt

Features of a belt sander:
- Belts are available in course to fine grades.
- It removes a lot of material quickly, which can cause damage.
- It is often used for stripping paint.
- Can sand larger flat surfaces.

137

Orbital sander

The orbital sander has a flat pad that vibrates in tiny circular motions at speed. Two spring-loaded clamps hold the sandpaper in place against the sander's pad. This lightweight sander is easy to manoeuvre, so it is useful for ultra-smooth sanding.

- Smooths flat surfaces quickly.
- Sandpaper is easily replaced.
- A high quality finish can be achieved.
- Care must be taken not to over-sand, as rounding of edges will result.

Orbital sander

Drills

Drills are used to bore holes in metal, plastic, or wood. When drilling any materials with a power drill, whether light or heavy, the workpiece must be held firmly. Drills can be mounted in drill stands for more precise drilling. Screwdriver bits are often used with drills and cordless drills to drive in screws easily and quickly.

Drills can be hand held or mounted in a drill press (see Chapter 17)

Special drill functions include:

- a keyless chuck for quick drill bit replacement
- hammer action for drilling masonry
- variable speed trigger switch
- speed selector (high/low)
- forward and reverse action for driving screws
- adjustable torque setting for driving screws, etc.

Driving screws with a drill attachment

Drill/Hammer/Torque ring

Speed selector

Keyless Chuck

Trigger Switch

Forward/Reverse Button

Battery

A drill with parts labelled

Iron

The ordinary clothing iron is a tool often found in the Wood Technology Room. It is used to apply iron-on veneers that cover the edges of sheet material. The iron is also used for removing small bruises from the surface of wood.

Oak edge banding veneer

Clothes iron

Oak edge banding veneer

Shelf front

Iron-on edging being applied

Jigsaw

The jigsaw has a narrow blade that is driven in an up and down motion by the motor. While it is usually used to cut curves, it can be fitted with a fence that acts as a guide for cutting straight lines.

⚠ Eye protection must always be worn.

⚠ The workpiece should be held firmly.

⚠ Disconnect the tool before making adjustments.

⚠ Always keep the power cable away from the blade.

Jigsaw cutting a curve

Trigger switch

Trigger lock button

Dust collection port

Blade guard

Sole plate/shoe

Blade

Jigsaw with parts labeled

A jigsaw can be used to cut through the centre by first creating a starter hole with a drill

USES

- for light work and sheet material
- to cut curves and large holes

Advantages	Disadvantages
• Base plate can be adjusted to cut at an angle. • The narrow blade is easily replaced. • Uses different blades for different materials.	• The depth of cut is limited. • They can be difficult to control, since the lower end of the blade is unsupported.

Biscuit joiner

The **biscuit joiner** is a modern power tool used to make a special joint. It has a small circular saw that cuts a slot in the two pieces of wood to be joined. A biscuit, which is usually made from pressed beech, is glued and put into the grooves to act like a loose tongue.

Using the biscuit joiner

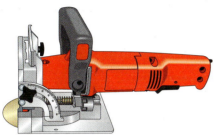

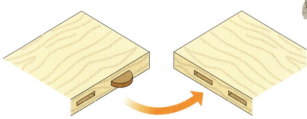
Biscuit Joiner and a biscuit joint

 USES

- for joining edges of boards together
- to make a simple, strong joint

Router

The **router** is a very versatile, portable power tool used for cutting mouldings in timber. Its various cutting attachments will cut joints such as mortises, rebates, housings, and dovetails. The router can be mounted on a special router table for cutting smaller pieces or when using larger router bits. However, the router is a particularly dangerous tool and should only be used by the teacher.

USES

- for making decorative mouldings on the edges of timber
- has replaced moulding planes
- for rebating and grooving

Router

141

⚠ Always wear eye protection.

⚠ Always keep the cutter facing away from yourself and others.

⚠ Always keep the power cable away from the cutter.

⚠ Always disconnect from power supply when not in use.

⚠ Disconnect before making adjustments.

⚠ Allow the cutter to stop before placing the router on the bench.

Cutter shank

Cutter edge

Rebate

Roller bearing

Router in use

Router table

The cutter sticks out below the base plate which can be raised and lowered to allow the depth of cut to be adjusted. A plunge mechanism allows the cutter to be raised and lowered quickly.

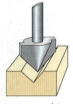      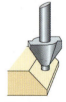 

| V-groove bit | Ogee bit | Beading bit | Cove bit | Dovetail bit | Rebate bit | Chamfer bit | Ovolo bit |

Some router cutters and the mouldings they produce

Circular saw

While this power tool is not widely used in schools, it is commonly used on sites for cutting sheet material and other work. The circular saw has a fence that keeps the blade running parallel to an edge.

Circular saw

- ⚠ It is a very dangerous tool.
- ⚠ Keep hands away from the blade.
- ⚠ It should always be disconnected when not in use.
- ⚠ It has a spring loaded guard that covers the blade when it is not cutting.
- ⚠ The depth and angle of cut can be varied by adjusting the base plate.

Planer

The planer has cutters that remove material quickly and easily. It is used by carpenters on site.

Planer

 USES

- smoothing rough timber quickly
- removing excess material

 CHAPTER QUESTIONS

1 Explain some safety rules associated with power tools and give examples of each.

2 Describe three advantages of modern power tools.

3 Describe two disadvantages of cordless power tools.

4 Name two advantages of a cordless drill over a drill with a plug.

5 The photo shows a bit used to cut a decorative moulding. With which power tool would it be used?

6 Name the mouldings given in the diagram below.

  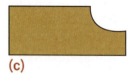

(a)   (b)   (c)

7 Name the parts of the power tools shown in the diagrams below.

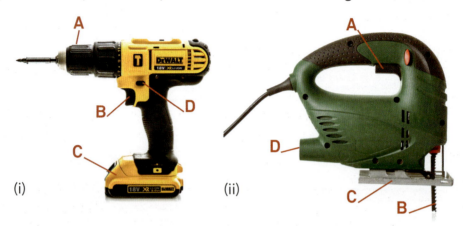

(i)   (ii)

8 What is the function of the fuse in an electric plug?

9 Name the parts (A), (B), and (C) of the plug shown right and explain their functions.

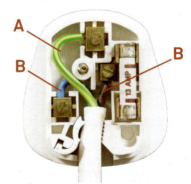

10 Many electrical power tools use a 110V power supply rather than 220V. Why is this voltage preferred?

 PowerPoint Summary   Weblinks

17 Machines

KEYWORDS
- 3D printer
- bandsaw
- CNC router
- laser cutter
- lathe
- mortiser
- pillar drill
- planer
- scroll saw

LEARNING OUTCOMES
- 1.1, 1.2, 1.3, 1.5, 1.7, 1.8, 1.10
- 2.5

Benefits of machines

What do you think are the main benefits of machines? Which is the most important benefit?

Learning intentions

At the end of this chapter you will be able to:
- Identify and discuss the function, main features, and safety aspects of machines associated with Wood Technology.
- Be familiar with common machines used by students and be competent in using them safely.

Machines are generally larger and more powerful than power tools. They are more dangerous because of their power and speed. Machines are usually fixed in position, while power tools are portable. Great care must always be taken when using them. The teacher will instruct you on the correct use of machines that you are allowed to use in the workshop.

⚠ Personal protective equipment (PPE) must always be worn when using any machine.

Table saw
Wood Technology rooms have a circular saw or table saw that the teacher uses to cut wood and sheet materials to size.

USES
- cutting larger boards to size
- cutting sheet material like plywood to size
- cutting pieces to length

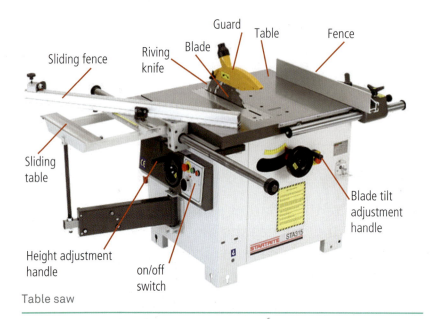

Table saw

Push stick in use

⚠ Keep hands clear of the blade at all times.

⚠ Never interrupt someone while they are using a saw or any machine.

⚠ Always ensure guards and safety equipment are used and in proper working order.

⚠ Keep working area around the saw clear to avoid trip hazards.

⚠ Always use a push stick to keep hands clear of the blade.

Scroll Saw

Scroll saws are very useful and are widely used in Wood Technology rooms for cutting curves in thinner wood, plastic and metal.

A thin blade held in place between two arms is moved by the motor up and down. The blade cuts on the downward stroke. The workpiece must be held firmly and your two hands press the piece against the table as you gently feed the line towards the blade. The blade is inserted and tensioned to keep the blade tight between the

Scroll saw. What safety precautions should you take when using this machine?

arms. This is done using the adjustment knob at the rear of the arm. The table can be tilted for angled cuts.

> ⚠ Keep hands clear of the blade.
> ⚠ Keep the material pressed down on the table.
> ⚠ Wear eye protection.
> ⚠ Always keep the guard in place.

Bandsaw

Bandsaws are very versatile. They are used to cut pieces to width and for cutting curves and angles. The bandsaw has a continuous blade that loops around wheels. The blade cuts downwards towards the table. The work is held firmly down against the table while it is pushed slowly through the blade. The table can be tilted to allow angled cuts. The fence can be used to guide pieces when making parallel cuts. A sliding mitre fence can be used for cross cutting and cutting mitres.

> ⚠ For safety the guard covers the blade. It can be adjusted to expose only enough of the blade to allow for the cut.
> ⚠ Keep hands clear of the blade at all times.
> ⚠ Always have the guard in position close to the wood.
> ⚠ Eye and ear protection should be worn.

Blade tensioning knob

Blade access door

Adjustable fence

On/off switch

Blade guard

Blade

Table (tilting)

Blade access door

Bandsaw

Pillar Drill

The **pillar drill** is used in the Wood Technology room to accurately drill holes in wood and other materials. Larger drill bits can be used safely. The depth of the hole is easily gauged using a depth stop or gauge. The pieces can be held safely and securely in the vice.

USES

- General precise drilling of vertical holes
- Larger diameter holes using forstner bits
- Drilling angled holes using the tilting table

⚠ Always wear eye protection.

⚠ Avoid wearing loose clothing or jewellery.

⚠ Keep long hair tied back.

⚠ Guards always in place.

⚠ Keep hands clear of moving parts.

⚠ Hold the work piece securely to the table or in the vice.

Pillar drill

Belt housing, On/off switch, Motor, Chuck, Feed lever, Chuck guard, Vice, Height adjustment lever, Tilting table

Forstner bit. What is the advantage of this type of bit?

Mortising machine

The **mortising machine** is widely used to cut square holes (mortises) to make mortise joints quickly and accurately and repeatedly. It cuts using a drill bit inside a hollow square chisel that trims the sides of the hole. The machine has a depth stop set to cut particular depths. Different sized chisels are used for various sized mortises.

The work piece rests on the moveable table and is secured against the fence with the clamp. The table can be moved from side to side or forwards and backwards using the adjustment wheel. When mortising a hole all the way through the piece, a hole is cut half way from one side, and then the piece is reversed and cut towards the middle from the other side.

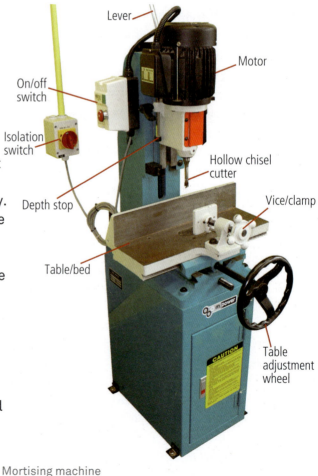

Mortising machine

Lever, Motor, On/off switch, Isolation switch, Hollow chisel cutter, Vice/clamp, Depth stop, Table/bed, Table adjustment wheel

148

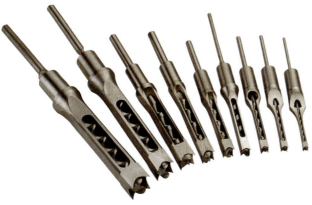

Hollow chisel and bit. What is the purpose of the opening in the side of the chisel?

Using a mortiser

> ⚠ Wear eye protection.
> ⚠ Keep hands clear of the cutter.
> ⚠ Report all faults immediately.

Planer/Thicknesser

A **planer** is used to prepare wood by smoothing the surfaces and planing the material to the required width and thickness. The teacher will prepare the wood for you. The top of the planer and the fence allow surfaces to be planed square to each other. Pieces are planed to thickness using the table underneath. Feed rollers pull the work pieces through. The feed table is raised or lowered to achieve the correct thickness.

> ⚠ Eye and ear protection should be used.
> ⚠ Keep hands clear of the cutters and guards in place.
> ⚠ Take care to keep hands clear when feeding material, as they can be easily caught.
> ⚠ Do not wear loose clothing and tie back long hair.

Fence — Blade guard — Feed table — Power and isolation switch

Planer/thicknesser

Sanding machines

Sanding machines are useful for smoothing surfaces and for finishing curved edges accurately. There are different types of sander in use. Some have a sanding belt or disk. A combination belt and disk sander is common in most Wood Technology rooms. Larger versions are available. A rotating bobbin sander is also common. They each use abrasive paper on a disk, belt or on a cylindrical bobbin. The abrasive paper leaves a smooth finish and removes material quickly and effortlessly. Sanders are useful for smoothing surfaces and sanding end grain. They allow curves to be smoothed easily.

The workpiece is held down on the table and pressed gently against the moving abrasive surface. When sanding curves, the piece is kept moving to a keep a smooth even curve. The bobbin sander is used to sand concave curves evenly.

Sliding fences can be used when sanding mitres and angles. The tables of the sanders can also be adjusted to various angles if needed.

⚠ Wear eye protection and a dust mask when sanding.
⚠ Keep hands away from the moving parts.
⚠ Secure loose clothing and jewellery.
⚠ Tie back long hair.
⚠ Use a mobile dust extraction unit.

Stop fence
Sanding belt
Sanding disk
Adjustable table
On/off safety switch

Belt and disc sander

Bobbin or Oscillating sander

Woodturning Lathe

The **lathe** is used for turning wood into decorative shapes. Some examples of turned items are shown. We will look at the lathe in more detail in the woodturning chapter.

Midi lathe with wood turned examples

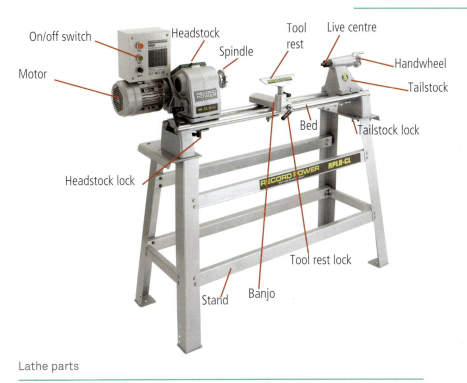

Lathe parts

Dust extraction

Dust extraction is an important part of every Wood Technology room. The extractors are vacuum devices that suck up dust and small particles into collection bags. The air is further cleaned as it passes through the extractor's filters, which help to keep the air in the room cleaner. Filters and bags must be cleaned regularly.

There are three types of extractor:

1 **Central or fixed systems**: These use ducts to remove dust from machines into large collection bags.

2 **Mobile extractor units**: These are used in smaller workshops and on sanding machines because of the finer dust.

3 **Air filter units**: These units filter dust particles in the air to purify the air further.

All modern machines and power tools are fitted with connections for extraction units.

Central dust system

Mobile dust extractor

Air filter unit

Investigating the machines

Divide into small groups. Each group is assigned the task of investigating a different machine. Look at the parts, uses, safety features, and safety rules of each. Members of each group present their research to the class so everyone can learn.

Computer-Aided Manufacture (CAM)

CAM is the term used to describe the process of making or processing items using computer-controlled machines. Computer-Aided Design (CAD) software such as SolidWorks® is often used with these machines.

CNC Router

CNC router machine

Benchtop CNC router

CNC machines are computer controlled. A **CNC router** is also computer controlled. The machine head holds a router bit that can be changed for different cuts and mouldings. The bit moves over the piece and follows a set design or pattern that has been drawn or programmed into the computer. They can reproduce an exact copy of any pattern numerous times. They can also engrave or carve complex 2D and 3D designs easily.

CNC:

Computer Numerically Controlled

▶ Hardwood Machining

Taking a look at technology

Break up into groups. Select one of the three areas below to research. Each group will produce a report, presentation, or video that further explains to the class how these emerging technologies are being used in industry throughout the world.

- **CNC Router**
- **Laser Cutter**
- **3D Printing**

St. Attracta's Community School BOOK RENTAL SCHEME

Laser Cutter

These machines use lasers to cut through thin materials and to burn or engrave complex image patterns onto materials like wood, aluminium, glass, plastics and stone. They can reproduce patterns with great accuracy and precision from computer-generated images or photographs.

Laser cutter

3D Printer

3D printing is a process of making a three dimensional solid object from a digital (computer) file. The **3D printer** lays down lots of thin horizontal layers of a plastic material (filament) in successive sheets or layers. These layers gradually build up to form the solid object.

3D Printer

3D printed object

3D printing allows you to produce complex functional shapes using less material than traditional manufacturing methods with very little waste material. A 3D model is first created on the computer using Computer-Aided Design (CAD) software. This model can then be printed quickly and used as a prototype to check and evaluate a design before you make the final piece. It allows you to correct mistakes and improve designs before manufacture.

CHAPTER QUESTIONS

1 What machine is used to smooth pieces of wood before you begin working on them?

2 Explain the function of a bandsaw.

3 Describe the safety features of the following?

(a) bandsaw
(b) table saw
(c) pillar drill.

4 Name the parts of the mortising machine labelled A, B, C, and D and state the use of each.

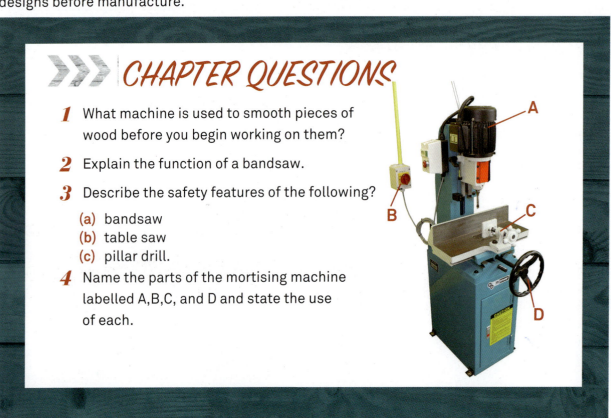

5 List three safety rules you would follow with each of the machines you might use in the Wood Technology room.

6 List three important safety precautions when using any machine in the Wood Technology room and give reasons for your choice.

7 Describe the steps you would use to drill a 30mm diameter hole through a piece of wood 50mm thick using a pillar drill.

8 Explain the following terms:

(a) CAD
(b) CNC
(c) CAM.

9 Draw a simple sketch of a scroll saw and label the main parts.

10 Sketch the safety signs displayed at the machines in your workshop. Describe the meaning of each.

11 (a) Name the woodworking machine shown in the diagram below.

(b) Describe the different work processes that would be carried out in each of the two areas of the machine shown by arrows A and B.

 PowerPoint Summary   **Weblinks**

18 Adhesives

KEYWORDS
- adhesive
- assembly
- catalyst
- contact glue
- polyvinyl acetate (PVA)
- resin
- soluble
- superglue
- synthetic
- water soluble

LEARNING OUTCOMES
- 1.3, 1.4 1.8, 1.10
- 2.3, 2.9, 2.11
- 3.7

Learning intentions

At the end of this chapter you will be able to:
- Identify different adhesives and describe where they would be used.
- Understand the properties of different adhesives and compare them.
- Use adhesives appropriately and efficiently in your project work.

There is a wide range of **adhesives** or glues available to suit different materials such as wood, plastic, cloth, and metal and for various other purposes. For example, glues are used to make wooden joints stronger and when veneering. While polyvinyl acetate (PVA) is widely used in the Wood Technology room, other types might be better in certain conditions.

⚠ Always read and follow the instructions.
⚠ Always get the teacher's permission when using glues.
⚠ Use glues in a well-ventilated area and avoid eye contact or inhaling fumes.
⚠ Always clean up excess glue and any spillages carefully.
⚠ Wash hands properly after use.

How adhesive works

Most adhesives, like PVA, take time to set. The pieces being glued must be held in position using cramps for 8–12 hours while the glue hardens. Once the glue has set, the bond is stronger than the wood itself. Try this experiment in class.

Testing the bond

Bond two pieces of wood using PVA glue. When the glue has set (24 hours), try to break the joint. Describe the result. Consider and discuss the strength of the glue.

Glue holds pieces together in two ways:

Specific adhesion	Mechanical adhesion
• This is the holding power of the glue itself, holding the surfaces together.	• Glue also gets into the cracks and pores of the wood, which creates a key or gripping effect.

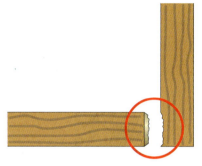

Adhesive can be stronger than wood

The glue area should be as large as possible

In order for the glue to work effectively, the surfaces must be in contact. This is why good fitting joints are important. When gluing a joint, all surfaces in contact should be lightly covered in glue. The greater the area of glue in contact, the stronger the joint will be.

Different adhesives set in different ways. Some contain solvents and they set when the solvent evaporates. Thermo glues are softened by heat and set when they cool down. Some dry slowly and need cramps to hold them while they set. Other glues come in two parts: glue and a hardener. The hardener is a **catalyst** which causes a chemical reaction, triggering the glue to set.

Selecting the right adhesive

The choice of glue will depend on the materials being bonded, the speed and strength of the bond needed, and also the location of the piece (indoors or outdoors).

While most glues give a strong permanent joint, some adhesives, like superglue, bond very quickly while others harden slowly, allowing time for final adjustments. **Water soluble** glue is not suitable for external situations. As most glue is made from chemicals, you must follow instructions. Some glue is

Examples of adhesives

harmful, so particular care must be taken when using those types.

Types of adhesive

Scotch glue (animal glue)

Scotch glue pre-dates modern adhesives. Made from the bones and hides of animals, it is obtained as small beads or pearls. The pearls are soaked in water overnight and heated in a special glue pot that prevents the glue from burning.

It is suitable for veneering and furniture restoration because it is **soluble** (dissolves) in water and the bond is broken by heating.

Scotch glue pearls

- water soluble (dissolves in water)
- strong, unpleasant smell
- not heat resistant – heat will break the bond
- long preparation time

Casein Glue

Casein glue is made from milk protein mixed with other chemicals. It is strong and durable glue that is non-toxic. It is obtained as a white powder and is easy to prepare. It is water resistant but can be affected by fungi.

It is prepared by mixing the powder with water in a non-metallic container. It is stirred to a thick creamy consistency and left to stand for 15 minutes before use.

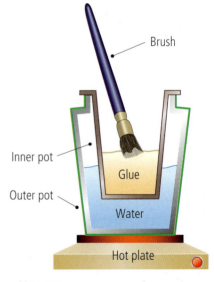

Glue pot

- very strong glue
- non-toxic
- long shelf life
- heat and water resistant
- simple preparation required before use
- stains certain woods
- must be used quickly once mixed

Synthetic Adhesives

PVA (polyvinyl acetate)

PVA is a synthetic resin glue. It is the most widely used glue in the wood technology room because it is safe, cheap and easy to use. It is a type of thermoplastic.

PVA wood adhesive in use

- strong
- very versatile – has many uses
- safe to handle with no toxic fumes
- water soluble (water resistant forms available)
- can be used from the container
- long shelf life
- must be cramped for 4–12 hours (usually left overnight)

Urea formaldehyde resin

Urea formaldehyde **resin** is very strong glue. This glue is very suitable for laminating and bending projects. It is used for making MDF and plywood. Care must be taken when using this glue, as it is harmful if inhaled and can damage your skin. It is important to work in a well-ventilated area and to wear a respirator.

Epoxy Resin

Epoxy resin glues are usually obtained as a resin and a hardener (**catalyst**) mixed together, so the two liquids are packaged separately. When they are mixed, a chemical reaction causes the glue to set. The glue mixes into a stiff paste and must be applied quickly. There are a number of types of epoxy

- expensive
- very strong
- set quickly
- glue and hardener must be mixed in correct proportion
- bonds metal, wood, glass, and ceramic

Epoxy resin glue

resin with many applications. They are especially suitable for bonding non-porous materials such as metal and glass as well as wood and plastic. Care should be taken to avoid skin contact and to avoid inhaling the fumes; work should be done in a well-ventilated area.

Superglue (cyanoacrylate glue)

Superglues are popular adhesives for a variety of small bonding tasks. They can be used on wood, metal, plastic, and ceramic. The bond is strong and it sets in seconds. Superglue is expensive and sold in small containers. Care must be taken with superglues: do not allow skin to get stuck together or to the piece as the bond forms quickly and is difficult to break.

Superglue. Consider and discuss the disadvantages of superglue.

Contact glue

Contact or impact adhesive is made from natural or synthetic rubber. Contact glue is widely used for veneering projects and for bonding leather and fabric to wood. The bond forms very quickly (on contact), so accuracy when positioning the pieces is most important.

- bonds on contact
- used for veneering
- very little adjustment possible
- strong smells – work in well-ventilated space
- solvent-based – harmful if inhaled
- harmful to skin – avoid skin contact

Contact glue

The glue is applied to both surfaces to be bonded using a special spreader. The glue is allowed to become 'tacky' before the surfaces are brought into contact. Contact glue contains a solvent which has a strong smell so must be used in a well-ventilated area. Contact glue can be obtained in a spray-on version.

Applying veneer

Create a simple instruction sheet or presentation to explain the steps used to apply a veneer panel to a wooden base.

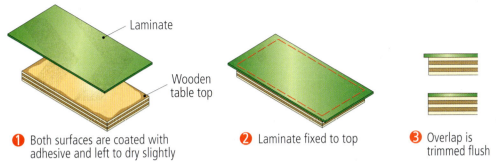

1 Both surfaces are coated with adhesive and left to dry slightly

2 Laminate fixed to top

3 Overlap is trimmed flush

Gluing a laminate with contact glue

Polyurethane glue

Polyurethane glue is strong water resistant glue that will bond wood and other materials. It is a gap filling glue expanding as it dries to fill small gaps in a joint. It is expensive so is not commonly used. It is also messy and is difficult to clean up.

- strong bond
- expensive
- will bond wood and other materials
- water resistant
- expands to fill small gaps
- messy to work with and clean up
- ready to use from the container

Polyurethane glue (Gorilla Glue)

Hot melt glue (Thermo glue)

Hot melt or **thermo glues** are applied using a special heated glue gun. The glue is inserted in the back of an electrically heated gun which heats the glue stick to melting point. As the trigger is pulled, it releases the correct amount of melted glue. The glue sets quickly as it cools. It is very useful for gluing card, light materials, fabric, and when assembling small models or to tack pieces together.

⚠ Safety! Take care when using this glue, as both glue and nozzle of the gun are very hot and can burn.

Hot melt glue gun

Assembly

Glue is used in assembling the parts of your projects. It is important that **assembly** is executed carefully. First, make sure that the pieces fit together without glue. Then, give yourself enough time to prepare, apply the glue, assemble the parts, put on the cramps, make adjustments, and clean off excess glue. Finally, check that the pieces are aligned and square.

Apply a thin and even layer of glue with a spreader or brush to all surfaces being joined. Do not apply too much, as the excess will squeeze out, causing a mess.

When the surfaces are glued, assemble the parts carefully and put on the cramps. Place pieces of wood against the work to protect it from being bruised by the pressure of the cramp. Tighten the cramps to put firm pressure on the work, but do not over tighten.

Clean off any excess glue with a damp cloth. Excess glue can set on the surfaces of the piece, which will form an unsightly light coloured stain when you apply the final finish to the piece.

Brush

Spreader

Roller

Stick

Methods for applying glue

Sash cramps on a frame

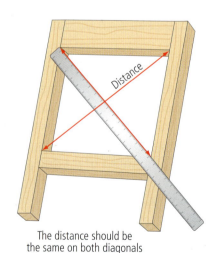

Distance

The distance should be the same on both diagonals for the piece to be square

Check that the pieces are aligned correctly and that the pieces are checked for squareness

CHAPTER QUESTIONS

1. Explain the term 'water soluble' in relation to wood glue.

2. What do the letters PVA stand for?

3. Give two safety precautions that should be followed when using synthetic glue.

4. When using PVA glue to assemble a door frame, how long is it best to leave the frame in the cramps for?

5. What is thermo glue used for and how is it usually applied?

6. List three features of PVA glue.

7. Give one unique feature of polyurethane glue.

8. What is the main use for contact adhesive?

9. Outline the steps you would take when gluing and cramping the joints in a small wooden frame.

10. Describe in detail how you would check that the frame was square.

 PowerPoint Summary   Weblinks

19 Finishes

KEYWORDS

- abrasive
- applied finish
- arris
- denibbing
- finish
- lacquer
- microporous
- scraper
- surface finish

LEARNING OUTCOMES

- 1.1, 1.2, 1.3, 1.4, 1.8, 1.10
- 2.3, 2.11
- 3.3, 3.7, 3.12

Learning intentions

At the end of this chapter you will be able to:
- Demonstrate how to achieve a high quality surface finish on a completed task.
- Select an appropriate applied finish for a task and justify your choice.
- Compare various applied finishes in terms of their durability and sustainability.

Completed projects must look attractive and they will only look attractive if they are well-finished. Giving a project a good overall appearance will involve applying some type of **finish**. There are a number of reasons for this.

Purpose of the finish
- It seals the wood and protects it from wear.
- It helps prevent decay (from insects and fungi).
- It enhances the natural beauty, grain, and colour of the wood.
- It gives a nice smooth finished surface.
- It can add colour (with stains and paints).

Selecting the finish
Considerations when choosing a finish for the task:
- the function of the final piece
- the location (indoors or outside)
- whether the piece is likely to get wet (in a bathroom, for example)
- how the item will be cleaned (items for serving food will need to be washed)
- whether it needs to be painted for colour or protection
- other health and safety considerations (food container, child's toy).

Discuss how sanding improves the surface finish

Two stages of finishing

1 **Surface finish** – preparing the wood before putting on the final finish layer.
2 **Applied finish** – putting on the final finish product (varnish, paint, etc.).

Surface finish process and tools

Before a piece can have an applied finish, it must be prepared. The surfaces should be clean and smooth. Planes, **scrapers**, filler, and **abrasive** papers are used to achieve a suitable surface finish.

Steps to a surface finish

- Pencil lines and marks are removed.
- Marks and scratches are removed using a cabinet scraper or sandpaper.
- Nails and pins are punched below the surface.
- Nail and pin holes and small gaps are filled with wood filler.
- Sandpaper is used to smooth surfaces and clean up excess filler.
- Start with 120 grit sandpaper (medium) then use 180 grit and finally 320 grit.
- Sand surfaces 'with the grain'.
- Sand end grain smooth also.
- Brush off all dust with a tack cloth.

Finishing in practice

Working in groups of three or four, make a list of the steps you'd need to take to prepare the surfaces of a simple artefact finished with varnish. How could you tell it was ready? Compare your results and discuss before reading on.

Cabinet scraper in use

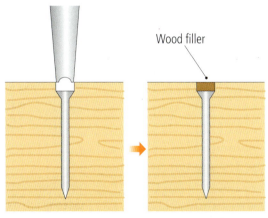

Wood filler

Nails are punched below the surface and the holes are neatly filled and sanded smooth

Wood Filler

Wood filler, a soft paste that is obtained in a variety of wood shades to suit different timbers, is used to fill small gaps and nail holes. A thin layer of filler is applied with a putty knife and is then scraped level with the surface. It dries to form a hard filling. Take care to clean off the excess and wipe with a damp cloth because the excess can cause staining under varnish and other finishes.

Types of wood filler

Applying wood filler. The surface is scraped level.

Sandpaper

Sandpaper is made using fine abrasive grits bonded to a paper, card or cloth-based backing sheet. It can be obtained in sheets, rolls, belts, and special pre-cut shapes suitable for sanders.

Sandpaper. The size of the grit used is printed on the back of the paper

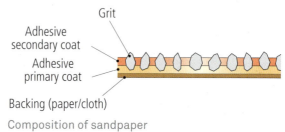

Composition of sandpaper

Examples of abrasive grits are crushed glass, aluminium oxide, and silicon carbide. The grit used to make the abrasive paper is put through a fine sieve to achieve different grades. The size of the grit determines the fineness of the sandpaper from coarse to very fine, as seen in the table right.

Grit size	
Coarse	40–60
Medium	80–120
Fine	120–180
Very fine	180–320
Super fine	400–600

Depending on the initial condition of the surface, it is best to start with 120 grit. For most tasks in softwood, working from 120 grit up to a 180 grit is sufficient. 320 grit is generally used as a maximum grade for preparing hardwoods.

Steel wool

Steel wool can be used to polish the edges of acrylic and also for smoothing varnish between coats. It is obtained in grades of fineness ranging from 0 grade (coarse) to 0000 grade (very fine).

> ⚠ Always use a knife or scissors to cut steel wool as small particles of steel can get into your skin.
>
> ⚠ Take care with steel wool as it is easily combustible.

Steel wool

Sanding

Sanding should be a brief task. Aim to smooth the surfaces without changing their shape. Sand your pieces with a sander or by hand with sandpaper wrapped around a cork sanding block. A cork sanding block is used because cork is solid enough to sand evenly but also has some give to absorb any imperfections without tearing. Always sand in the direction of the grain. Particular attention should be paid to sanding of mouldings and end grain so they are smooth.

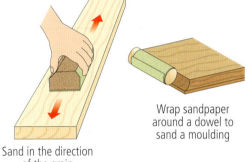

Wrap sandpaper around a dowel to sand a moulding

Sand in the direction of the grain

Always sand with the grain

Important when sanding

- Always sand in the direction of the grain.
- End grain can be sanded in any direction.
- Sanding should be brief. Do not over sand the pieces.
- For smoothest results, use 120 grit paper, then 180 grit, and finally 320 grit.
- Sand surfaces smooth without changing their shape.
- Any tiny scratches will be highlighted by your finish.
- Sanding creates fine dust, so always use a dust mask to avoid inhaling dust.

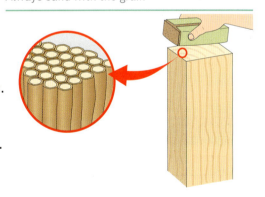

Why is it ok to sand end grain in all directions?

Sanding checklist

What is the aim of sanding and how do we know when to stop? Make a checklist to guide the class when doing project tasks.

When you have finished sanding, you will notice sharp edges. This is known as an **arris**. These sharp edges are easily damaged, so it is best to break the edge with one or two passes of sandpaper.

It may be easier to sand surfaces of some items before assembly, as it is difficult to get into all areas after gluing. Take care of smooth surfaces, as they can easily get damaged on rough bench surfaces.

Aims of sanding
- Surfaces are clean, even, and smooth.
- All marks and pencil lines are removed.
- All scratches are removed.
- All filler is sanded back to the wood surface.
- All end grain is smooth.

Arris

Arris slightly rounded

Sharp edges are removed with a light pass of sandpaper

Applied finish process and tools

An applied finish is a coating or covering applied to protect the wood surfaces and improve its appearance. Finishes are made from chemicals or oils mixed in a solvent such as water or white spirit. The solvent allows the finish to be spread over the surface easily. As the water or solvent dries, it leaves a coating on the wood.

Oil finishes are spread onto the surface. They soak into the wood and dry slowly, giving deep protection. Brushes or equipment are cleaned using the appropriate solvent (see table).

⚠ Always read and follow instructions on containers of finish.

Solvents used for finishes

Finish	Solvent
• emulsion paint • water based varnish	• water
• polyurethane varnish • gloss paint	• white spirit
• bees wax	• turpentine
• French polish • sanding sealer	• methylated spirit

Solvent:

A liquid used to dissolve other substances. The most common solvents in wood finishing are water, acetone, turpentine, and toluene.

Paint

Paint is a good protective finish available in a variety of colours. It can be applied to wood, metal, and other materials. Like varnish, it is available in three surface finishes: gloss, satin, and matt. Gloss is shiny, while matt gives a dull finish. Satin is between the two.

⚠ It is important to choose lead-free paint, particularly on items made for children.

Advantages	Disadvantages
• Good for exterior and interior work • Variety of colours available • Durable protective finish • Easily cleaned • Long lasting • Covers scratches and imperfections	• Hides the natural grain and beauty of the wood • Difficult to apply well • Needs a lot of preparation • Can blister or crack over time

Paint is usually applied on wood with a brush in a number of different layers, each one adding to the protection.

Steps to applying paint

- Prepare wood surfaces well.
- Seal knots with wood knotting solution to prevent seepage from knots and help minimise discolouration of the final finish.
- Apply a primer with a brush.
- Fill all cracks and holes with filler and sand smooth.
- Apply undercoat (1-2 coats).
- Apply final finish coat (gloss).
- Allow each coat to dry before applying the next.

Wood knotting solution

Wood fillers come in various colours

169

Primer

Primer is a special light paint that seals and protects the wood. Primer acts as a base for the undercoat layer and helps it adhere well.

Undercoat

Undercoat is applied next. Its dull matt finish covers the surfaces, fully covering the grain and providing a base for the final gloss coat. The colour of undercoat must blend with the final coat.

Paint primer

Finish coat

This final coat can be gloss, satin, or matt. It is applied evenly to avoid drips or streaks. The finish coat is applied evenly, avoiding brush marks, drips, runs, or dirt. The surfaces are checked after a short time and any drips or runs are brushed out carefully.

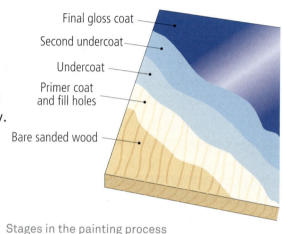

Final gloss coat
Second undercoat
Undercoat
Primer coat and fill holes
Bare sanded wood

Stains

Stains and dyes are used to darken or change the colour of the wood. They enhance the colour but do not protect the wood. They consist of pigments or dyes mixed in a solvent or water.

Stages in the painting process

Solvent and water-based wood dyes

1 Brush on the stain over the whole piece quickly and evenly

2 Wipe off excess with a clean, lint-free cloth

Applying a stain or dye

Stains can be difficult to apply evenly. They are brushed on evenly and left for a few minutes to let the stain be absorbed and then the excess is wiped off with a clean dry cloth.

Varnish

Varnish is a protective coating for wood available for indoor and outdoor use. It is the most popular finish used in the Wood Technology room. It is usually applied as a clear finish but can be obtained with a stain or pigment that darkens the wood. Modern varnish is made from polyurethane resin in a spirit-based medium, although water-based varnish is available. Water-based varnishes reduce the need for solvents and chemicals for cleaning brushes, so they are safer and friendlier to the environment. A spray-on varnish can be obtained in an aerosol can for smaller items. Varnish is available in a gloss, satin, and matt finish. A special high-gloss 'yacht' varnish (used on boats) can be obtained that is hard wearing.

A selection of varnishes

- water resistant
- durable
- enhances the grain of the wood
- heat resistant
- easily cleaned
- available in clear and wood shade forms

Brushing on varnish

Varnish is applied onto the surfaces in a thin even layer with the grain using a brush, but a cloth or roller can also be used. All surfaces are covered to seal the wood and prevent swelling. The varnish must be checked for drips or runs which should be brushed out evenly.

The varnish soaks into the wood and dries overnight. When the first coat dries, the surfaces will be slightly rough. The roughness is lightly sanded (denibbed) using 320 grit sandpaper. Then, the dust is cleaned off and a second coat is applied and will dry again overnight. The second coat is sanded lightly and a final coat is applied and allowed to dry.

Applying varnish with a cloth

Microporous finishes

Microporous finishes function as a breathable skin on the wood. They are used outdoors on furniture, decking, and fences to protect the wood from the rain. Small microscopic holes in the finish allow water vapour inside the wood to evaporate out through the varnish, but they do not allow water to penetrate the finish. Therefore, the wood can breathe naturally. These finishes are environmentally friendly and available in a variety of wood shades.

Ronseal fencelife

Danish oil

Like other oil finishes, Danish oil soaks into the wood and dries to give a protective finish. Made with tung oil, it is applied evenly with a cloth or brush, then allowed to soak into the wood surface. Any excess is wiped away with a cloth.

⚠ Danish oil is flammable. Cloths used to apply Danish oil should be spread flat and allowed to dry before they are disposed of safely.

Danish oil

Applying oil
- Apply with a brush or clean cloth, working well into the grain.
- Put on two or three coats and let it soak in before wiping away any excess.
- Leave overnight to dry and lightly sand with 320 grit sandpaper to make smooth.
- Repeat this process to gradually build up a soft sheen.

Advantages of Danish oil
- Oil is easy to apply.
- It doesn't raise the wood grain.
- Application results in a nice soft sheen finish.
- It is suitable for indoor and outdoor use.
- You can re-oil as needed.
- The treated wood is washable
- When dry, the wood is food and child safe.

Other oil finishes

Tung oil, teak oil, and linseed oils are all penetrating oils that are used to finish wood or applied to deepen and enhance the grain before applying varnish. They are applied using a cloth and will need time to dry naturally.

A selection of finishing oils

Wax finish

Wax finishes are applied to wood to give a nice shine. Beeswax is the main ingredient in most wax polishes. Wax is a soft finish and not water resistant, so it is easily marked and is only used indoors.

Applying wax

- Wax can be applied to sealed or unsealed wood.
- Apply the wax using a clean, dry cloth rubbing it well into the grain.
- Build up a number of coats before allowing it to dry for 30 minutes before polishing.
- Polish the surfaces using a separate clean cloth to bring up a shine.
- This process can be repeated to build up a soft lustre.

Wax finish

- easy to apply
- gives a nice shine with a natural finish
- does not raise the grain
- easy to renew the finish
- no sanding between coats
- not heat or water resistant
- easily damaged soft finish

Finishing a child's chair

You have been asked to select a finish for this small chair made from pine, pictured. It is to be used by a young child. In small groups, think about the most suitable finish and the reasons why you selected it. Share your thoughts, first with the group and then with the class.

Lacquer

Lacquer is a hard and durable professional finish applied to wood furniture using special spray equipment. A spray gun and air compressor are used to finely coat finish onto the wood.

Spray gun with parts labelled

Using a spray gun

This finish is built up in two coats. First, a coat of sealer is applied. It dries quickly and is lightly sanded. Then, the final lacquer finish is applied. The fast speed at which the finish dries is a great advantage in producing furniture.

Lacquer is mixed with harmful solvents that evaporate very quickly. Special spray equipment is needed to apply lacquer. Spraying is done in a special spaying area with proper face mask and extraction.

⚠ Full respiratory protection must always be used with lacquer finishes.

French polish

French polish is a high-quality traditional finish applied by hand using a special pad called a rubber. The polish is made from shellac dissolved in methylated spirit. Shellac is a crust surrounding an insect that lives in trees in countries such as India and Thailand. A variety of different polishes were used to polish furniture, such as button polish, clear polish, and white polish.

French polishing is a specialist process where the wood is sealed. The pad, or rubber, made from cotton wool wrapped in cotton, is soaked in polish and used to rub it onto the wood surface. A finish is gradually built up.

French polish

Three stages of applying French polish:

1 Bodying in   2 Building up   3 Spiriting off

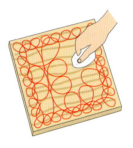

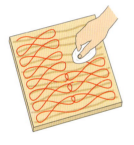

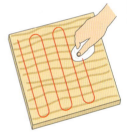

❶ Cover the panel with circular strokes

❷ Continue with figure-eight strokes

❸ Finish with straight, parallel strokes

Applying French polish

1 Bodying in

- A loaded pad is used to apply polish.
- Circular motions are used.
- Work from outside towards the centre.
- Several layers are applied.
- Leave to dry overnight.

2 Building up

- De-nib the slightly rough surface with very fine steel wool.
- Dust off the surfaces.
- Reapply polish as before: 5 – 6 coats.
- Repeat a number of times to build up a soft shine.
- The pad can be kept moist overnight in a sealed jar with some methylated spirit in the bottom.

3 Spiriting off

- As a layer of polish builds up, the finish becomes streaky and uneven.
- A new clean pad charged with methylated spirit is used along the grain direction to even out the marks.
- The spirit melts the top layer of the polish as it moves across the surface.

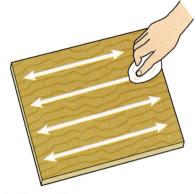

Spiriting off

CHAPTER QUESTIONS

1 Name a finish that is suitable for use on a park bench.

2 List two finishes suitable for a bathroom cabinet project and give reasons for your choices.

3 Describe what is meant by the term surface finish.

4 Explain why it is necessary to sand wood in the direction of the grain in wood.

5 Nails and panel pins are punched below the wood surface and filled. Why is this necessary?

6 Explain the following terms associated with finishing:
   (a) end grain
   (b) arris
   (c) abrasive grit
   (d) steel wool.

7 Why is it necessary to apply a final finish on a wooden artefact?

8 List four stages you would take to prepare a piece before applying a varnish.

9 List four steps you would take to apply the varnish to a wooden table top.

10 Describe how you would clean up after varnishing a project.

11 List three advantages of paint as an applied finish.

 PowerPoint Summary   Weblinks

20 Hardware: Fixtures and fittings

Learning intentions

At the end of this chapter you will be able to:
- Identify a range of fixtures and fittings used in common wooden artefacts.
- Explain the appropriate function of common hardware fittings.
- Describe how common fixtures and fittings are used in project tasks.

Fixtures, fittings, and other hardware are widely used in project tasks. For example, a door for a cabinet will need hinges, a handle, and a catch or locking device. You will become familiar with a range of different fittings, from nails and screws to handles and hinges. You should be familiar with the main types of hardware fittings and where they are used.

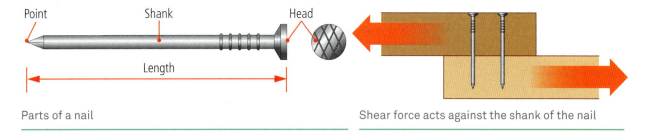

Parts of a nail

Shear force acts against the shank of the nail

Nails

Larger nails are used by carpenters when constructing buildings, floors, and roofs. There are over 20 categories of nails that come in different sizes and shapes to suit their function and use. Smaller nails and panel pins are often used in Wood Technology to secure wooden pieces together. Nails work best when the force acting on them is a shear force (at 90° to the shank).

Round wire nail

This general purpose nail made from steel has a round head and is available in sizes from 25mm to 150mm. They are used for flooring and constructing timber walls and roofs.

Round wire nail

Oval nail

Oval nails are lighter and their shank and head is oval in section. This shape allows the head to be driven below the surface without splitting the wood. The oval nail is inserted with the oval in line with the grain.

It is used for nailing two small pieces together and where the nail is close to the end of a piece. It leaves a smaller nail hole that can be covered with filler.

Oval nail

Consider why the oval nail is inserted with the head in line with the grain

Panel pins

These are smaller nails used for light work. They are the most common in the Wood Technology room. **Panel pins** are coated (galvanised) to prevent corrosion. They are available in lengths between 18mm – 40mm. They can bend easily. Bent pins should be pulled out using pincers. They are used for fixing plywood to the back of cabinets and for securing mouldings.

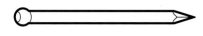

Panel pin

Tacks

Tacks have a sharp point and wide head. They are used for securing cloth and laying carpet.

Tack

Upholstery nail

This decorative round-headed nail is used to secure the edge of upholstery to a stool or chair. They are bronze or black in colour.

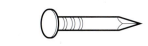

Upholstery nail

Clout nail

These short nails with a wide head are used outdoors to attach roofing felt. The nail is galvanised to resist corrosion.

Clout nail

U-shaped nail

U-shaped nails or staples are nails shaped in a 'U'. They are galvanised to prevent rust. They are used outdoors to secure fencing and wire to wooden posts.

U-shaped nail

Nailing

Care should be taken to drive nails correctly. Hit the nail squarely or it may bend. Different methods of inserting nails is given below.

Staggered Nailing

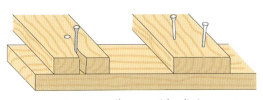

Stagger nails to avoid splitting the end of the wood

Dovetail Nailing

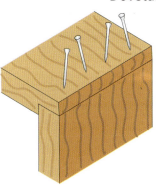

Dovetail nailing will add grip to the joint

Secret Nailing

Tongued and grooved floorboards – secret nailing

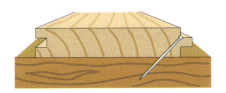

Clinched-over nail – strong but unsightly

Nailing methods

179

Staples

Special staples are used with a staple gun to fix fabric to wood. They are obtained in different lengths. Be careful when using a staple gun. Do not discharge staples into the air as they can injure someone.

Staples and staple gun

Screws

Screws are used to join two pieces of wood together. As the thread screws into the wood, it pulls the pieces tighter. Screws are also used to attach handles, hinges, and other fittings to wood.

Screws are identified by the shape of their head (**countersunk**, raised head, and round head) and also according to the type of screwdriver used to drive them. The diagram right shows the common types.

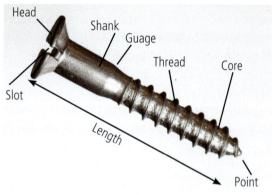

Parts of a screw

Screw types

Make sketches of these different screw heads. Which types are most common in the wood technology room?

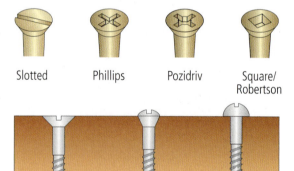

Slotted   Phillips   Pozidriv   Square/Robertson

Countersunk head   Raised head   Round head

Screw heads

When driving a screw, the correct size screwdriver or bit must be used. Philips head and Pozidriv screwdrivers are available in different sizes.

Phillips screwdriver

Pozidriv screwdriver

Examine screwdriver heads and bits and discuss their shape, sizes and use.

Screws are made from steel or brass. The thread of a modern screw continues the length of the shank, which gives added grip. Often, screws are coated with zinc, brass, or chrome to prevent them corroding. Brass is a soft metal and is easily damaged or may break if forced.

Phillips head screws

Choosing screws

To ensure the screw has an adequate grip, a screw should be at least twice as long as the piece it is securing. A small pilot hole is drilled before inserting a screw. For most screws used in wood technology, a 3mm pilot hole is sufficient. This makes sure the screw can be driven with ease, preventing the screw splitting the wood and not damaging the head. The hole is usually countersunk to leave the head of the screw flush with the surface.

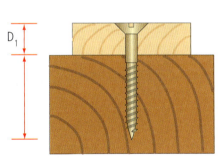

D_1

The screw should be at least twice as long as the piece it is securing

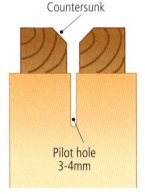

Countersunk

Pilot hole
3-4mm

A pilot hole should always be drilled

Screws are ordered according to:
- Length required
- The diameter (gauge) of the screw
- Type of head
- Material

Reading labels

The pictures show the labels on two boxes of screws. Identify the details of each type.

SPAX
Z 2
200
3.5 x 40

REISSER®
R2 Csk Head
Part Thread
PZD 2
Hardened Steel
5.0   70
Yellow Tropicalised, Lubricated
200 Pcs. (approx)

Other screws

Coach screw: A heavy duty screw with a hexagonal head driven with a spanner or socket spanner.

Cup hooks and screw eyes: small fittings used for hanging cups, keys, and curtains

Coach screw   Cup hook   Screw eye

Angle Brackets

Angle brackets are L-shaped pieces of metal that are secured with screws. They come in various shapes and sizes: larger types are used to hold shelves on a wall, while smaller types are often used to secure table tops to frames and to strengthen joints.

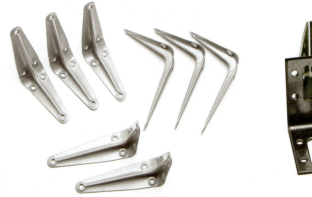

Selection of metal brackets and supports

Knock-down fittings

Joiner blocks and knock-down fittings are designed to connect wooden pieces or panels quickly and without using a regular joint. They are typically made from plastic or metal in two parts. They are easily attached with screws, allowing the joints to be quickly taken apart if needed. Wooden joiner blocks are also easily made and these can be used to add strength to a joint if needed.

Plastic joiner block

Knock-down fittings

Clamping bolt

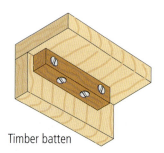

Timber batten

Hinges

Hinges allow doors, windows, and lids to open and close easily. Your choice of the many types and sizes will depend on the task, the appearance, and where they will be used. You will need to consider and investigate the hinge type as you design and plan your work.

Hinges are mainly made from steel and brass. They are often coated (galvanised) for outside use. Small butt hinges and ornamental hinges can be sourced for projects like small boxes.

Butt hinge   Parliament hinge   Rising butt hinge   Flush hinge   Cabinet hinge

Decorative tee hinge   Tee hinge   Decorative butt hinge

Concealed cabinet or Blum hinge   Strap hinge   Cranked hinge

Sliding stays

Piano hinge

Common hinges

Hinge uses

Create a well presented investigation/research sheet to show where each of the hinges pictured are used.

Fitting a butt hinge

- Mark out the position of the hinge on the two pieces using a rule and try square.
- Set a marking gauge to the width of the hinge and mark on each piece.
- Set the gauge to the thickness of the hinge, again marking each piece.
- Mark the waste to be removed and begin removing it with a sharp chisel as shown.
- Taper the recess, as this prevents 'pinching' of the hinge (door or lid fails to close fully).
- Fix hinge in place using screws.

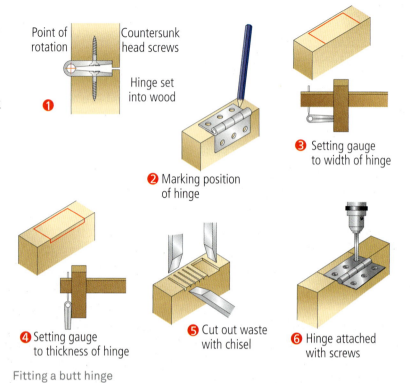

Point of rotation

Countersunk head screws

Hinge set into wood

❶

❷ Marking position of hinge

❸ Setting gauge to width of hinge

❹ Setting gauge to thickness of hinge

❺ Cut out waste with chisel

❻ Hinge attached with screws

Fitting a butt hinge

Catches & Locks

Cupboard lock

Cut-door lock

Box lock

Door handle and lock

Lock

Keyhole

Locks

Various escutcheon plates

Uses of Locks, catches, and bolts

Create an investigation/research sheet to show examples of these locks, catches, and bolts in use.

Double ball catch   Roller catch   Magnetic catch   Barrel bolt   Box clasp

Catches

Locks and catches are used to secure doors and lids on boxes. A catch may be used to hold a door, gate, or lid in a closed position. The type, style, material, and size of a lock will depend on its function and location. Some locks, like the mortise lock and the box lock, are recessed into the wood. Cupboard locks are fitted to the surface of the wood.

There are a wide range of barrel bolts made for securing large gates, cupboard doors, etc. They can be made from brass or steel and they are galvanised for outside use.

Handles

Handles are used on drawers, cabinets, boxes and doors of every kind. They are made from wood, brass, steel, aluminium, plastic, and other materials. They are secured to the wood using screws or bolts. Choose handles carefully; select the correct size and style for your particular door, drawer, etc.

Selection of decorative handles and fittings

A simple handle function incorporated into the piece can be very effective. A hole drilled in a drawer can be efficient, decorative and a sustainable alternative that reduces waste.

Examples of self-handled drawers

Lamp fittings

When making a lamp, you will need to use a plug, a lamp holder, and a ring (called a nipple) to connect the holder to the top of the wooden stem. Lamp holders are made of Bakelite or brass.

> ⚠ Always use 3-core electric flex with a brass or metal holder.
>
> ⚠ Always wire the plug and holder correctly and have it checked by a competent adult.

3-pin plug

Nipple

Switched bulb holders

Lamp fittings

CHAPTER QUESTIONS

1 Make neat sketches of the following nails and outline where they would be used.
  (a) oval nail   (c) u-shaped nail/staple
  (b) panel pin   (d) tack.

2 Make a neat sketch of a screw and label the parts.

3 Name the following common fittings:

(a)   (b)   (c)   (d)

4 Name each type of screw in the diagram below.

  (a)   (b)   (c)

5 Describe the purpose of the following fittings:
  (a) strap hinge
  (b) tee hinge
  (c) piano hinge.

6 Explain why it is necessary to drill a small pilot hole into the timber before inserting a screw.

7 Describe the steps you would take when preparing a piece to take a screw.

8 Make a sketch to show how you would connect the top of a table to its frame.

PowerPoint Summary   Weblinks

21 Joints

Learning intentions

At the end of this chapter you will be able to:
- Identify and compare different types of joints.
- Create basic drawings or sketches of joints.
- Evaluate and decide where particular joints may be suitable.

Joints in wood and other materials are used when we want to make connections stronger. However, joints can also add a decorative element often used in design. The most effective pieces use simple jointing techniques that are well made to give strength and durability.

There are many ways wood can be joined. Nails and screws can be used, but joints formed in the wood are strong and show off your skill. Adhesives are usually used to add strength to many joints.

What makes this joint strong?

Consider the reasons strong and decorative joints look well

WOOD JOINTS	
Advantages	**Disadvantages**
• Strong, solid and long lasting. • Can be a decorative feature (dovetails and finger joints). • Joints resist forces well.	• They take time to make. • They are often hard to make well. • Specific tools required.

Creating joints

Create simple sketches of each joint as you proceed through the chapter. Try to sketch the 3D view if you can also.

Butt Joints

Basic joints like the **butt** joint or rebated butt joint are easy to make. Nails, pins, or screws are used to give added strength to these joints. The rebate will add strength or grip because of the extra glue area. They might be used in simple box construction.

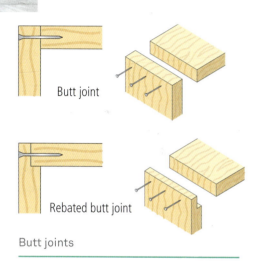

Butt joint

Rebated butt joint

Butt joints

Edge Joint

Wider boards often shrink and are prone to cupping. Often, a wide board made from solid wood is required for a table top, for example. A wide board is made by joining a number of narrow boards edge-to-edge. A number of edge joints can be used. Alternating the end grain direction helps to avoid cupping.

Alternating grain helps to prevent warping of the board

The edges must be planed flat to prevent gaps and to ensure a strong glue bond. The boards are slightly thicker than required so that slight inaccuracies can be planed after the glue has set.

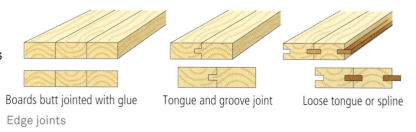

Boards butt jointed with glue   Tongue and groove joint   Loose tongue or spline

Edge joints

189

Housing Joints

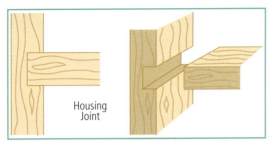
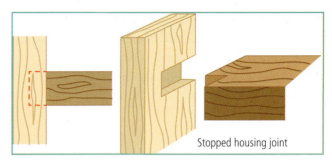
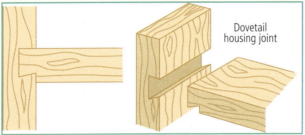

Types of housing joints

Housed joints or **housing** joints are simple and effective. They are used in shelving units or for securing dividers in boxes. Housed joints are glued and often strengthened using panel pins. The stopped housing joint is used where you wish to hide the joint which would have been visible in a basic housing joint.

Choosing joints

A simple tool caddy made from contrasting woods is shown in the sketch. Working in pairs, discuss and brainstorm which joints might be suitable for joining the pieces at the junctions (a) and (b) as well as the corners (c). Name the joints and make simple sketches of your solutions.

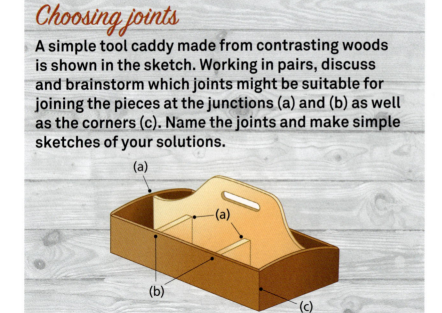

Halving Joints

Halving joints are created when half of the thickness of each piece is removed. When the two halves come together, they make up one full thickness. Used in frame construction, these joints are strong, yet easy to make. They are often strengthened using glue and screws.

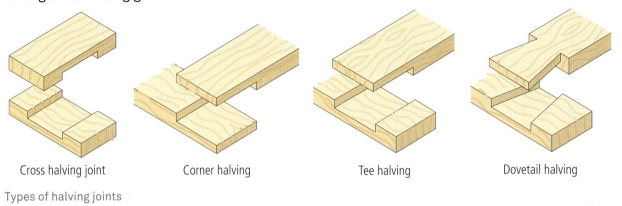

| Cross halving joint | Corner halving | Tee halving | Dovetail halving |

Types of halving joints

Bridle Joints

The **bridle** joint likely gets its name from its resemblance to the way a bridle and bit slips into a horse's mouth. With a large glue surface to give a strong bond, this strong joint has many uses. It is often used as an alternative to the mortise and tenon joint. It is used in frame construction, tables, and chairs. As a decorative feature, the bridle joint is usually made of an uneven number (usually three) of interlocking tenons. The tenons are usually of equal thickness.

Bridle joint

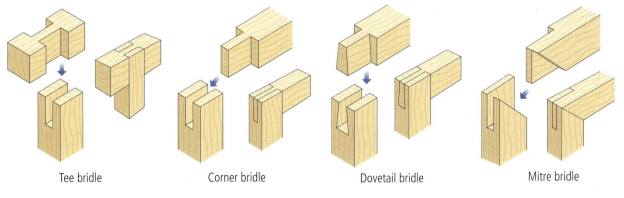

| Tee bridle | Corner bridle | Dovetail bridle | Mitre bridle |

Types of bridle joints

Finger Joint

One form of bridle is often used in the corners of boxes, trays, and containers. The large glue surface makes this attractive joint strong. When planning this joint, it is important to have an odd number of fingers (5, 7, 9, etc.) which will give a symmetrical appearance.

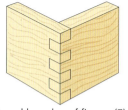
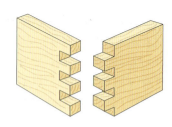

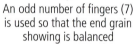
An odd number of fingers (7) is used so that the end grain showing is balanced

Finger joint

Mortise and Tenon Joint

Mortise and **tenon** joints are widely used and very strong. While there are different types, each mortise and tenon consists of a hole cut into one piece (the mortise) through which the tenon, cut from the other piece, fits exactly. Often, the tenon goes all the way through the piece, which can act as a decorative feature. Sometimes the mortise is purposely stopped or hidden so the tenon is not seen. This is sometimes known as a stub tenon or blind tenon.

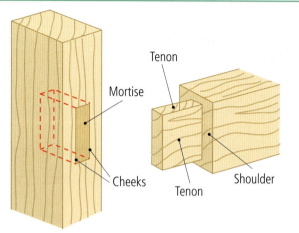

Mortise and Tenon

Usually, the mortise is one third the width of the piece to ensure the tenon is not weak.

In wider pieces, twin tenons are used. A single, wide tenon would shrink and become loose, so two tenons are more secure.

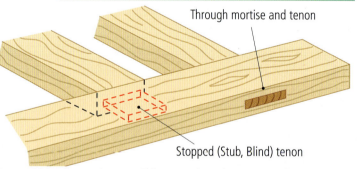

Through mortise and tenon

Stopped (Stub, Blind) tenon

Stopped Mortise and tenon. What are the advantages of this joint?

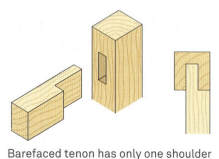

Barefaced tenon has only one shoulder

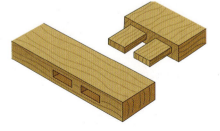

Twin mortise and tenon joint

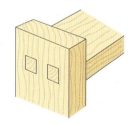

A **wedged** mortise and tenon is used when the joint is likely to receive a lot of stress or forces trying to move it – for example, in a chair leg. The wedges secure the joint firmly and make sure it doesn't loosen.

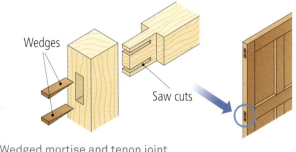

Wedged mortise and tenon joint

A **haunched** mortise and tenon is used in the corner of a frame like a door. It gives extra width to the tenon and prevents twisting of the joint.

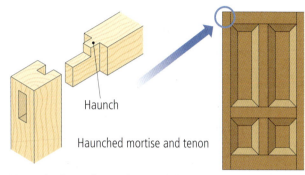

Haunched mortise and tenon joint

Dovetail joint

Dovetail joints are widely used. They resist pulling forces very well, so they are especially suited for making drawers. They are attractive and strong. The slope of the dovetail is usually greater in soft wood than hardwood. Variations of dovetail joints are pictured here.

Dovetail Slope	
Hardwood	1 : 8
Softwood	1 : 6

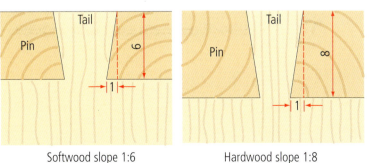
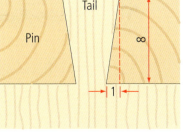

Softwood slope 1:6
Hardwood slope 1:8

Slope of dovetails

Consider what happens to the dovetail joint as the drawer is pulled

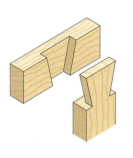

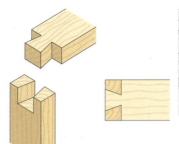

Tee dovetail halving joint   Single through dovetail joint

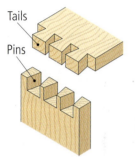

Tails

Pins

Through dovetail
Box, carcases
and drawers

Lapped dovetail
Often used in fronts of drawers where
strength is needed but joint must be hidden

Types of dovetail joints

Mitre Joint

A **mitre** joint or mitre is a simple joint where two pieces meet
with a 45 degree bevelled corner. A plain mitre is weak so it is
usually strengthened with pins, loose tongues, or biscuit
joints. A mitred bridle joint is used to give a strong joint that
retains a clean mitre in the front.

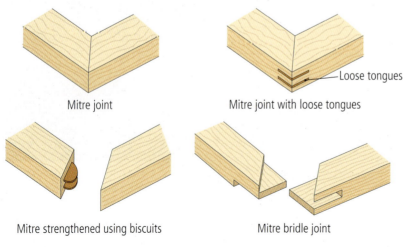

Loose tongues

Mitre joint   Mitre joint with loose tongues

Mitre strengthened using biscuits   Mitre bridle joint

Mitre joints

Screw Joints

Screws are often used to join pieces together effectively. They can add strength to simple joints. Screws are usually countersunk into the wood so the head is **flush** with the surface, which gives a neat finish. A brass screw cup can be used to give a decorative appearance.

Although a screwed joint is secure, it can be unattractive on quality work. One method to hide a screw is to drive a wooden plug below the surface to cover the head of the screw. Plugs are cut from scrap wood using plug cutter bits, as shown.

Wooden plugs and cutter

Method for creating a wooden plug.
- Drill a small pilot hole for the screw.
- Using a larger drill bore a hole suitable for the plug.
- Cut a plug using a plug cutting bit (same diameter as the larger hole).
- Secure the screw, then glue and insert the plug using a pin hammer.
- Sand off the excess material so the plug is flush and smooth with the wood surface.

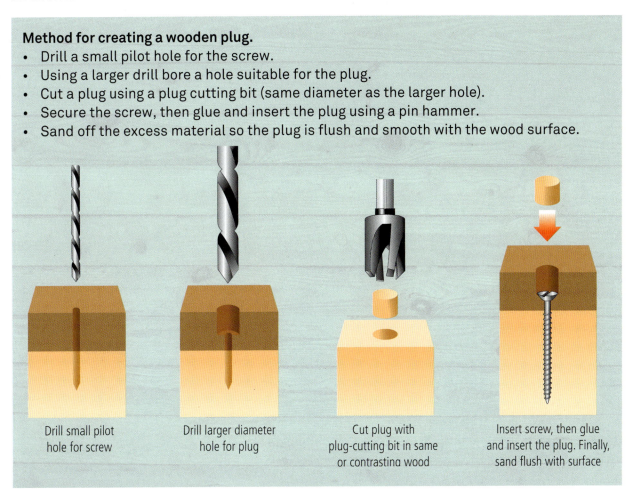

Drill small pilot hole for screw

Drill larger diameter hole for plug

Cut plug with plug-cutting bit in same or contrasting wood

Insert screw, then glue and insert the plug. Finally, sand flush with surface

195

Joiner blocks

Simple butt joints are sometimes strengthened using blocks made from wood or plastic. Plastic blocks are often called knock-down fittings because they enable pieces to be assembled and taken apart easily. Wooden blocks are often used to joint tops to tables or for reinforcing joints at the sides of a box.

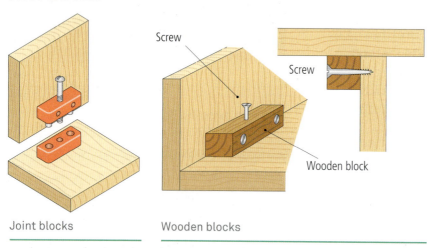

Joint blocks

Wooden blocks

Dowel Joint

A **dowel** is a piece of wood shaped in a cylinder. They are obtained as long pieces or as short ready-made dowels. The grooved sides allow air and glue to escape from the holes as the joint closes.

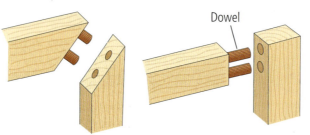

Dowel Joints. Why are two dowels needed in the joint rather than just one?

Dowels. What do the grooves on the sides do?

A dowel joint is similar to a mortise joint. The holes for the dowels must be very accurately marked. A dowelling jig is very useful to drilling the holes accurately.

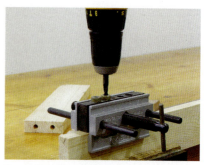

Dowelling jig. Explain briefly how this device helps to position the holes accurately

196

Biscuit Joint

As we have learned, a biscuit is an oval-shaped piece of compressed beech wood. They are used when making biscuit joints. Biscuit joints are quick and easy to make using the biscuit joiner and they form a strong joint.

Method for creating a biscuit joint
- Mark the centre positions for the biscuits on both pieces.
- Set the joiner for the appropriate size of biscuit and depth of cut.
- Using the joiner, cut slots into both pieces.
- Apply glue to the slot and edge before inserting the biscuit.
- Fit the two glued pieces together and cramp them firmly.

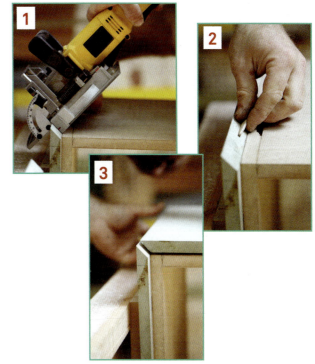

Biscuit joints are strong and can be made quickly, but what are possible disadvantages?

Joints in use

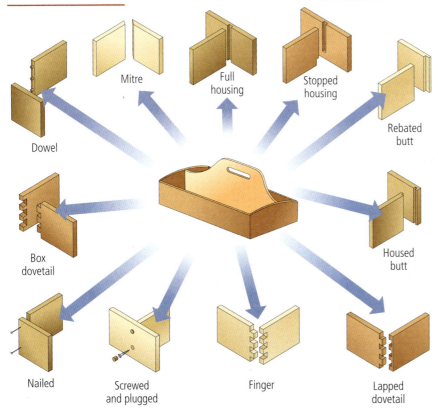

Mitre
Full housing
Stopped housing
Rebated butt
Dowel
Box dovetail
Housed butt
Nailed
Screwed and plugged
Finger
Lapped dovetail

Joints used in boxes

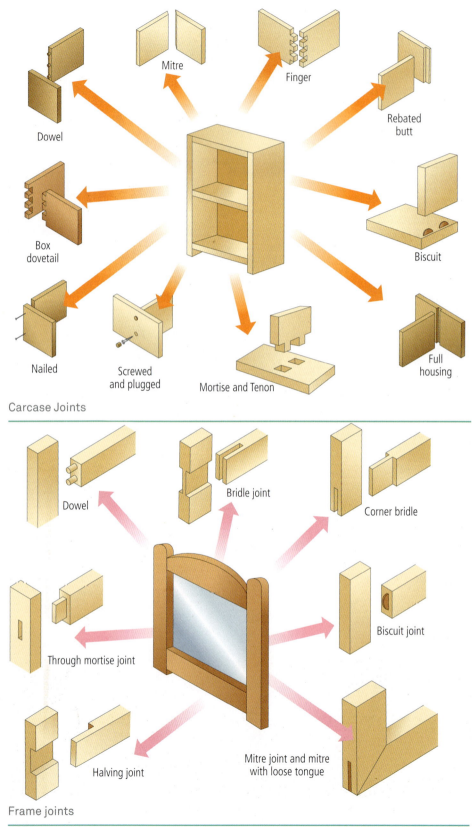

Mitre

Finger

Rebated
butt

Dowel

Box
dovetail

Biscuit

Nailed

Screwed
and plugged

Mortise and Tenon

Full
housing

Carcase Joints

Dowel

Bridle joint

Corner bridle

Through mortise joint

Biscuit joint

Halving joint

Mitre joint and mitre
with loose tongue

Frame joints

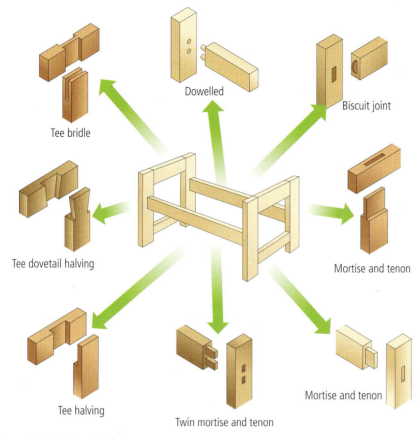

Tee bridle

Dowelled

Biscuit joint

Tee dovetail halving

Mortise and tenon

Tee halving

Twin mortise and tenon

Mortise and tenon

Stool and table frame joints

Joints in Metals

Metals can be joined to wood using screws (as with a hinge). Metals are joined to other metals using nuts and bolts, rivets, soldering, and welding. Special glues may also be used.

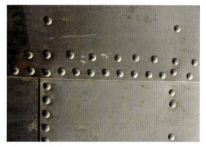

Riveted joint

Soldered joint

Nut and bolt

Welded joint

Joining plastic

Plastic is joined using glue. Super glue is often used to bond acrylic. We also use screws and bolts to secure plastic to wood and other materials.

Gluing plastic

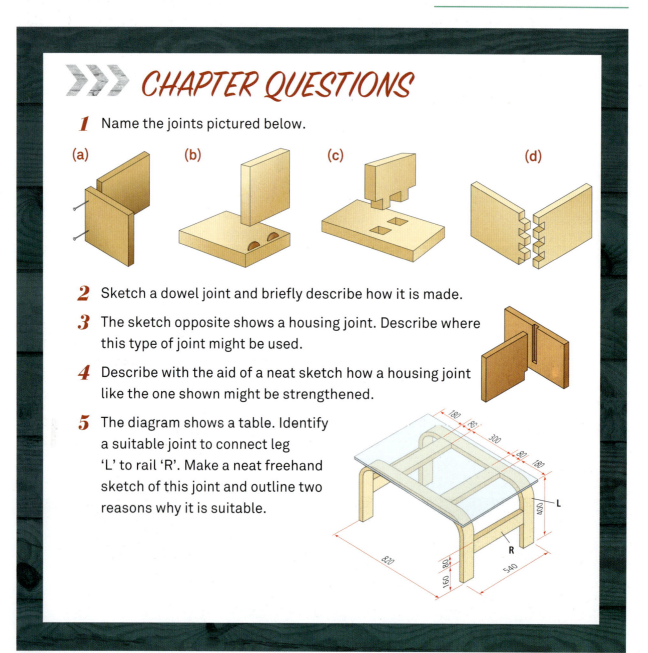

CHAPTER QUESTIONS

1 Name the joints pictured below.

(a) (b) (c) (d)

2 Sketch a dowel joint and briefly describe how it is made.

3 The sketch opposite shows a housing joint. Describe where this type of joint might be used.

4 Describe with the aid of a neat sketch how a housing joint like the one shown might be strengthened.

5 The diagram shows a table. Identify a suitable joint to connect leg 'L' to rail 'R'. Make a neat freehand sketch of this joint and outline two reasons why it is suitable.

6 One piece of a tee-halving joint is shown in the diagram. Make a neat sketch to show the other half of the joint.

7 Describe with the aid of notes and neat freehand sketches the steps you would follow to mark out and remove the trench shown in the diagram.

8 The diagram below shows a wooden planter for displaying flowers on a window sill. Using notes and sketches, describe two methods of joining the front 'S' to the sides 'A'.

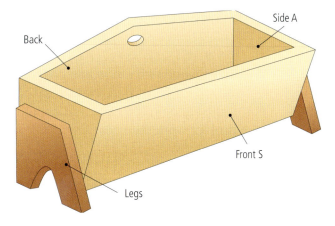

Side A

Back

Front S

Legs

9 Describe using sketches how you would connect the legs of the planter to the sides using screws and plugs.

PowerPoint Summary · Weblinks

22 Carving and Shaping

KEYWORDS
- chip carving
- gouge
- relief carving
- skew chisel
- sweep
- veiner

LEARNING OUTCOMES
- 1.3, 1.4 1.8, 1.10,
- 2.3, 2.11

Learning intentions

At the end of this chapter you will be able to:
- Identify different carving tools and state their use.
- Describe types of carving and compare them.

Carving in wood and stone has been used as a form of art and decoration for centuries. Wood carving can be decorative and culturally specific. You can add decorative touches to your own project work using carving.

Carving chisels

Examples of carving

Chisels

Basic shaping may be done using regular chisels, but there are a variety of shaped chisels, **gouges**, and tools used for carving wood. Descriptions of the common types are given here. Palm chisels fit into the palm of the hand. Other carving chisels and gouges are used by hand pressure or by tapping with a carver's mallet.

Carving chisels and palm chisels

Skew chisels

The **skew chisel** has a high quality blade and a hardwood handle. They come in different sizes. The edge of the skew chisel is angled back, enabling it to fit into tight spaces.

Gouges

Gouges have U-shaped blades used for carving shapes in wood. The blades of carving chisels are made from high quality steel and they have a hardwood handle.

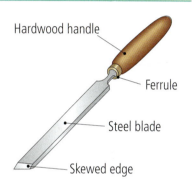

Hardwood handle

Ferrule

Steel blade

Skewed edge

Square edge

Skewed edge

Skew chisel

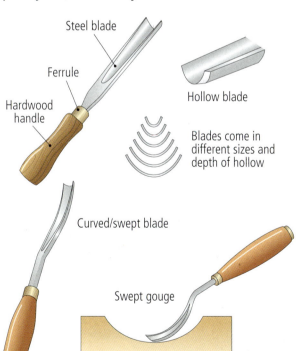

Steel blade

Ferrule

Hardwood handle

Hollow blade

Blades come in different sizes and depth of hollow

Curved/swept blade

Swept gouge

Carving gouges

Carving gouges come in a variety of curves and blade sizes, from very shallow to a deep curve. Each curve or **sweep** is identified by number. A number 1 is a flat chisel. The blades are wider at the cutting end.

Veiner

A **veiner** is a small gouge with a deep narrow U-shaped blade. It has a straight blade and is used to make narrow U-shaped grooved cuts into the wood surface.

Gouge can be used with hand pressure or, with difficult wood, using a carver's mallet

Carver's mallet. Consider why the mallet is round

Veiner

Vee tool. Where does it get its name from?

Vee tool

The Vee tool can be obtained in various sizes. Its v-shaped blade is used to carve v-shaped grooves, lettering, and tight cuts. It is used for incised carving and for defining an outline of a carving.

Types of carving

Whittling

Whittling is a form of carving shapes from wood using sharp knives. It is often done on branch wood or sticks. Special carving knives can be used for whittling that allow you to make delicate cuts more easily.

Incised carving

This is where a simple shape or outline is transferred onto the wood. The outline is then carved into the wood using a veiner or vee tool.

An example of whittling

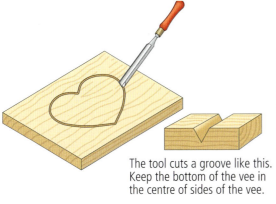

The tool cuts a groove like this. Keep the bottom of the vee in the centre of sides of the vee.

Incised carving

An example of incised carving

Chip carving

Chip carving uses cuts in the wood to make attractive patterns. The cuts are often formed using special carving knives. Chip carving patterns can be very elaborate. Some simple carved cuts like triangles and diamonds can be done using a chisel. They are a simple way to add decoration to a piece of work.

 'My Chip Carving – Proper Technique' by MyChipCarving.com

Mark out the triangle and find the centre

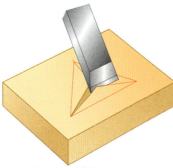

Outline the middle lines down to the centre point

Example of elaborate chip carving

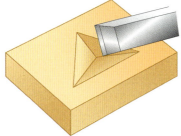

Carefully finish the angled cuts using the chisel

Completed triangular cut

Method for chip carving

1 Plan the pattern on paper.
2 Carefully transfer the design onto the wood surface.
3 Carefully outline the slopes to the centre point.
4 Carefully make the angled cuts to complete the three side slopes.

205

Relief carving

Relief carving involves outlining and highlighting a shape or design on a piece of wood by removing material surrounding it. Removing the surrounding wood reveals the shape clearly and makes it stand out. There can be low relief (shallow) carving or deeper (high) relief carving, depending on how much you wish the shape to stand out.

Relief carving example

1 Draw the outline pattern on to the wood.

2 Use a chisel or knife to cut around the outline of the pattern.

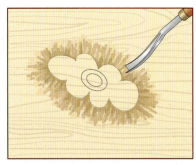

3 Use a gouge to remove the wood around the outline (setting in).

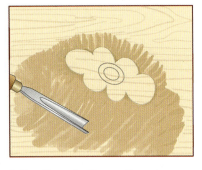

4 Continue to lower the area around the outline (grounding).

5 Use a fine chisel or gouge to shape the fine details; work in the direction of the grain.

6 Sand lightly and apply a finish to complete the carving.

Stages in relief carving

Transferring a pattern

Patterns from photos, books, or printed from the internet can easily be transferred to the wood. You can use carbon paper or draw the pattern out by hand. Another method is to use a soft pencil (2B) to transfer graphite onto the back of the photocopied or printed pattern. Then tape the pattern onto the wooden piece so it doesn't move about. Carefully draw over the pattern, pressing the graphite underneath onto the wood surface. If the lines are too light when the sheet is removed, you can darken them with a pencil before carving.

1   2   3   4

Transferring a pattern onto wood

Texturing punch

The grounding or texturing punch is a piece of steel with a textured end. The textured point produces a textured effect on the wood. These tools are often used on the background of relief carvings. They can be made from a piece of steel bar and triangular file. Texture can be added to any surface to create a decorative look.

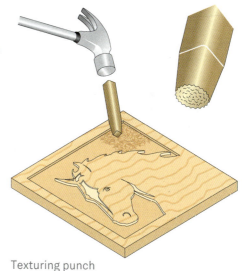

Texturing punch

Texture design

Research and then create a design to decorate the top of a wooden jewellery box using a textured effect.

Sculpture and 3D carving

Three dimensional carving or sculpture is where a figure is carved from a block of wood called a blank. Rasps, files, gouges and chisels are used to produce simple or complex shapes.

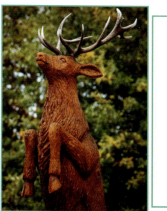

Examples of wood sculpture

207

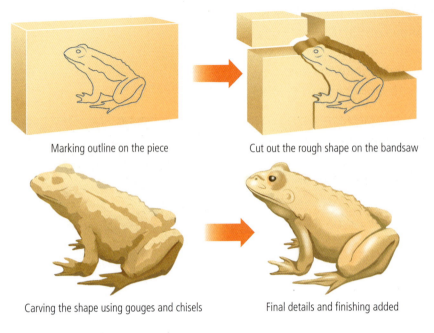

Marking outline on the piece

Cut out the rough shape on the bandsaw

Carving the shape using gouges and chisels

Final details and finishing added

Stages in 3D carving

Shaping

Surform tools (short for surface forming) and shapers can also be used to create successful shapes in wood. Surforms, rasps and files produce a rough finished surface which can be further smoothed by sanding on a sanding machine and details added using a multi-tool.

https://www.
crystaldriedger.
com/tutorials-tips/
dremeltutorial

Shaping with a rotary multi-tool

Sharpening

When carving, having a sharp cutting edge is vital. Chisels and gouges must be sharpened often using a sharpening stone and slip stone.

Gouges must be sharpened in the outside bevel using a sweeping, rolling motion

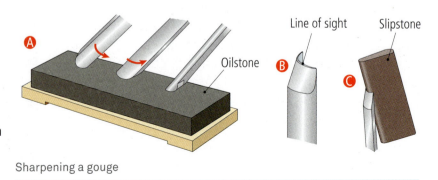

Ⓐ   Oilstone   Line of sight   Slipstone   Ⓑ   Ⓒ

Sharpening a gouge

along the oilstone. The burr from sharpening is removed using the slipstone and the edge is given a final polish on a leather strop.

Suitable woods

Most woods are suitable for carving. However, having an understanding of the characteristics of different wood will help in choosing the most suitable wood for your project.

The best wood should be easy to work with a uniform grain pattern that is not too pronounced.

Characteristics
- Free from knots and defects
- Straight uniform grain
- Suitable colour (light/dark)

Light woods	Dark woods
Sycamore Pine Lime Poplar	Mahogany Walnut

Medium density fibreboard (MDF) is a man-made wood suitable for carving because of its uniform consistency and absence of grain. It is easy to work with and to cut in any direction, so the chisels will follow the lines easily. Carving a veneered board of MDF allows the facing veneer to be left exposed, revealing a good contrast to the MDF below.

Finishes

All carvings should be properly finished. The wood may be sanded lightly to remove slight imperfections. Care must be taken to avoid sanding out the fine detail. The chosen applied finish should seal the wood but not take away from the detail of the carving. Stain is often used to highlight the shadow areas. Varnish may be used, but avoid gloss finishes because shiny surfaces distract from the visual appearance. Danish oil is often used, as it seals and protects the wood while giving a nice matt or satin finish.

CHAPTER QUESTIONS

1 Name the following tools used in carving wood.

(a)  **(b)**  **(c)**

2 Draw a sketch describing a skew chisel and briefly explain what the skew chisel might be used for when carving.

3 Briefly explain the term 'sweep' as it applies to wood carving tools. Use a simple sketch to aid your explanation.

4 Name three methods of carving wood you have learned about for the examples (a), (b), and (c) below.

(a)  **(b)**  **(c)**

5 Name one light coloured wood and one dark coloured wood which might be suitable for carving piece (b) above.

6 Using notes and sketches, describe how you would transfer the pattern onto the wooden blank for the piece pictured right.

7 Describe, using notes and sketches, the basic steps that you would use to carve the piece.

 PowerPoint Summary **Weblinks**

23 Woodturning

Learning intentions

At the end of this chapter you will be able to:
- Identify parts of the woodturning lathe and describe their purpose.
- Name the common tools and safety precautions associated with woodturning.
- Briefly outline how simple pieces are prepared and mounted on a lathe.

People have been turning wood for many years using simple pole lathes that were manually operated. Woodturning uses simple tools and skills to produce beautiful rounded artefacts based on a cylindrical shape using special gouges and chisels.

Examples of wood turning

Lathe

The woodturning lathe is used in wood technology for rotating wood. Depending on the type and size (length) of the lathe, it may be freestanding or mounted on a bench. The parts of the lathe are the same on most machines. You should be familiar with the parts before you use the lathe.

Parts of the lathe

The distance from the centre of the **spindle** to the bed of the lathe (a half **swing**) will limit the diameter or size of bowl that may be turned. The length of the bed is important, as it will determine the maximum length of piece that may be turned.

Headstock

The **headstock** is where the motor and drive centre is located. It is usually where the on/off buttons are found, as well as the belts and pulleys that drive the spindle. The pulleys and drive belt can be adjusted to change the speed at which the wood turns.

Lathe drive belt

Initially, larger pieces such as large bowls should be turned at a slower speed. The speed can be increased as needed. Smaller pieces and finer work might need faster speeds to achieve a better finish.

⚠ Students shouldn't adjust the belts in the headstock, as it could cause an accident.

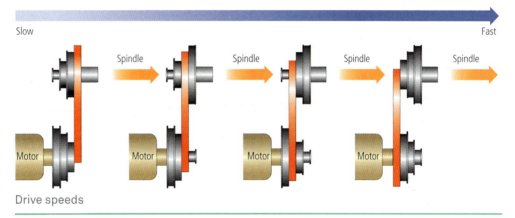
Slow   Fast
Spindle   Spindle   Spindle   Spindle
Motor   Motor   Motor   Motor
Drive speeds

Centres

When turning spindles on a lathe the wooden piece known as a **blank** is held between two centres: a drive centre and a revolving centre.

Drive centre

The drive centre fits into the drive spindle. It is set into the centre of the wood and it turns the wood as it spins.

Drive centre

Live or revolving centre

This is held in the **tailstock** end and revolves with the wood as it turns. It must be tightened against the wood to ensure the piece is held firmly in position.

Tool rest

The tool rest for a lathe is set into a block that can be moved along the bed. The block is called a **banjo** and can be locked into position. The tool rest can be adjusted for height and position and is locked into position by the tool rest lock.

Revolving/live centre

Tool rest

RECORD POWER

Locking screw for height adjustment

Banjo or tool rest holder

Locking screw for lateral adjustment

Tool rest and banjo

Consider why the tool rest needs to be so adjustable

Faceplates

The drive centre can be removed and replaced with a **faceplate**. These can be used when turning bowls, dishes or bases. The piece or blank is fixed to the faceplate using screws.

Faceplates

Chucks

Chucks are used to grip the wood without the need to screw into the piece. The chuck is attached to the drive spindle. The jaws of the chuck hold the wood tightly and can adjust to different diameters.

Chucks screw onto the spindle

Turning tools

There are a number of basic tools used for woodturning. They have sturdy blades and longer handles compared to other chisels and gouges. Their size makes them easier to hold when turning. The blades are made from high speed steel (HSS) and the handles are usually hardwood.

Woodturning tools: chisels, gouges, and parting tools

The basic tools are:

- gouges
- parting tools
- scrapers
- skew chisels.

Gouges

The gouge is used for turning bowls and also on spindle work (between centres). There are two basic types of gouge used for woodturning: the shallow-fluted gouge and the deep-fluted gouge.

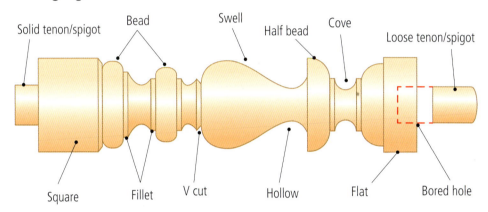

Woodturning profiles

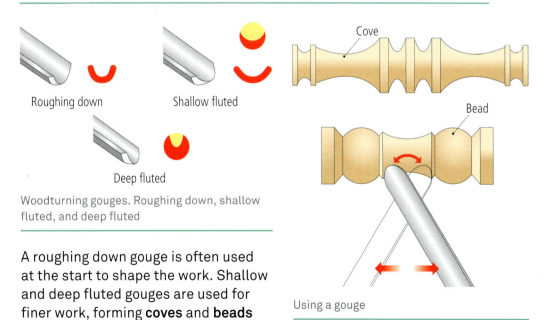

Woodturning gouges. Roughing down, shallow fluted, and deep fluted

A roughing down gouge is often used at the start to shape the work. Shallow and deep fluted gouges are used for finer work, forming **coves** and **beads** in the wood.

Using a gouge

Skew chisel

The skew chisel has an edge that is swept back or 'skewed'. The edge is bevelled on both sides unlike a firmer chisel. The blade of the skew chisel can be rectangle or oval in section. It is used to cut 'V' grooves and beads on the work piece. The chisel is used to make a paring cut which leaves a very smooth finish on the wood.

Skew chisels

Skewed back

Skew chisel with edge swept back

V groove

Bead

Skew chisel

Beading cut

Beads and 'v' grooves

Parting tool

The parting tool is used to 'part' or make deep cuts that divide the wood into separate sections and also to turn spigots for joining a stem to a base or to secure a piece in a chuck.

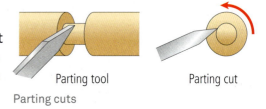

Parting tool

Parting cut

Parting cuts

There are two basic forms of parting tool, found in a variety of sizes: rectangular and diamond (shown below).

25° angle

Rectangular   Diamond

Parting tool types

Scrapers

Scrapers have a flat blade and their edge is bevelled. Some have a square edge while others have a curved edge. They work by scraping away at the wood as it turns, leaving a roughly shaped surface. This rough surface must be sanded smooth with sandpapers.

Square and rounded scrapers

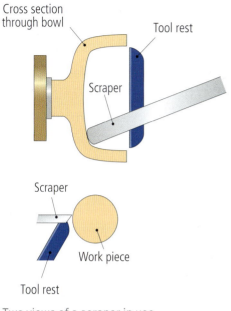

Two views of a scraper in use

Measuring on the lathe

Taking accurate measurements of rounded pieces can be difficult. Callipers are used by turners to ensure accuracy. Callipers are used to measure the inside diameters and outside diameters of turned work. The Vernier calliper also has a depth gauge to measure the depth of holes and is also available with a digital readout.

Vernier callipers

Dividers can also be used to take accurate dimensions from a drawing.

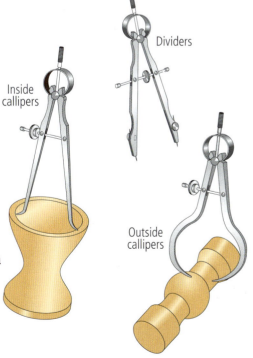

The dividers, inside callipers, and outside callipers

Lathe safety

Using any machine can be hazardous, so it is important that you follow safety guidelines when using the lathe.

⚠ Always wear full face visor.

⚠ Remove jewellery and tie up loose clothing and long hair.

⚠ Only work as instructed and with permission of the teacher.

⚠ Make sure the work is always securely held on the lathe.

⚠ Keep the tool rest close to the work.

⚠ Check the clearance – rotate the work by hand before switching on.

⚠ Avoid touching the rotating wood with your hand.

⚠ Use face mask when sanding and finishing.

Turning techniques

The two basic forms of turning are spindle turning (between centres) and bowl turning (faceplate & chuck).

Spindle turning
Prepare the piece

- Select a piece (also called a blank) with no defects.
- Mark the ends to find the centre and position the drive centre as shown in the diagram.
- Insert the drive centre using a mallet (a hammer will damage the drive centre).

Mounting the piece

- Insert the piece and drive centre in the headstock end.
- Slide the tailstock to meet the centre at the other end of the piece.
- Tighten the centre against the end of the piece.

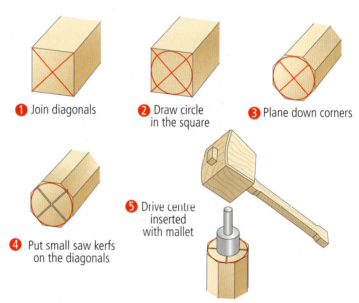

❶ Join diagonals   ❷ Draw circle in the square   ❸ Plane down corners

❹ Put small saw kerfs on the diagonals

❺ Drive centre inserted with mallet

Steps to prepare and mount a piece (blank) on the lathe

A blank mounted on a spindle

Spindle turning

Profiles

Designs of turned work are drawn as an outline or **profile** of the shape. A profile template can be made in light hardboard or plywood. A profile only needs to show half of the object, since the other half is created automatically. The profile template is used to check the accuracy of the shape against the drawing and when making several pieces with the same shape.

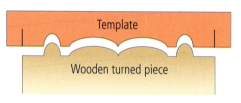

Profile template

Profile design

Draw a profile of a small candle stand and make a profile template of your design.

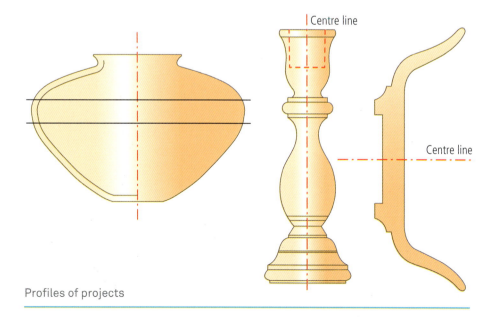

Profiles of projects

Boring a hole

Sometimes you will need to bore a hole through the centre of a turned piece. For example, a hole is needed to thread electric flex through the stem of a lamp. There are three ways to accomplish this:

Method 1

- Before turning, prepare the blank.
- Groove two sections in the centre using a saw or router.
- Glue both pieces together to form the blank for turning.
- The groove (hole) is now in the centre of the piece.

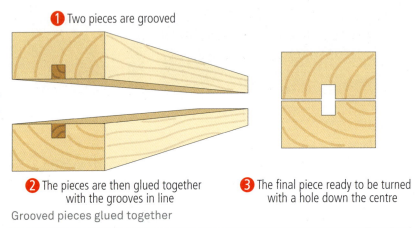

1 Two pieces are grooved

2 The pieces are then glued together with the grooves in line

3 The final piece ready to be turned with a hole down the centre

Grooved pieces glued together

Method 2

- Secure the piece using a hollow centre in the tailstock.
- Drill the hole carefully through the hollow centre to halfway, removing shavings regularly.
- Reverse the piece in the lathe and repeat boring through the other half.

Long hole boring kit

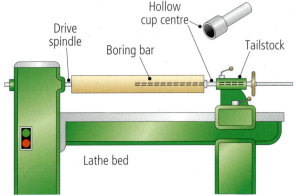

Drive spindle

Hollow cup centre

Boring bar

Tailstock

Lathe bed

Boring a long hole on the lathe

Method 3

- Using a long auger bit in the drill, bore a hole at the centre and go halfway through the length of the piece.
- Reverse the ends and repeat the boring process, taking care that you are drilling straight and accurately.

Auger drill bit

Joints

Joints are used in woodturning to connect pieces together to make longer sections and to connect a stem to a wider base. This is useful and prevents wasting valuable timber.

A **spigot** and socket joint is used to create a strong bond between the pieces. A hole is first drilled in one piece. Then, the spigot is turned while gradually checking for the correct diameter to ensure a tight-fitting joint. The joint can be glued to fix it permanently in place.

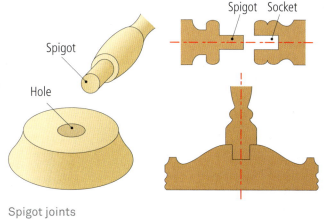

Spigot joints

Bowl turning

When turning a bowl or dish on the lathe, a faceplate or chuck is used to hold the piece firmly. A bowl is turned in two stages. The bottom is turned first and finished, then the piece is reversed and the top or inside is hollowed out and finished.

Bowl turning

Preparing and mounting the blank for bowl turning

- Draw the diagonals on the faces of the wooden piece to locate the centre.
- Draw the outline of the largest circle on the blank with a compass.
- Draw tangents to the line to give an octagon.
- Use a saw to remove the corners, making it safer to turn.
- Locate the faceplate on the centre of the face and screw it down. The screws should secure the piece, but not be too long to interfere with the turning.
- Mount the faceplate on the lathe and tighten by hand.
- Adjust the tool rest to the work piece with adequate clearance. Check that the piece rotates without touching the tool rest.

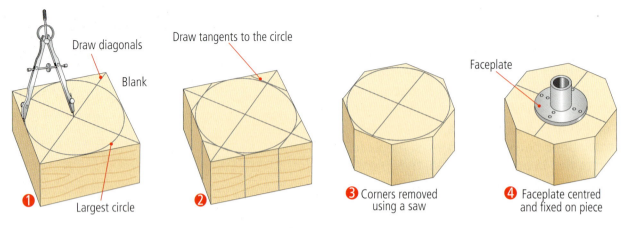

① Largest circle · Blank · Draw diagonals

② Draw tangents to the circle

③ Corners removed using a saw

④ Faceplate · Faceplate centred and fixed on piece

Preparing and mounting a blank on a faceplate for bowl turning

Turning a bowl with an auxiliary faceplate

An auxiliary faceplate may be used to avoid damaging the piece with screws or when there is a possibility that the lathe tool may catch on a screw.

Wood for turning

Most wood can be turned on the lathe. Close-grained hardwoods are best. Softwood like pine is ideal to start with because softer wood is easier to work with. The wood you use should be free of defects such as knots and splits which are unsightly and can get snagged by the chisel or gouge.

Popular woods for turning are:

- Beech
- Ash
- Oak
- Sycamore
- Elm
- Cherry
- Yew
- Walnut
- Maple.

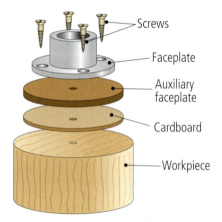

Screws · Faceplate · Auxiliary faceplate · Cardboard · Workpiece

Attaching work to an auxiliary faceplate

Turning a bowl attached to a faceplate

Finishing

Sanding and finishing of work is usually completed while the piece is on the lathe.

The wood is sanded through different grit sizes of sandpaper (120, 180, 320), ensuring that any scratches and blemishes are removed with each successive grade. Avoid spoiling the appearance of the piece by paying careful attention not to round the edges while sanding.

Sanding a piece on the lathe

⚠ Sanding and finishing on the lathe creates fine dust, so always wear a dust mask.

⚠ Take care while sanding and finishing, as the friction can cause burns.

⚠ Use non-toxic finish on artefacts that will have contact with food.

A variety of finishes can be used on turned work. Oil finishes like Danish oil are very popular because they can be applied on the lathe and they soak into the wood. Friction polish and beeswax is also a popular finish. Objects like fruit bowls and other artefacts in contact with food must be finished with a non-toxic finish.

⫸⫸⫸ *CHAPTER QUESTIONS*

1 Label the parts of the lathe pictured.

2 Name the parts of the lathe pictured below and outline their purpose.

(a)   (b)   (c)

3 List three safety precautions you should take when using the lathe.

4 Using sketches explain the following terms:
(a) cove   (b) bead   (c) fillet.

5 Draw a sketch of the cutting end of the following woodturning tools:
(a) parting tool   (b) roughing down gouge   (c) skew chisel.

6 Describe how you would ensure that the candle sticks pictured were copied on the lathe accurately and name the device that could help you.

7 Describe the purpose of a live centre.

8 Outline the steps you would use to prepare and mount a piece to be ready for spindle turning.

9 List two safety rules to follow when sanding on the lathe.

10 Make a neat sketch to show how you would join the stem of the lamp in the diagram to its turned base.

 PowerPoint Summary   **Weblinks**

24 Veneering

Learning intentions

At the end of this chapter you will be able to:
- Understand how veneers may be used to create attractive designs.
- Appreciate and describe how veneers are a sustainable alternative to solid wood panels.
- Incorporate simple inlay designs into a basic task.

Veneer is a thin layer of wood cut from the log. High quality veneers are used to cover cheaper boards to enhance their appearance. Veneers are also used to make plywood. They are layered together and bonded to produce this man-made board. Decorative patterns and even pictures can be created using combinations of different veneers.

Veneers are usually bonded with glue to a solid wood base called **groundwork** made from man-made wood such as plywood or MDF. The veneers taken from different parts of the tree give different patterns.

A veneer is a thin layer of wood

Sustainability
Tropical hardwood trees and other rare woods are used to make veneers. This is an environmentally sustainable way to use wood efficiently because an object can have the look of the tropical wood while using much less of it. Therefore, using veneers ensures that scarce natural resources are not wasted.

Advantages of veneering
- Large areas of wood and sheets can be covered with veneer (stable, no splitting).
- Different veneers can be used to create a wide range of pictures and patterns.
- Veneering uses rare and expensive woods efficiently with minimum waste.

Veneer production

The veneer is cut from the log in one of two ways: rotary cutting or slicing.

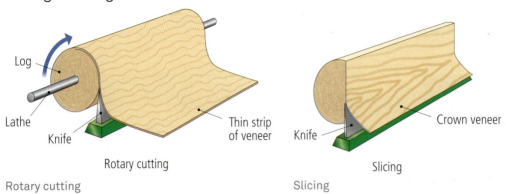

Rotary cutting

Log
Lathe
Knife
Thin strip of veneer
Rotary cutting

Slicing

Knife
Crown veneer
Slicing

The thickness of the veneer is usually between 0.6mm – 1.0mm. The slicing method usually results in an attractive grain pattern. Some parts of the tree unsuitable for solid timber will yield attractive small veneer pieces.

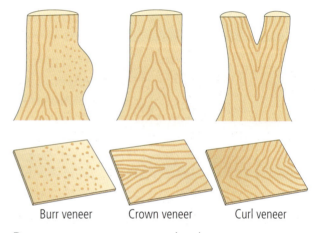

Burr veneer

Crown veneer

Curl veneer

Burr veneer, crown veneer, and curl veneer

Using veneer

Veneers for project work can be obtained in school in small sheet sizes or rolls as pictured below. Variety packs are also available that include a small range of wood shades.

Sheets of wood veneer

Veneered boxes use burr veneers and coloured veneers decoratively

Veneer is bonded to a solid base (known as groundwork) of plywood or MDF using contact adhesive. Contact glue bonds very quickly when the two glued surfaces are brought together. Veneers with a self-adhesive backing can also be bought. This type is easy to apply by peeling away the backing paper before sticking the veneer down.

Groundwork

Plywood or MDF are used for the groundwork because they will not warp. A backing veneer is always applied to the underside of a veneered panel to provide a counter balance to the board and prevent warping.

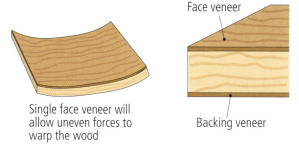

Single face veneer will allow uneven forces to warp the wood

Face veneer

Backing veneer

Counter veneering prevents warping

Veneers must be flat before they are glued to the groundwork. Any buckling can be flattened by dampening the veneer with a damp cloth and clamping the veneer between two boards overnight.

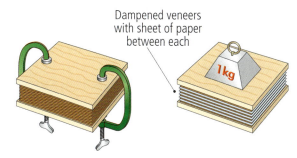

Dampened veneers with sheet of paper between each

1 kg

Flattening veneers. Why do you think veneers must be flat before bonding?

Cutting

The join between each veneer must be accurately cut. A sharp scalpel or craft knife is used. A cutting mat or clean cutting board will support the work. Straight cuts are made with the aid of the steel rule. Cutting along the grain is generally easy. When cutting through harder veneer or across the grain, press gently on the knife and repeat the same cut several times until you cut through.

⚠ When using sharp knives, take care to keep hands away from the edge.

Cutting veneer

Applying the veneer

The veneer or pattern is bonded to the groundwork using contact glue. In past times, animal glue was used. While animal glue could be lifted again by heating the veneer with an iron if needed, contact glue bonds in seconds, so you must be accurate when placing the veneer. Contact veneer doesn't require cramps. A rubber roler or veneer hammer is used to press the veneer to the groundwork and to press out all air pockets, ensuring good contact between the veneer and the base. Contact glue is available in a spray can, which allows an even application of the glue.

Contact glue. Why is it most suitable for veneering?

Step-by-step veneer application

- The groundwork is first sealed using a thin layer of contact glue. Allow the glue to dry.
- Next, apply a thin film of glue on on both surfaces to be bonded. This requires a few minutes to become 'tacky'.
- Then, the veneer is positioned above the groundwork and aligned carefully.
- The centre of the veneer is glued first, gradually working towards the outside edges to avoid trapping any air under the veneer.
- Squeeze out any air pockets using a veneer hammer or roller.
- When the glue has set, trim off the overhanging veneer.

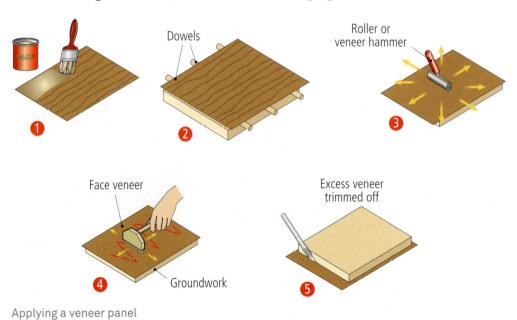

Applying a veneer panel

Veneered designs

The colours, grain patterns, and grain direction of veneers can all be used in a creative way to give an attractive effect. Regular patterns and geometrical designs can also be used to create effective results.

Example of a veneered design

Matching veneers

Simple decorative patterns can be created using the grain of the veneer with basic matching techniques shown in the diagram below. Lining up the edges and angles is crucial with these patterns.

Book matching

Quartered

Diamond

Diagonal

Aligned   Not properly aligned

Matching veneers

Marquetry

This is the art of making decorative pictures from wood veneers. The grain pattern, grain direction and the different types of wood are used to give the shades of colour and texture which create the picture. Even simple designs can give effective results.

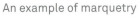

An example of marquetry

Sketch this simple leaf motif

There are a number of ways to create a **marquetry** picture using veneers. The window method is popular because it allows you to align the grain direction as you build up your picture as shown in the example below.

Steps of the window method

Step 1

- Draw or copy a design onto a piece of paper and transfer the design onto the veneer using a sheet of **carbon paper** as shown.
- Cut out the shape using a sharp craft knife or scalpel.
- Place the opening over a second veneer and line up the grain pattern as desired.

Step 2

- Cut through the gap or 'window' or mark the second piece through the window and cut out the second shape.
- Carefully fit piece into place and then tape this second piece into the gap with masking tape. In this example the leaf surface is cut in two separate sections
- Use this process to cut out and build up the different parts of the design or picture.

Step 3

- Each section is taped in place. When ready add a veneer frame. Bond to the groundwork, remove the tape, sand and finish.

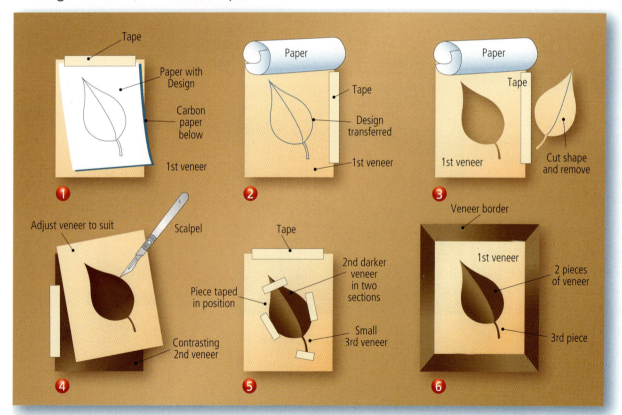

Creating a simple marquetry picture

Parquetry

Parquetry uses contrasting veneers and grain patterns to create regular geometrical designs. A chessboard is a simple form of parquetry. Each piece must be evenly and precisely cut. The diagram shows steps used to create a chessboard in veneer.

Veneers or solid pieces can be used for this. Solid pieces are used to incorporate these designs into a floor, for example. By using the grain direction, a clever 3D effect can be achieved.

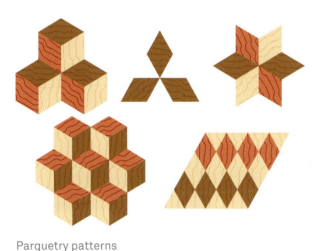

Parquetry patterns

❶ Cut parallel strips of contrasting veneer – 5 light and 4 dark

❷ Tape together in alternate strips to form a sheet

❸ Cut this sheet to the same width to form light and dark squared strips

❹ Stagger the joints and tape to form the chessboard effect

❺ Tape together, apply border, bond to groundwork and finish

Veneering a chessboard

Borders

Photographs and pictures have frames. Veneered pictures and panels can be greatly enhanced by adding a border of decorative veneer.

Plain mitred border

Crossbanding grain direction changed to give effect

Using a contrasting colour veneer to give effect

Consider the use of veneered borders to create a framed effect on the pieces above.

How to create a border with veneer

Border

Panel

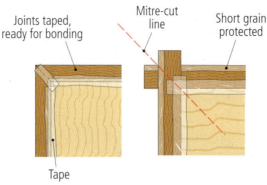
Joints taped, ready for bonding

Mitre-cut line

Short grain protected

Tape

1 Cut and match the strips of veneer. The strips should be long enough to overlap the corners.

2 Carefully mark and cut the mitres at the corners of the border, remove the waste veneer and tape the joints of the mitres.

3 Tape the border to the veneered panel with care to ensure tight joint lines.

4 When you are happy with the panel bond it to the groundwork.

Creating a veneered border

Inlaying

Inlaying involves inserting a strip of contrasting wood or standard line inlay into a recess in the solid wood surface. **Motifs** or standard preprepared veneer patterns can be bought. These can be inserted as a center focal point of a decorative piece.

Inlay lines of contrasting woods are attractive

Veneer designs

A variety of expensive hardwoods are used for inlay (boxwood, ebony, walnut, purpleheart). Other materials such as mother of pearl, tortoise shell, ivory, and bone can be found in antique

Designing inlay

Work in pairs to plan and sketch three possible inlay patterns that could be used on the top of a small wooden jewelery box. Use the internet to generate ideas.

pieces. Coloured plastic can be used as a colourful addition to your design work. Even a small strip can enhance the design.

Inlay strips or bandings are inserted into a shallow groove in the wood. The groove can be created using a router or a **scratch stock**. The scratch stock is made from an old hack saw blade secured between two pieces of hardwood as shown below. It is used like a marking gauge, to scratch a shallow groove into the wood.

Inlay mitred at corners

Scratch stock

Using the scratch stock

Patterns and angled corners can be done using a template to assist the removal of the material using a chisel. A sharp chisel is used to cut and join inlay and create mitre cuts.

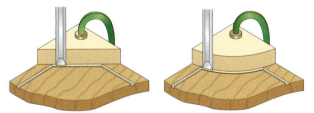

Using an inlay template at corners

Pre-made inlay bandings are available in different patterns, as shown here. They are bought as 1 m lengths and come in different widths. A variey of prepared motifs are also available from specialist suppliers.

Wood veneer bandings

Finishing

A veneered or inlaid piece will be slightly uneven. Scrape away any remaining glue or gum from tape. Sand the surfaces smooth using light sandpaper. Take care not to over-sand veneered pieces, as is easy to sand through the thin veneer. Always sand in the direction of the grain. This will take great patience on a marquetry piece with different parts, particularly with grain going in different ways.

Applied finish depends on where the piece will be used and personal taste. Varnish or wax is commonly chosen.

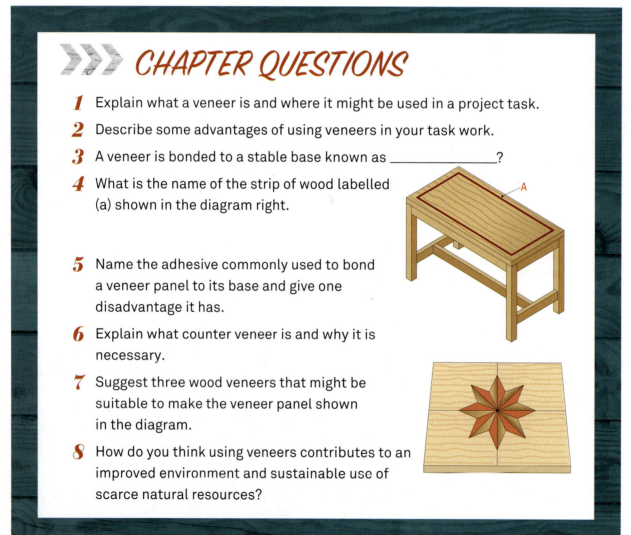

▶▶▶ CHAPTER QUESTIONS

1 Explain what a veneer is and where it might be used in a project task.

2 Describe some advantages of using veneers in your task work.

3 A veneer is bonded to a stable base known as _____?

4 What is the name of the strip of wood labelled (a) shown in the diagram right.

5 Name the adhesive commonly used to bond a veneer panel to its base and give one disadvantage it has.

6 Explain what counter veneer is and why it is necessary.

7 Suggest three wood veneers that might be suitable to make the veneer panel shown in the diagram.

8 How do you think using veneers contributes to an improved environment and sustainable use of scarce natural resources?

 PowerPoint Summary · Weblinks

25 Laminating, Scroll Saw Work, and Pyrography

Learning intentions

At the end of this chapter you will be able to:
- Understand short grain in wood.
- Describe the process of laminating to create a curved piece for a task.

Creating curved work in wood can be a challenge, but the results are beautiful. Curves cut from a solid piece can improve the appearance of a project, although it wastes a lot of wood. Care must be taken to avoid **short grain**, which can break away easily when cutting curves in wood.

Wood can be bent by first heating it with steam and then gradually bending it into shape. Curves in wood can also be formed through the **laminating** process.

Chair featuring curved wood

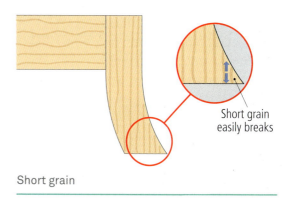

Short grain easily breaks

Short grain

235

Laminating

Laminating is the process of gluing together small thin sections of wood to form larger sections. Thin sections of wood will bend into gentle curves without splitting, so curved pieces can be created by laminating thin sections. The laminated pieces will be stronger than one solid piece of the same size. Laminating is used in construction to create very strong beams that can be formed into interesting shapes.

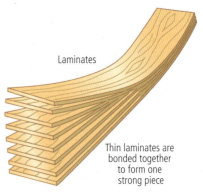

Laminates

Thin laminates are bonded together to form one strong piece

What makes laminated pieces strong?

Glu-lam beams are strong and are used in construction. Discuss and identify the advantages of laminating in modern building and project work.

Laminating process

Thinner wooden laminates are used in the wood technology room, as they bend quite easily and they hold their shape when the glue sets. Most woods have some elastic properties, but woods like ash, elm, beech, and oak as well as pine can be used for laminating in project work. Veneers may be used very successfully for laminating because they are easily cut and there is little waste.

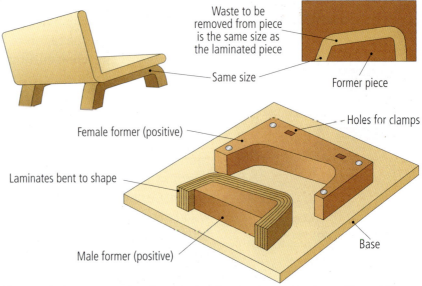

Waste to be removed from piece is the same size as the laminated piece

Same size

Former piece

Holes for clamps

Female former (positive)

Laminates bent to shape

Male former (positive)

Base

Formers help to create the shape by holding the laminates in position while glue sets.

The laminates are bent around wooden shapes called **formers**. The laminates are first glued and are then cramped between these shaped formers until the glue sets.

You will need to over-bend the pieces slightly because the parts will spring back a little when the cramps are removed. Allow for this when you are planning your bend.

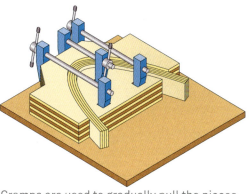

Cramps are used to gradually pull the pieces together and hold the formers together while the glue sets.

Laminating can greatly enhance your project work.

You must also be careful not to over-bend the wood so much that it cracks. Softening the wooden laminates in hot water for a few minutes will help to make them less brittle.

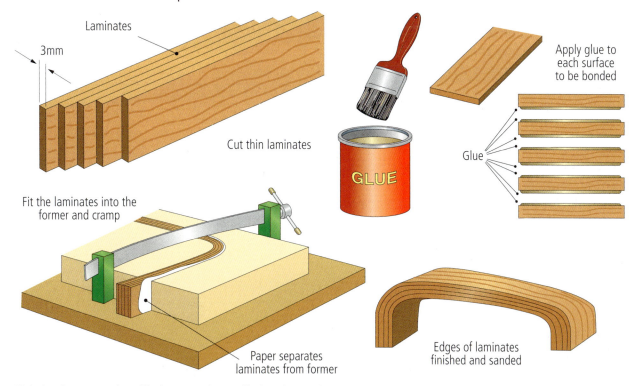

Laminates

3mm

Cut thin laminates

Apply glue to each surface to be bonded

GLUE

Glue

Fit the laminates into the former and cramp

Paper separates laminates from former

Edges of laminates finished and sanded

Thin laminates are less likely to crack or split. Laminates between 1-4mm work best.

Using laminates

- Prepare thin laminates (1mm – 4mm thick).
- The total thickness of the laminates should equal the thickness of the piece required.
- Soften laminates in hot water so they bend more easily.
- Glue is thinly applied to each surface to be bonded (not the two outside faces).
- Position the laminates in the former with paper around them to prevent them from sticking to the former.
- Tighten the clamps and allow the glue to set fully.
- Clean and plane the edges square.
- Remove any paper and sand the piece smooth with sandpaper.

Steam bending

Slight curves can be created in solid wood by first softening the wood using hot steam. The softened wood fibres are easier to bend. This is done by slowly bending the heated wood around a former. The wood may require heating and reheating a number of times before the piece is fully shaped.

The wood is heated in a special steaming box. The wood is left steaming for a number of hours to heat the wood all the way through. When it is fully hot, it can be taken out and bent by clamping it around the former.

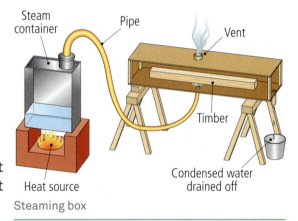

Steaming box

Saw Kerfing

Another method of creating curves in wood is known as saw kerfing. Saw cuts or kerfs are sawn into the wood, leaving the front face intact. The cuts allow the piece to bend, as seen in the diagram.

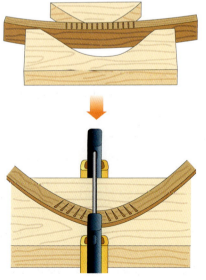

Saw kerfing

Scroll saw work

The scroll saw is used to cut interesting shapes in order to create visually appealing pieces or to add attractive elements to project work. Scroll saw work is sometimes referred to as **fretwork**. A hand-held fret saw was used to do this type of work, but a scroll saw or laser cutter is now used, as it is quicker and more accurate.

Always keep hands clear of the blade when using the scroll saw.

Examples of fretwork

> ⚠ Keep hands clear of the blade.
> ⚠ Keep the work pressed firmly down on the table while sawing.
> ⚠ Wear eye protection.

Pictures can be created using different woods and grain patterns similar to marquetry. This is known as **intarsia**. The wooden pieces are selected carefully according to the colour or type of wood and the grain pattern. The pieces are carefully cut on the scroll saw to fit closely together. The upper edges of each piece are rounded slightly and sanded to give a 3D effect and illusion of depth. The pieces are then bonded into place before finishing.

Introduction for Basic Intarsia Seashell Series Tutorials

Intarsia

Cutting a pattern

Thinner pieces of material (6mm – 15mm) are easier to cut with the scroll saw.

Solid wood, plywood, and other thin manufactured boards are used.

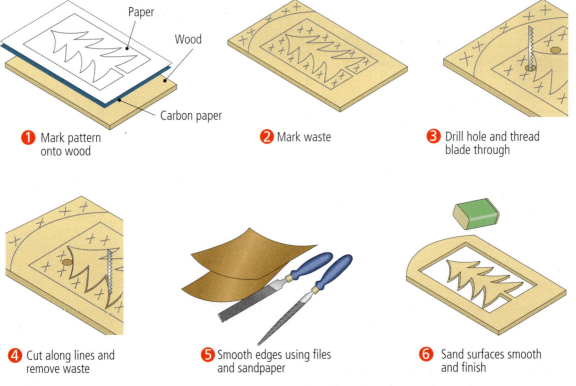

❶ Mark pattern onto wood

❷ Mark waste

❸ Drill hole and thread blade through

❹ Cut along lines and remove waste

❺ Smooth edges using files and sandpaper

❻ Sand surfaces smooth and finish

The process of making a scroll saw pattern

Steps to cutting a pattern with a scroll saw

- Mark out the pattern on the wood surface.
- Mark the waste to be removed.
- Drill relieving holes in the waste using a suitable drill bit.
- Thread the scroll saw blade through the hole and secure to the saw.
- Carefully and accurately cut along the lines, keeping to the waste side.
- Remove the piece and replace the blade.
- Smooth the edges using a file and sandpaper.
- Finish by sanding all surfaces smooth.

Pyrography

Pyrography is the art of burning a pattern or design onto the surface of a piece of wood. Simple designs can improve the appearance of any artefact. An electrically-heated tool is used for burning the design into the wood. It is similar to a pen or soldering iron, but it has an electrically heated wire. The wire or point can be easily replaced when worn or damaged.

Pyrography tool

Pyrography works best on light coloured wood like pine, beech, ash, lime or plywood. Designs should be planned carefully and marked out before you begin. It is important to sand the surfaces smooth before you do any burning as sanding later will remove the burning effect.

⚠ The wire and tool are very hot.

⚠ Be careful not to touch the hot element of the tool.

⚠ Switch off and unplug the tool when not in use.

Using a Pyrography tool

Pyrography design

Investigate and collect 3 simple designs that might be used for a pyrography task.

241

CHAPTER QUESTIONS

1 Explain what a laminate is.

2 Name two hardwoods that you could use for a laminating task.

3 Describe what a former is and how it might be used.

4 When gluing laminates, why is it necessary to put paper between the former and the laminates?

5 The diagram shows a child's chair with laminated legs.

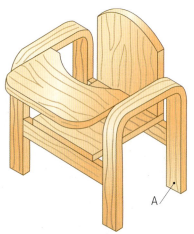

   (a) Describe how you would prepare the laminates to make the legs, labelled (a).

   (b) Sketch the former you would use to create the laminated leg sections.

   (c) Describe the steps you would take to glue and finish the leg sections.

6 The diagram shows a letter box made from lightcoloured hardwood. It is suggested that a design should be crafted with the aid of a scroll saw and applied to the piece to improve its appearance.

   (a) Investigate and suggest ideas for 3 suitable designs that might be used. Select one and give reasons for your choice.

   (b) Describe the steps you would take to complete the scroll saw design chosen.

7 The design shown opposite was cut from a piece of wood using a scroll saw and bonded to a darker background piece. Outline the steps necessary to transfer the design to the piece and cut out and finish the piece.

 PowerPoint Summary   **Weblinks**

26 Forces, Mechanisms, and Structures

Learning intentions

At the end of this chapter you will be able to:
- Identify and describe different forces.
- Name and describe simple mechanisms and where they may be used.
- Demonstrate an understanding of forces, structures, and mechanisms.

Forces

A force is something which causes change in an object (motion or shape). Different forces have different effects. There are pushing forces, pulling forces, twisting forces, shear forces, and bending forces. Understanding these different forces can help you to plan your projects, understand how joints work and to use equipment effectively.

Compression is a pushing force

Compression

Compression is a pushing force. The vice holds wood pieces in place using compression. Sash cramps use compression force to hold joints firmly in position while the glue sets.

Tension

Tension is created by a pulling force.

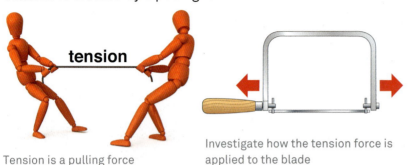

Tension is a pulling force

Investigate how the tension force is applied to the blade

Forces in the room

Working in pairs, examine the Wood Technology room to find examples of the forces mentioned here. Present your findings as a poster.

The chain of a swing is in tension as a person sits on it. The blade in a coping saw is held securely by a tension force created by the frame.

Shear

Shear force works when two forces are not aligned and this results in two objects trying to move in opposing directions. Nails are designed to work best under a shear force.

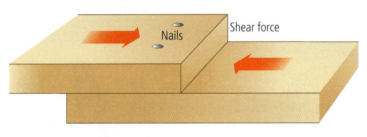

A shear force. Unaligned forces in opposite directions

A scissors is an example of shear force working.

Bending

When a force is applied to a piece, it will cause it to bend. If elements or parts of an item are weak or if the load is too great, they may bend out of shape and even break. We have already learned how bending acrylic or wood laminates to create interesting shapes can add to the appearance of a task.

Torsion

Torsion is a twisting force. Torsion is used to tighten a bolt or when driving a screw with a screwdriver.

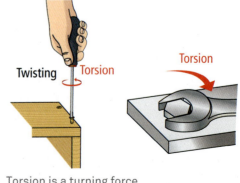

Torsion is a turning force

Mechanisms

Mechanisms are simple mechanical devices. They are all around us and make daily tasks easier. We use them without noticing their usefulness, importance, or how clever they are.

Levers

When you pull the brake of a bicycle or open a tin of varnish with a screwdriver, you are using a lever. **Levers** are simple mechanisms that that allow work to be done more easily. A simple lever is a bar that pivots at a **fulcrum.** There are three classes of lever. The first has the fulcrum in the middle, the second has the load in the middle, and the third class has the force or effort in the middle.

Finding levers

Identify some examples of levers in the Wood Technology room.

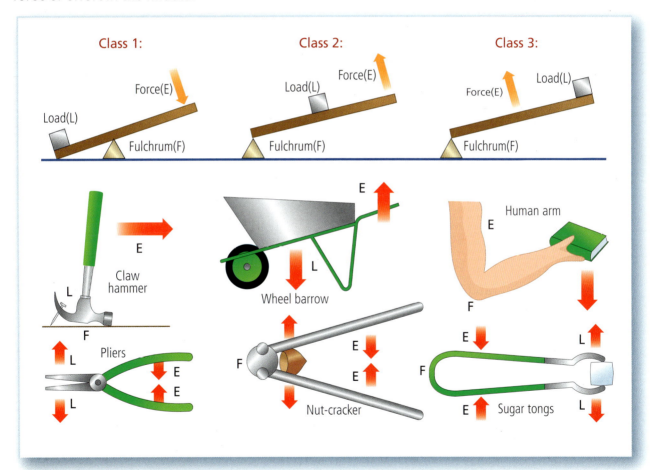

Three classes of lever

Gears

Gears are wheels with teeth. The teeth are designed to interlink (mesh) together to transfer rotary motion and torque. Gears of different sizes are also used to speed up or slow down the motion in machinery. A number of gears connected together is called a **gear train.** The diagram shows simple spur gear trains. The speed or velocity of the gears are increased or reduced by the ratio between the teeth. This is known as the **velocity ratio**.

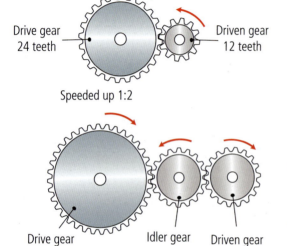

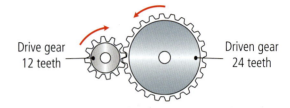

Drive gear bigger than driven gear – speeded up

Drive gear smaller than driven gear – slowed down

The rotation in the drive gear will reverse the rotation of the driven gear.

Gear trains

Velocity ratio

The velocity or gear ratio is the ratio between the speed of one gear compared to another. It can be calculated using a simple formula.

$$\text{Velocity (gear) ratio} = \frac{\text{number of teeth on driven gear}}{\text{number of teeth on drive gear}}$$

Example:

Velocity ratio = $\frac{12}{36}$ = $\frac{1}{3}$ = 1:3

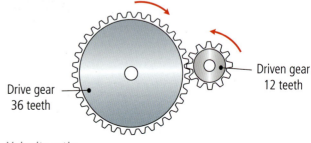

Velocity ratio

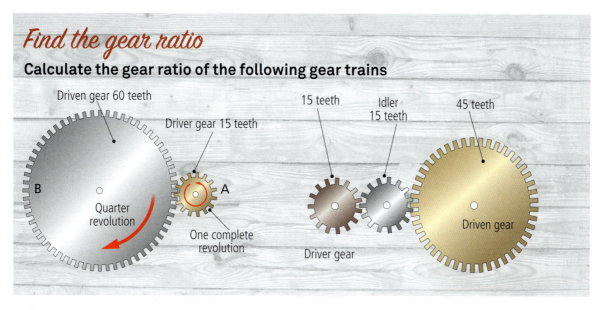

Find the gear ratio
Calculate the gear ratio of the following gear trains

Driven gear 60 teeth

Driver gear 15 teeth

B

Quarter revolution

A

One complete revolution

15 teeth

Idler 15 teeth

45 teeth

Driver gear

Driven gear

Different gear types are used in a range of different situations.

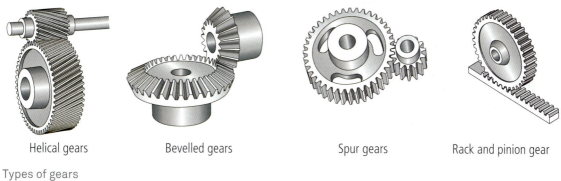

Helical gears

Bevelled gears

Spur gears

Rack and pinion gear

Types of gears

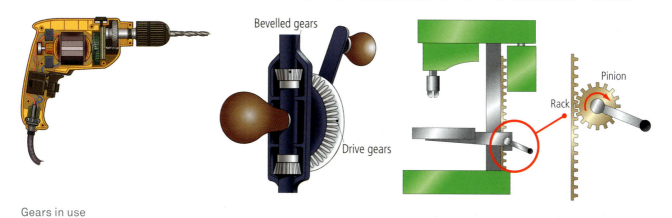

Bevelled gears

Drive gears

Rack

Pinion

Gears in use

247

Pulleys

A **pulley** is a wheel that carries a belt or rope and they are used to transmit motion. They can also assist in lifting heavy loads by giving a mechanical advantage. Pulleys are found in the drive mechanism of a woodturning lathe or pillar drill where they transfer motion from the motor to the drive spindle and also regulate the speed of rotation.

Change in speed is achieved by using pulley wheels of different sizes. They usually drive in one direction only, but if the belt is crossed it can be used to reverse direction of rotation.

Pulleys are used to drive a lathe and change its speed

Block and tackle pulley systems used to lift heavy weights easily

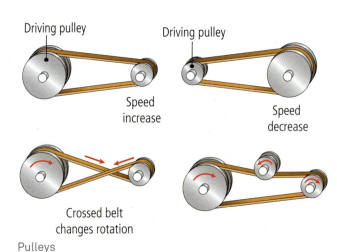

Driving pulley

Driving pulley

Speed increase

Speed decrease

Crossed belt changes rotation

Pulleys

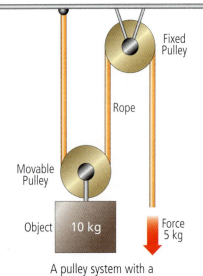

Fixed Pulley

Rope

Movable Pulley

Object   10 kg

Force 5 kg

A pulley system with a mechanical advantage of two

Effort 5 kg

2:1   10 kg

If you have 2 pulley wheels, the effort needed to lift the load is reduced by 2

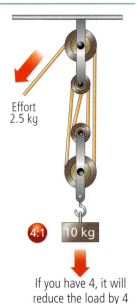

Effort 2.5 kg

4:1   10 kg

If you have 4, it will reduce the load by 4

Pulleys in a block and tackle can help to lift weights

Velocity ratio

The velocity ratio for pulleys can be calculated using a simple formula.

Velocity ratio $= \dfrac{\text{Diameter of the driven wheel}}{\text{Diameter of the drive wheel}}$

The output speed (OS) $= \dfrac{\text{Input speed}}{\text{Velocity ratio (VR)}}$

Example:

The diagram shows a pulley system. Wheel A is the drive wheel with a diameter of 160mm and wheel B is the driven wheel with a diameter of 40 mm. Calculate the output speed of wheel B if wheel A rotates at 120 rpm (revolutions per minute).

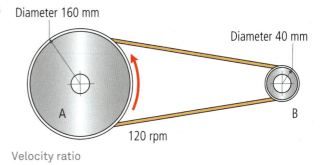

Diameter 160 mm

Diameter 40 mm

A

120 rpm

B

Velocity ratio

$\text{VR} = \dfrac{40}{160} = \dfrac{1}{4} = 1{:}4$

$\text{OS} = \dfrac{120}{1{:}4} = 120 \times \dfrac{4}{1} = 480 \text{ rpm}$

Linkages

When levers are connected together with moveable joints, they are known as **linkages**. Like levers, they allow tasks to be carried out more easily.

Examples of linkages. Can you find more examples?

Structures and stability

The project tasks you make must be strong and stable. They must have good structural strength to carry the loads or to do their job effectively and safely.

Evaluate stability

Working in groups, discuss why the artefacts shown here might be unstable and suggest how improvements could be made.

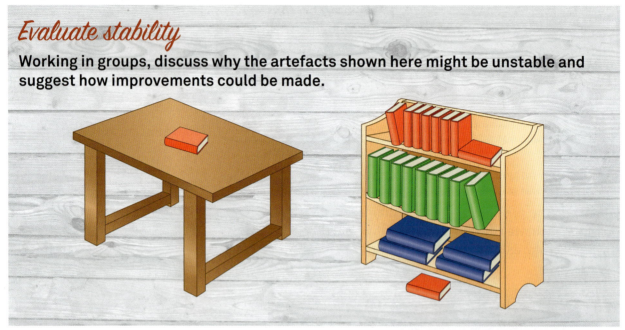

Frames

Frames are strong structures. Most efficient pieces will have structures such as frames included to make the piece sturdy. Triangles are the simplest and strongest frames. This is why electricity pylons and roofs use them in their construction.

Frames are used to add strength to items such as tables and chairs. Adding a rail can give a table greater strength and stability.

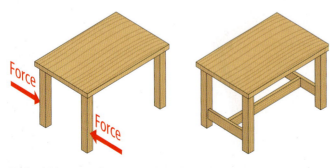

Rails add strength

Triangles are strong structures

As you design artefacts, you must make sure they are structurally stong without being too heavy in appearance. Using too much material or very large sections is wasteful and will not look well.

Stablility of items is also important when designing. Being aware of the centre of gravity of an object is important. Keeping the weight of the piece low helps to keep the centre of gravity low. A wider base will also aid the stability if this lamp, for example.

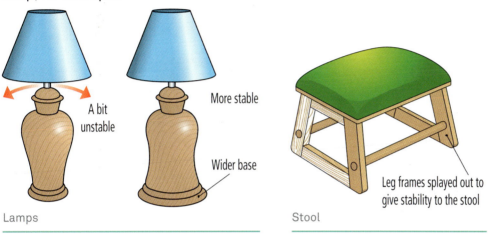

A bit unstable

More stable

Wider base

Lamps

Leg frames splayed out to give stability to the stool

Stool

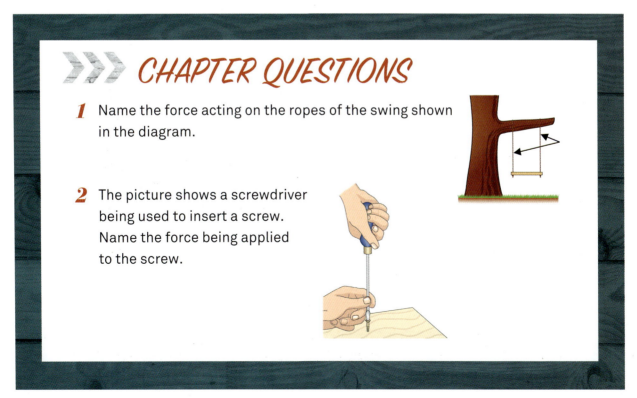

CHAPTER QUESTIONS

1 Name the force acting on the ropes of the swing shown in the diagram.

2 The picture shows a screwdriver being used to insert a screw. Name the force being applied to the screw.

3 Give an example of another force and where it might be applied in the Wood Technology room.

4 Name the gear mechanism shown in diagram and name a common woodworking machine that uses this type of mechanism.

5 In the diagram, gear A is the drive gear in a gear train and rotates anticlockwise, as shown. Gears C and B both have 12 teeth. Gear A is the driven gear and has 36 teeth.

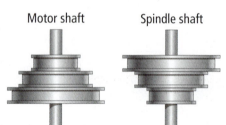

12 teeth

A
B
C

   (a) Describe in which direction gears B and A will rotate.

   (b) If gear C rotates at 45 rpm, what will be the rotational speed of the gear A?

6 The diagram shows the pulley system of a pillar drill. Reproduce the sketch into your copy and indicate where the belt will be positioned to get the maximum speed from the drill.

Motor shaft   Spindle shaft

7 A right angle drill is used when drilling in confined spaces. Bevel gears, as shown, are used in these drills.

   (a) If the smaller gear rotates clockwise as shown, use another arrow to clearly indicate the rotational direction of the larger gear.

   (b) If the small gear has 10 teeth and rotates at a speed of 80 RPM and the larger gear has 50 teeth, calculate the rotational speed of the large gear.

8   In the gate pictured here, what is the correct name for the force acting in member A?

9   If pulley X in the illustration rotates clockwise, which direction will pulley C rotate?

10 The small pulleys pictured here are 100mm in diameter and the large pulley is 200mm in diameter. If pulley X rotatoes at 180 revolutions per minute (RPM), what is the rotational speed of pulley Z?

11 Identify one design defect in the wooden book shelf pictured here and describe a possible remedy.

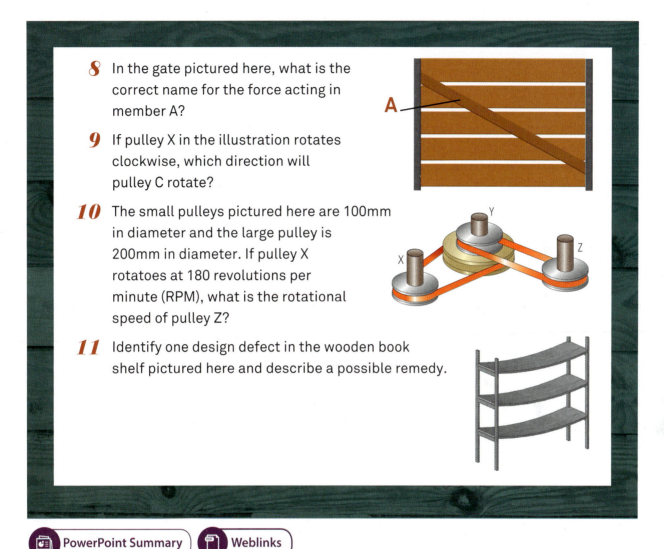

PowerPoint Summary   Weblinks

27 Simple Electronic Circuits

Learning intentions

At the end of this chapter you will be able to:
- Name the basic components of a simple electronic circuit.
- Describe the functions of simple electronic components.

Electronic **circuits** are all around us in things we use every day. They help to control most of the appliances in our homes, such as phones, electronic games, TVs and calculators. We will examine some simple electronic circuits you could use in your projects. For example below is a design for the electronic circuit of a portable bedside light.

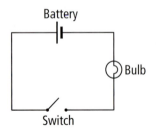

Circuit diagram for the bedside light

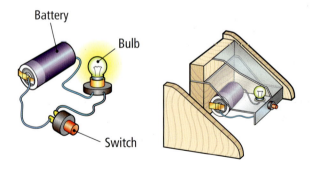

Bedside light

Electronics

In electronic circuits, electrons move along conductors (wires). A conductor is a material that allows electrons to move along it easily. Many materials conduct electricity, although some are better than others. Copper is the most common electric conductor used.

A simple electronic circuit lights the bulb

Circuits

In the light example above, the electronic circuit is formed when the terminals of a **battery** are connected to the bulb or any other set of components. To stop or break the circuit, a **switch** is inserted that can be opened to stop the flow of current or closed to connect the circuit and allow electrons to flow.

A battery has two terminals: one positive and one negative. When a conductor is attached to each terminal, the electrons in the conductor are pushed by the negative terminal and attracted to the positive one. This causes a **current** to flow through the conductor. Current is measured in amps. The **voltage** is the force that makes the electrons move and is measured in volts. A component (e.g. a bulb) must be included in a circuit or the battery may be damaged.

Circuit diagrams are drawings of electronic circuits. Like any working drawing, they follow agreed standards. Components such as batteries, light, and measuring devices all have specific individual symbols so they can be easily recognised. The table below shows some of the more common ones.

Assorted batteries

🗋	Component	Symbol	Description
Battery			Provides the power or voltage in the circuit
Bulb			Small light bulb
Fuse			Component with a resistance wire used to protect the circuit
Motor			Driven by the current, it provides movement
Resistor			Controls current by resisting the flow of electrons
Variable resistor			The resistance can be adjusted within a certain range
Ammeter			Device for measuring current
Switch			Allows the current to be turned on and off in the circuit
LDR Light-dependent resistor			Light-dependent resistor whose resistance varies with light intensity
LED			Light-emitting diode
Thermistor			Resistor whose resistance varies with temperature
Transistor			Acts as switch or amplifier

Table of components

Electric Symbols	
Current	Amps (A)
Voltage	Volts (V)
Resistance	Ohms (Ω)

The current between the terminals of a battery depends on the voltage. A larger current is generated with a larger voltage (battery). Voltage is also referred to as the potential difference or PD. This is the difference of electrical pressure between the terminals of a battery. For example, a 6 volt battery has a PD of 6 volts between its terminals.

The best way to build a circuit is on a special circuit board. The components of the circuit are soldered to the board using a soldering iron. The solder is heated and melted on to the joint. When cool, it forms a bond between the pieces.

Heat solder pin then apply solder

Hold the component in place while the solder sets

Fixing a component with solder

Resistance

Components called **resistors** are used to restrict and control the flow of current. The level of resistance to the flow of current is measured in **ohms**. Resistors are obtained with a predetermined or set resistance or you can get a variable resistor where the level of resistance can be adjusted by turning a dial, for example.

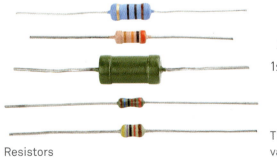

Resistors

Tolerance

No. of zeros

2nd digit

1st digit

Resistor symbol

The coloured lines of a resistor indicate the value of the resistance

Values	Black	Brown	Red	Orange	Yellow	Green	Blue	Violet	Grey	White
	0	1	2	3	4	5	6	7	8	9

The strength of the resistor is calculated using the coloured bands found on each resistor. In a variable resistor, the resistance is changed by turning a dial. When resistors are connected in a line within a circuit, they are said to be in series. As can be seen in the diagram, the total resistance is equal to the combined resistance of all the resistors. This will weaken the light.

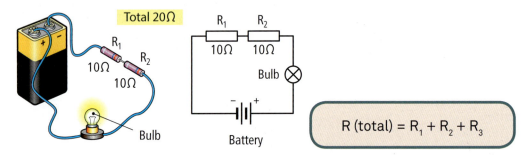

$$R\ (total) = R_1 + R_2 + R_3$$

Resistors in series

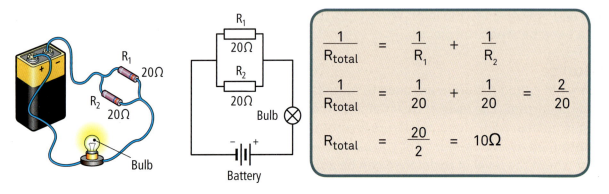

$$\frac{1}{R_{total}} = \frac{1}{R_1} + \frac{1}{R_2}$$

$$\frac{1}{R_{total}} = \frac{1}{20} + \frac{1}{20} = \frac{2}{20}$$

$$R_{total} = \frac{20}{2} = 10\Omega$$

Resistors in parallel

If the resistors are connected side by side, they are connected in parallel. In this case, the bulb will be brighter because the resistance is shared, giving a lower overall resistance.

Ohm's law

$$Voltage = Current \times Resistance$$

Ohm's law is an important basic law of electric circuits. Using the formula for Ohm's law, it is possible to calculate the missing value when given any other two.

Light-dependent resistors (LDR)

Light dependent resistors are components that sense changes in light. They are connected in a circuit to detect light or to detect darkness. They are often used to switch on a light automatically.

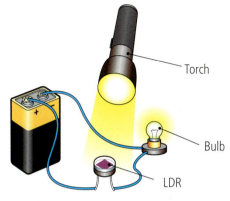

LDR – light-dependent resistor

Light-emitting diodes (LED)

The light-emitting diode or LED is a small bulb. LEDs come in various colours (e.g. red, green and yellow). They must be connected in the correct position, as the current flows in one direction only. A resistor is used alongside an LED to prevent it from overloading.

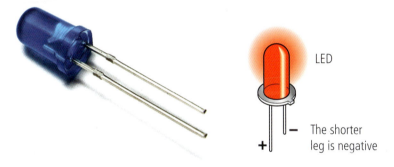

LED

The shorter leg is negative

Light-emitting diode (LED)

Thermistors

The thermistor is a component whose resistance changes with variations in temperature. As the temperature decreases, it acts as a switch, for example, to turn on heating. They are used in temperature sensors, thermometers, and many electronic devices.

Thermistors

Transistors

A transistor acts like a switch or an amplifying device. Transistors used in schools are generally (bipolar) NPN types that have three legs: an emitter, collector, and base.

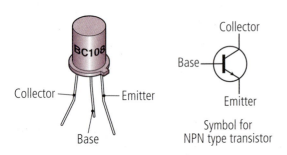

Transistor

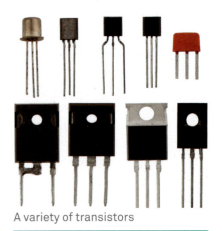

A variety of transistors

When a small current is applied to the base, the transistor is ON and current flows from collector to emitter. When no current is present on the base, the transistor is OFF and there will be no current flowing between the collector and emitter. In the same way, as a push switch is controlled by your finger, the transistor is controlled by the small current on the base.

Capacitors

Capacitors store electrical energy when connected to a power supply. They are a commonly used component in electronic circuits. They are used in the flash units of cameras and other devices. The charge capacity of small capacitors is measured in microfarads (uF).

Capacitors

Symbol for
ordinary capacitor

Circuits

Why not try making this circuit for an alarm buzzer? An alarm can be added to the door of a small cabinet. This could be done using a switch that activates when the door is opened. It is also possible to create a circuit that can detect water or try making a circuit that could be incorporated into a model car to make the lights go on in the dark; it uses a light-dependent resistor to activate the circuit and LEDs as lights.

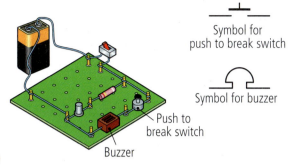

Symbol for push to break switch

Symbol for buzzer

Push to break switch

Buzzer

Alarm buzzer circuit

CHAPTER QUESTIONS

1 What is the most common conducting material used in electrical circuits?

2 What makes this material suitable for use in electrical circuits?

3 A battery is used in simple electronic circuits. Name the two terminals.

4 Current is the flow of _____ in an electronic circuit.

5 Sketch the symbols for the following basic components found in electronic circuits:
   (a) battery
   (b) led
   (c) resistor
   (d) transistor.

6 Explain the following in basic terms:
   (a) voltage
   (b) current
   (c) resistance.

7 State a formula for Ohm's law.

8 Describe the purpose of a resistor in a circuit.

9 Calculate the voltage of the following sets of batteries:

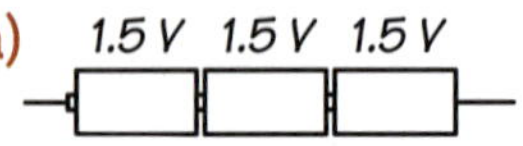

(b)

1.5 V

(a) 1.5 V 1.5 V 1.5 V

1.5 V

1.5 V

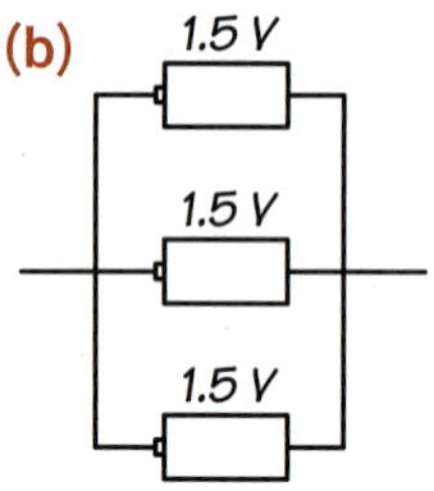

10 Describe how the following might be used in a circuit:

(a) switch

(b) thermistor

(c) LDR

(d) LED.

PowerPoint Summary

Section 3

DESIGN THINKING

28 Sketching

Learning intentions

At the end of this chapter you will be able to:
- Use sketches and drawings to present your ideas.
- Create sketches using a variety of media.
- Explore a problem using sketches.

Sketches and drawings help you to communicate your ideas to others. Sketches, often produced **freehand**, are used in Wood Technology and many other subjects to quickly record details. They are essential for presenting your thoughts, ideas, and solutions in your project folio. Knowing and practising basic principles will let you develop your sketching over a period of time.

Drawings, which will be discussed in the next chapter, are more formal than sketches. They are done with board and tee square and set-squares. Usually a drawing will include different views of an item or object with measurements.

USES

- Enhance your presentations greatly
- Help communicate your ideas and solutions
- Assist you to record your work
- Assist you to explain your thoughts
- Aid explanations in exams

Paper

Plain white paper is usually the best to use but you can begin with lined or graph paper which can give a guide. There are many standard sizes and qualities of paper but A3 or A4 paper is generally used. Each size is double the area of the one smaller.

Special ruled grid paper will help with sketching. These pre-printed papers have ruled grids (squared or isometric 30°) which aid 2D and 3D sketching. Grid papers can be used while you get better at sketching.

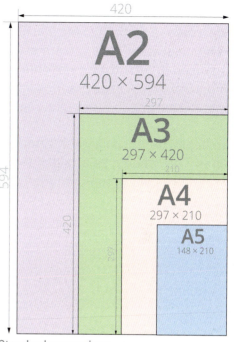

Standard paper sizes

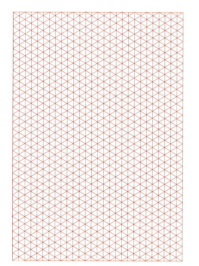 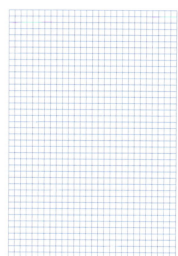

Isometric grid and regular squared paper

Pencils

The pencils used for sketching and drawing vary. They can be found in different grades according to the hardness of their lead. The grade is usually printed at the top of the pencil. Sketching is usually done using a HB or 2B pencil, while a 2H is used to mark out wood and for drawing.

Grading of pencils

Freehand sketching

You can use a ruler to help you sketch, but sketching freehand is much quicker once you are used to it. Freehand sketches are used to record your work and for documentation in your project folios. A little practice is the key; after a time you will find it is easier and your sketches will improve.

To begin, practice sketching **horizontal** lines and **vertical** lines. They should be straight and **parallel** to each other. Practice moving your hand from your elbow and not your wrist.

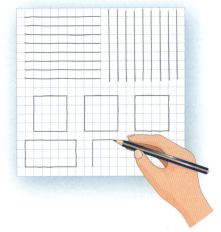

Practice sketching horizontal and vertical lines. Focus on making them straight and parallel

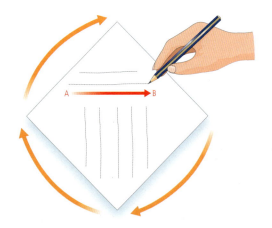

Drawing straight lines freehand. Move the sheet around to help draw angles

Draw the lines lightly at first and then go over the correct one to heavy it in. Grid paper can be used and you could move the paper to help you.

Proportion

Proportion is the relationship between two measurements (e.g. an object's height compared to its width). As you sketch, look at what you are drawing and be aware of its length, width, and height. Compare the sizes to each other. The height of the memory stick opposite is about 4 times its width. This will help you to gauge its proportion.

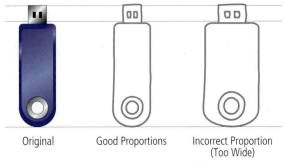

Original   Good Proportions   Incorrect Proportion (Too Wide)

Comparison of proportions. Always draw proportions correctly

To help with sketching proportions, practice with squares.
When you sketch a square, make sure that all sides are equal.
Incorrect use of proportion will not look as well.

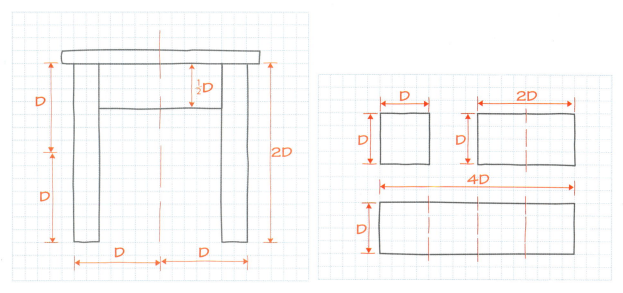

Notice the proportions of the items you see

Practicing squares

Using a squared grid paper or plain white paper, practice drawing perfect squares and rectangles of different proportions. Repeat the process until you are happy with the result.

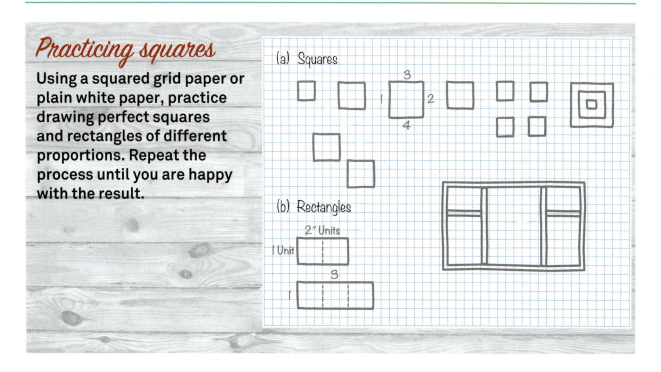

When you are sketching, make sure that squares are drawn square and rectangles keep their shape and proportion. Getting the proportion right can be a difficult skill to master.

Light and heavy lines

As you sketch, use light lines to create an outline of the piece, its divisions, and parts and details. Light lines are easily erased. Once you are happy with the light outlines, go over them with heavier lines.

Good sketches need not be complicated. It is important that straight lines are straight and parallel

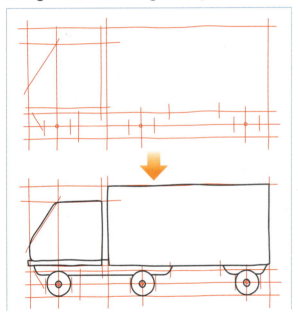

Use light lines to produce boxes or crates that can be finished off.

Crate:

When sketching, most objects may be fitted into a boundary, box, or crate. Sketching the outline crate lightly at first will help you to assess shapes and proportions before completing the details and going over the sketch with heavy lines.

2-dimensional (2D) sketching

Start with simple 2D sketches. Draw sketches of basic items around you in school or at home. Remember, you are not trying to be an artist; just try to represent what you see in a simple and accurate way.

Activity

Try to sketch the items shown opposite. When you have finished, discuss the result with a partner and try again to improve.

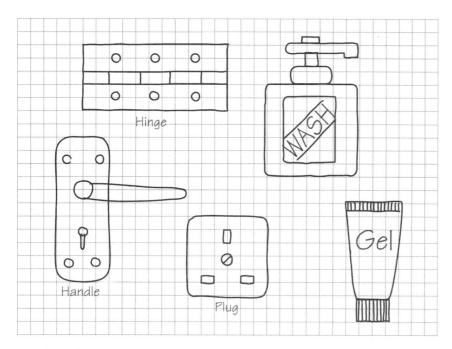

Use these shapes to practise sketching

Sketching 2D curves

Curves and circles are a little difficult, but they can also be drawn with the aid of crates. Draw a light box to outline the size of the curved element. Find the mid-point, as shown in the examples. Line in the curve lightly with the mid-point as a reference. When you are satisfied with the light curve, go over it with a heavy line as before.

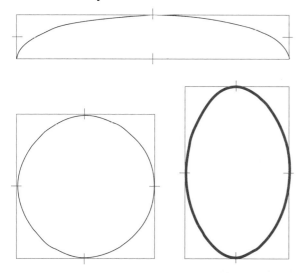

Light crate lines help in drawing curves and circles

3-dimensional (3D) sketches

3D or **pictorial** sketches are used to show three faces of an object. They require a bit more practice. A pictorial drawing or sketch will give a better view of how an object appears.

Grid paper can be used to assist the process. The views of a simple halving joint shown illustrate the two basic types of pictorial: oblique and isometric views.

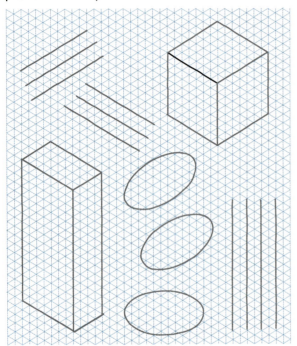

Start your 3D sketching by using isometric grid paper. Notice that the solid blocks are made up of parallel lines

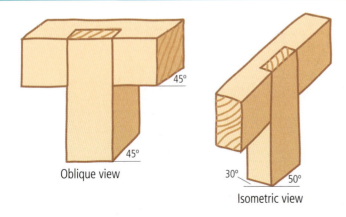

Oblique view

45°

45°

Isometric view

30°   50°

Two pictorial views of a tee halving joint

As before, sketch the shape lightly and then when you are happy with the result, go over the sketch using a heavy line. Light pencil lines are easily rubbed out if you make a mistake. As you improve, you can begin sketching on plain paper. Sketch simple views of projects or joints as you do them. Practising these simple sketched views will help you improve. They are a good record of your work.

Practice 3D

Complete the basic 3D sketches of the two simple exercises pictured below. Use the steps to guide you.

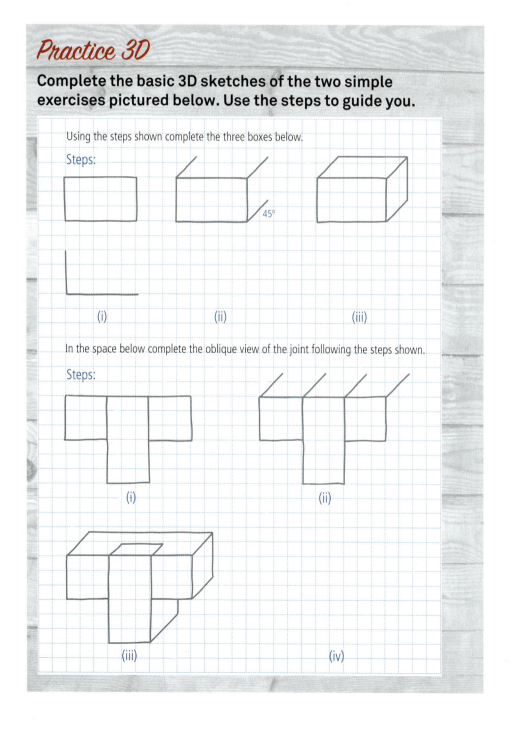

Using the steps shown complete the three boxes below.

Steps:

45°

(i)   (ii)   (iii)

In the space below complete the oblique view of the joint following the steps shown.

Steps:

(i)   (ii)

(iii)   (iv)

Exploded views

You can also sketch views of joints or pieces taken apart. These are called **exploded views.** They allow you to visualise objects more clearly and how they should go together.

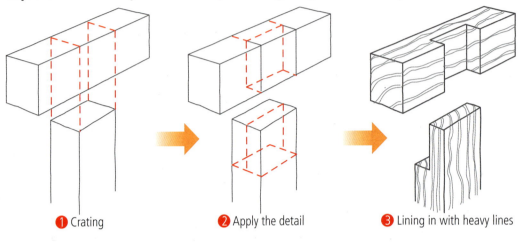

❶ Crating   ❷ Apply the detail   ❸ Lining in with heavy lines

Exploded view of joints

Practice and improve your sketching

Sketch some common items at home or select some of these objects. Compare and discuss your sketches with others and write three sentences to describe what you learned that can help you improve.

Sketching 3D Curves

Curves and circles are drawn using crates. Draw light lines to create a box that the curved shape will fit into. Line in the curves lightly and then draw the correct line more heavily.

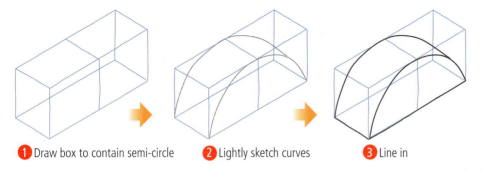

1 Draw box to contain semi-circle   **2** Lightly sketch curves   **3** Line in

Drawing curves in a box

Enhancing your sketches

Drawings and sketches can be greatly improved using basic **shading** and colouring techniques.

Search online for a 9:20 minute video called 'How to Shade Basic Forms – Pencil Tutorial' by The Virtual Instructor.

Shading

Practice changing how much pressure you apply to the pencil as you shade from side to side to control the amount or tone of the shading from light to dark. Using different shading methods such as line, cross hatching, or stippling can give slightly different effects.

Shading and coloured shading will lift a simple line drawing and improve its impact. Using shading will give your drawings and sketches a more realistic appearance. As you sketch, try to be aware of the different areas of light and shade or shadow generated by the light falling on an object. Adding shadow and shade in your sketches will help give a feeling of depth and realism. An estimated shadow will often be enough to improve the appearance of the sketch.

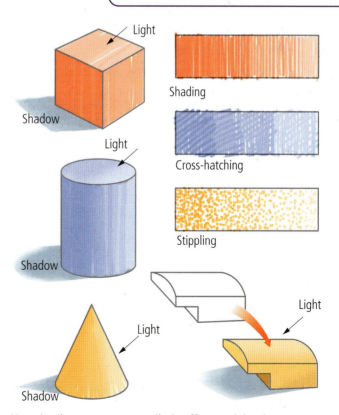

Use shading to create a realistic effect and depth

273

Texture

Texture describes how a material looks and feels (e.g. soft, coarse, smooth or shiny). Examples of texturing for common materials are shown below.

Shading can be used to show different textures and materials like metal, plastic and wood.

Add **grain** to show the surfaces of wood effectively. You can also add colour to indicate the material.

Draw a sketch of this bridle joint and include the grain texture.

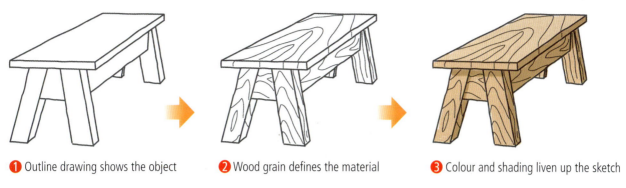

❶ Outline drawing shows the object ❷ Wood grain defines the material ❸ Colour and shading liven up the sketch

Build up sketches gradually. Add shading, texture, and colour

Reflective surfaces such as glass and acrylic (Perspex) reflect light. A simple way to show shininess in a sketch is to draw a number of parallel lines across the surface. Draw vertical lines on a flat horizontal surface and draw diagonal lines on a vertical surface.

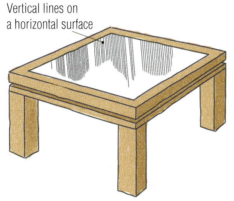

Vertical lines on a horizontal surface

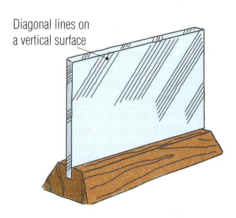

Diagonal lines on a vertical surface

Vertical or diagonal lines show shiny surfaces

Colour

Colour should be used to create a realistic effect on your sketches. Even a little colour will make a big difference. Colour can be added using a basic set of coloured pencils. They will allow you to vary the tone and depth of colour in your sketches. Specialist graphic markers such as the Promarker can also be used to add colour effectively.

Coloured pencils and markers can enhance your work

CHAPTER QUESTIONS

1 What are the advantages of using sketches in the Wood Technology room?

2 Produce a 2D sketch of:
 (a) your calculator
 (b) the front of the vice
 (c) a toaster
 (d) a microwave oven.

3 Draw a simple sketch (2D or 3D) of the following tools in the Wood Technology room. Use colour and shade to enhance your sketches.

 (a) bench hook   **(b)** try square
 (c) firmer chisel   **(d)** marking gauge
 (e) nail punch   **(f)** marking knife.

4 Complete 2D Sketches showing the details of these two joints

 (a) housing joint   **(b)** bridle joint.

5 Complete a shaded sketch of the coping saw shown here.

6 Draw a simple shaded sketch of the nail punch shown here.

 PowerPoint Summary   Weblinks

29 Drawing

Learning intentions

At the end of this chapter you will be able to:
- Read and understand information from basic drawings.
- Communicate information to others using basic drawings.
- Create working drawings using appropriate standards.

The purpose of drawings

Drawings and sketches are used in wood technology to communicate ideas and information about sizes, shapes, joints, and features of a solution to be made. Knowing about how information is presented on standard drawings will allow you to read and understand information clearly and communicate using your own drawings.

Getting started

Working drawings are more formal and usually done with a board and tee square, while sketches are drawn freehand. Begin by taping a sheet to the board. Line the sheet up level with the tee-square as shown in the diagram. Lines are drawn using set-squares resting on the tee-square as shown. Lengths are measured in millimetres along lines using your ruler or set-square. The compass is used for drawing circles accurately.

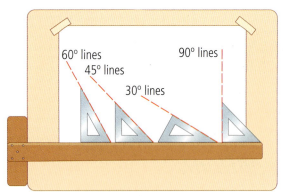

Use instruments to draw lines and angles

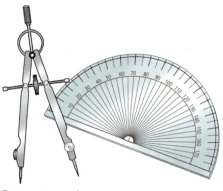

Protractor and compass

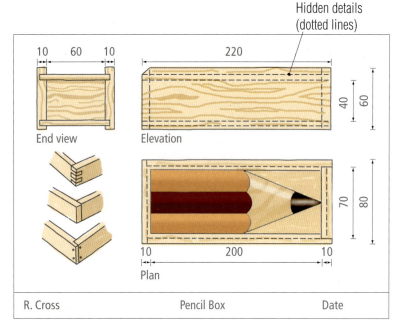

What kind of information do we find on a working drawing like this one?
Make a list and discuss

Simple drawings

Mostly, our drawings are made up of straight lines, squares and rectangles with some circles. Practice with simple shapes and joints to build up your drawing skills. As with sketches, draw outlines lightly at first and go over the lines heavily when you are happy with the result.

Hidden detail

Dotted lines are used on drawings to show **hidden detail**, which is something that is part of the object but cannot be seen in a particular view.

Find the hidden details

Examine the working drawing above and consider what the hidden detail shows and how this hidden detail helps you understand the parts of the box.

Scale

Often, objects are drawn full size (1:1), but when an object is too large to fit on a sheet, a **scale** is used to reduce or enlarge the size evenly so that the proportions stay the same. A half size (1:2) or a quarter size (1:4) drawing are often used. The drawing's scale is written clearly as a ratio on the drawing to tell anyone reading the drawing what scale was used.

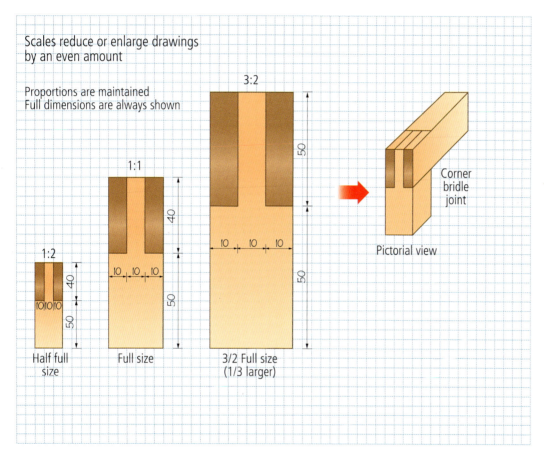

Scales are used to give a clear picture. Reproduce the images shown of a view of a corner bridle joint

Orthographic views

Orthographic views include elevation, end views, plans, and sections. **Orthographic projection** is the standard method used to present these as a working drawing. Orthographic projection is based on the principle that the view of each face (front, side, etc.) is projected onto a plane surface as shown in the diagram below. These planes are then rotated into a flat position, creating the views.

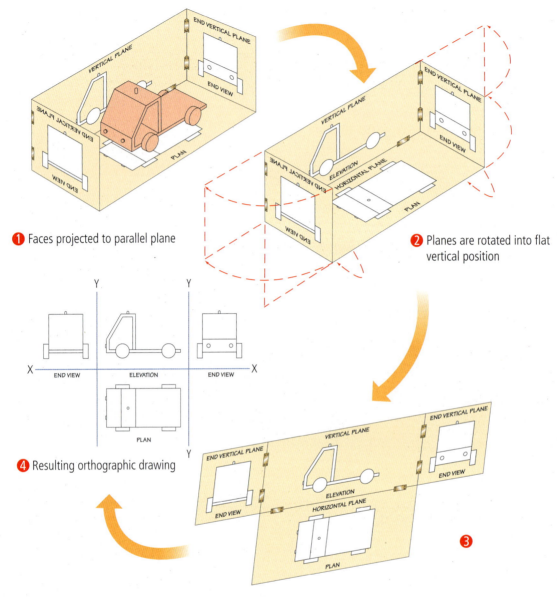

1 Faces projected to parallel plane

2 Planes are rotated into flat vertical position

3

4 Resulting orthographic drawing

Orthographic drawings are commonly used in project work

In Wood Technology, we might use an **elevation** (front view), **plan** (top view), and **end view** (side view) or perhaps only two of these may be needed to give the required information and measurements. These views will give us the length, width, and thickness measurements in a 2D drawing. Orthographic views of our solutions usually include measurements. Notes and descriptions may also be included.

Drawing a housing joint

The 3D pictorial view shown here shows a housing joint. The finished orthographic views are also shown. Complete the given elevation, plan, and end views.

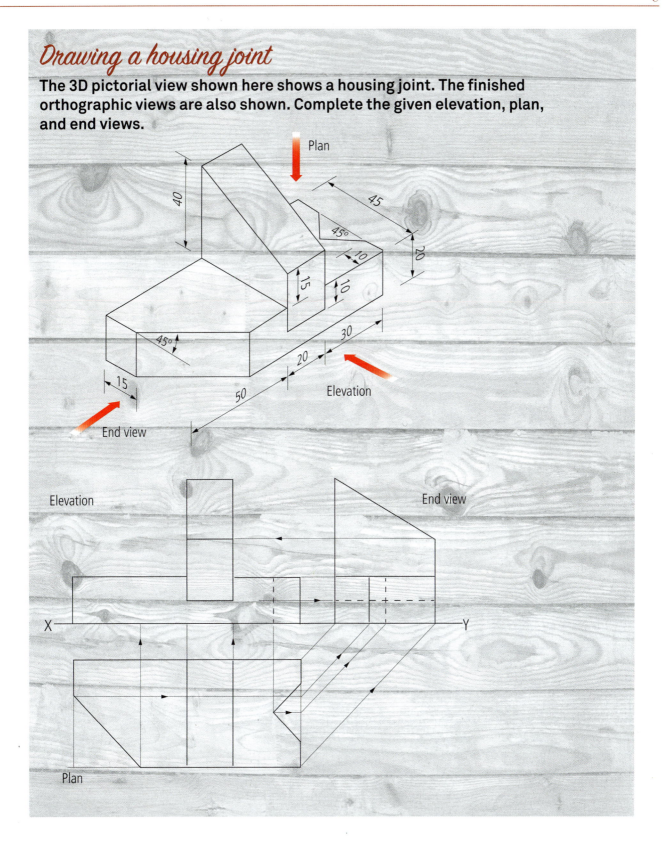

Sections

A **section** is the view obtained when an item or piece is cut and the exposed surface is viewed.

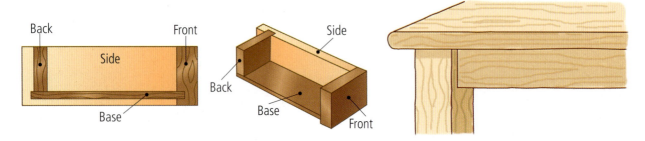

Section through a drawer

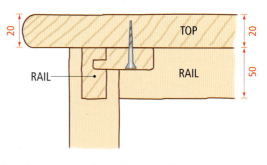

Sections are used to show detail

Pictorial drawing (3D drawing)

Pictorial drawing allows the viewer to see three faces or sides of an object at once, hence the name 3D drawing. There are different ways to draw or represent an object in 3D. Each one gives a slightly different view or appearance. Pictorial views give a good idea of how the object looks. As we have seen, they can be sketched freehand or accurately drawn using instruments such as Computer-Aided Design (CAD).

Oblique Drawing

Oblique is simply created by drawing the front view (elevation). Lines at 45° are then drawn from the main points. The length of each of these lines is measured along each one.

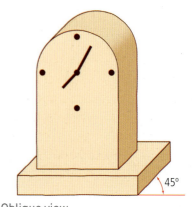

Oblique view

1 Set up structure lightly   **2** Outline detail lightly   **3** Line in and shade

A desk lamp with a desk tidy drawn in oblique

Circles in oblique

Draw circles in a vertical position using a compass. Circles on a horizontal surface are drawn using a series of ordinates to find the points on the curve before completing the curve freehand.

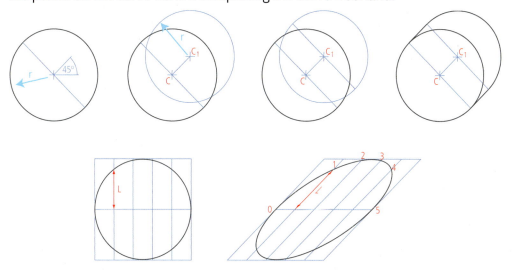

Circles in oblique. Vertical circles using a compass and horizontal circles using ordinates

Isometric drawing

Isometric drawings are constructed using axis lines drawn at 30° or vertical. When drawing an isometric, first form the isometric axis. Then, construct a frame on the isometric axis equal to the overall measurements of the item.

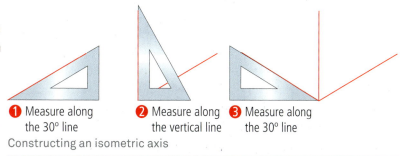

1 Measure along the 30° line   **2** Measure along the vertical line   **3** Measure along the 30° line

Constructing an isometric axis

Full measurements are only measured along the axis lines. The details are filled in on the frame. When the details are correct, the drawing is lined in.

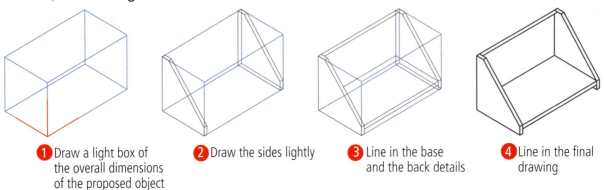

1 Draw a light box of the overall dimensions of the proposed object

2 Draw the sides lightly

3 Line in the base and the back details

4 Line in the final drawing

Steps in drawing an isometric view

Circles in isometric

When using instruments to draw curves or circles, a box is constructed first and then the circles are constructed using ordinates to find the points on the curve.

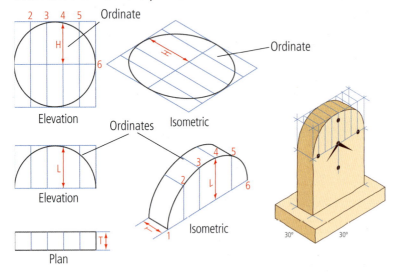

Using ordinates to construct a circle

Perspective

A **perspective** view is a more realistic view of something because it is how we might see it with our eyes. In perspective, lines appear to converge or vanish to a point called a vanishing point, as can be seen with the horizontal lines in the diagram of the table.

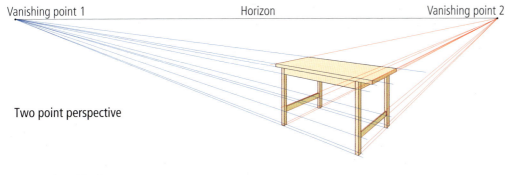

Two point perspective

Vanishing point 1   Horizon   Vanishing point 2

Perspective drawing

Standard Dimensions & Conventions

Drawings are a method of communicating ideas. All drawings follow similar standards called conventions that make them easy to understand worldwide. Your teacher will guide you further.

It is important that your drawings are properly **dimensioned**. Your drawings should show all measurements clearly so your design solutions can be made from the drawings.

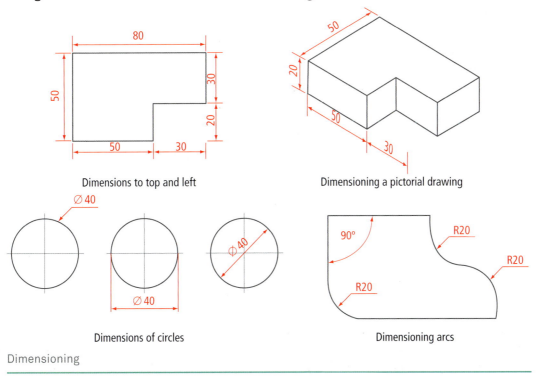

Dimensions to top and left

Dimensioning a pictorial drawing

Dimensions of circles

Dimensioning arcs

Dimensioning

CHAPTER QUESTIONS

1 Outline the purpose of orthographic drawings and pictorial drawings.

2 Make a drawing showing the elevation and end view of the simple wooden piece shown in the diagram right. Insert 4 main dimensions on your drawing.

3 Draw an oblique view of the piece shown in the diagram right.

4 If you were asked to draw a view of the object in the diagram above to an increased scale of 2 : 1, explain what this means and why drawing to a specific scale would be useful.

5 Explain the term hidden detail and why it is important when completing a drawing.

6 The diagram shows a candle holder made from hardwood. The holder is a 60mm cube and the supporting pieces are 15mm thick. Draw an elevation of the candle holder. Project a plan of the holder from the elevation. Insert 4 main dimensions on your drawing.

7 The diagram shown here illustrates a pictorial view of a letter holder. The thickness of all pieces is 12mm. Draw, full size, an elevation looking in the direction of the arrow A. Project an end view from this view. Insert the main dimensions on your drawing.

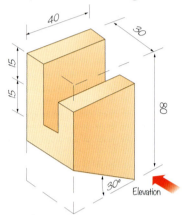

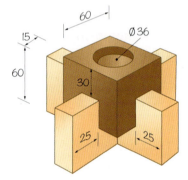

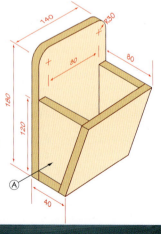

PowerPoint Summary

30 Planning and Presenting the Design Process

Learning intentions

At the end of this chapter you will be able to:
- Understand the key principles of design and ergonomics.
- Explore a topic using a mind map.
- Explore design problems in an informed manner.
- Communicate design decisions through a structured design folio.
- Critically evaluate design solutions.

Designers solve problems; they have ideas and solutions to create new things and make improvements to existing ones. In Wood Technology, you will also solve design problems and create your own artefacts. Designers often follow a process to assist them in creating items that are useful and attractive.

Designer drawings

287

Presenting your ideas, design, and process in a folio/report

A report is a written record of the work that you do in designing, researching, planning, and producing your project or artefact. A **folio**/report is presented with your artefact as part of the assessment process. Shorter reports or presentations may also be an element of your classroom based assessments (CBAs). Always make an effort to present your work neatly and well organised. Reports should contain a range of sketches, drawings, images, and photographs to support your written explanations. A project report will usually include a scale model of your chosen solution.

The best reports are clearly written and well-presented. They are usually presented or bound in a folder. The report may be typed, but clear written work is also acceptable. Folios will include details under all of the headings given in the instructions or **brief**. Complete sections of your folio as each stage of your project progresses. A project copy may also help you to record work as you go so you can update your folio each week.

Examples of project reports

Features of good design

Knowing the qualities of a successful design will help you when you design items of your own. Good designs often have some features in common.

Appearance/Aesthetics

Aesthetics are concerned with the beauty or appearance of something. Designs and projects should be attractive to look at. We can usually tell if something is attractive, but it can be difficult to design an attractive artefact. Following principles of good design and adding some simple decorations will help to make your work attractive.

Shape/Form

Shape and form are similar. Consider if the piece is curved or square, rectangular or triangular in shape, for example. Are there angled pieces in the object? The shape and form greatly affect the appearance of an object.

Proportion

Proportion concerns the visual relationship between the size and weight of different parts of a piece. In particular, the height, width, and depth of an artefact must be considered for both functionality and available space.

The Golden ratio

Designs based on the proportions of the human body are recognised as being close to perfect and are known as the 'golden ratio'. Leonardo Bonacci, aka Fibonacci, a 13th Century mathematician outlined a number series (1,1,2,3,5,8,13 and so on) where each number is the sum of the previous two numbers. A rectangle drawn using any two adjacent numbers in the series to form the sides will give a rectangle of **golden ratio** proportions. These proportions are found in nature and in classic architecture around the world. Using these proportions will make your designs look better.

Small wooden trinket boxes

Evaluating aesthetics

List the features of the boxes pictured above that make each one attractive. In small groups, discuss their shape and form. Then, consider which you would like best and why. Does everyone like the same things? Why is this?

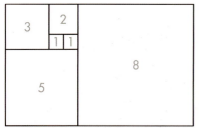

Rectangle constructed with the golden ratio

Golden ratio in nature

Golden ratio in architecture

Analysing proportions

In small groups, discuss and write a short comment about the proportions of the two lamps pictured opposite. Use the golden proportion to suggest an alternative design for the height and base of the lamp.

Two lamps using different proportions

Balance

Like the lamps pictured on this page, we all notice when there is balance or harmony in how something looks, or conversely, where balance is lacking. Successful designs usually have a balance in their shape or structure. This is related to proportion. Symmetry is an example of visual balance that can be used to aid your designs.

Style

Everyone has their own personal style and tastes. Just as there are different styles of writing and painting, designers are influenced by certain characteristics, aesthetics, or design movements. Some common styles include modern, contemporary, rustic, and art deco.

Colour

Colour can be introduced using wood stains or paints. Each type of wood has its own unique and attractive colour. Using woods with contrasting light and dark colours can enhance your work, as seen in the boxes above.

Using shelves to divide the height of this side table into parts creates symmetry, balance, and functionality.

Quality

The quality of the materials, the workmanship, and the finish will all affect the final design. Try to use the best materials available. For best results, take care to do your best work by paying attention to the small details.

Ergonomics

Ergonomics is about designing for comfort. It is the study of human proportions and how spaces and objects are designed to be comfortable and easy to use.

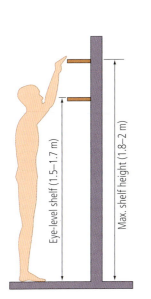

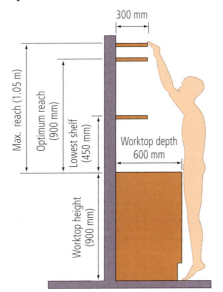

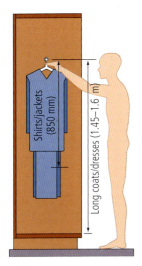

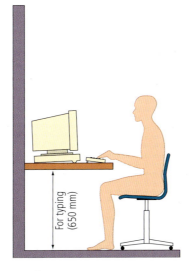

Ergonomics. Design sizes for human comfort

Ergonomics in practice

Do some research into ergonomics and produce a simple presentation about the main factors that must be considered when designing artefacts for use at home.

Safety

When designing, always consider how your designs will be used and who will be using them. Materials should be safe to use and used safely. If the artefact is for a young child, it should be easily cleaned and have no small pieces that could be swallowed. When making a lamp, follow wiring instructions carefully and always have the wiring checked before use.

Designing step-by-step

The **design brief** will outline details of the item to be made. It highlights conditions and instructions you must follow. You will select or be assigned a brief for a task or project. Always read the brief carefully, as it instructs you as to what is needed in the artefact. As you read the brief, highlight or underline the important words and phrases. Take the brief home and discuss the options with family. Your teacher will also advise you. When you are familiar with the requirements of the brief, you can begin the design **process**.

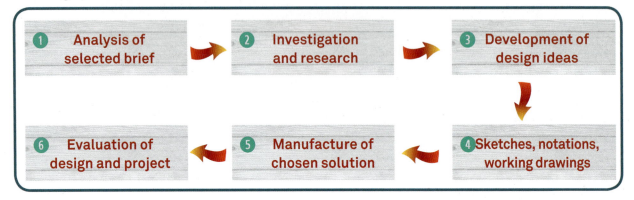

A design process helps when working through any design problem

Step 1: Analysis

A good and effective **analysis** is essential to a successful design. Analysis is a detailed examination of the brief in order to understand the different elements that must be investigated. It will help determine the features that must be included in the design and the artefact.

In your analysis, identify and list all the items required in the brief. Explore each item in turn and make sketches to help you. Look up the meaning of key words, list the possibilities and outline the problems you may need to solve.

You can use lists, diagrams, mind maps and spider diagrams to help you and to present your thinking clearly. Presenting a detailed exploration of the parts is important and will help you with the next step. You might include personal goals to aim for in your analysis.

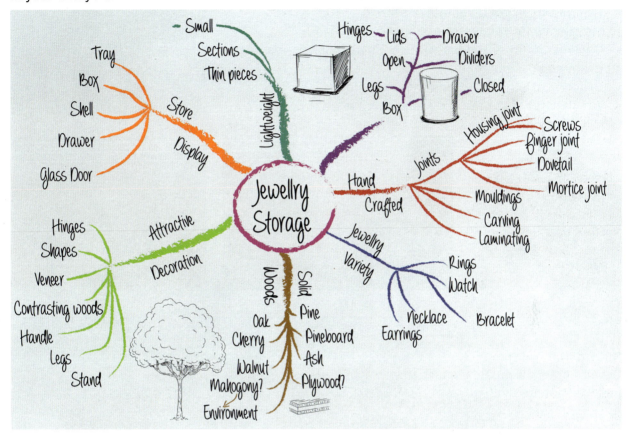

Mind map exploring features of the jewellery storage box

Step 2: Investigation/research

Once the analysis is complete, you will need to investigate features of the brief. The analysis will direct you to investigate certain parts further. For example, the materials, adhesives and finishes may need to be researched.

Research is done to find possible **solutions** to the design (existing solutions). Use the internet, books, magazines, and shop visits for your research. These may give you inspiration for ideas. You will also need to collect measurements to help with your design and record this in your folio. Sizes of existing pieces can be researched. Investigation of the size of items to be contained as well as size of available materials will contribute to the design.

293

Considerations for investigation:
- What is the artefact? What is its function?
- Where is it to be used? Inside or outside?
- Which materials might be suitable?
- What dimensions should it have?
- What items might it contain or store?
- List any limits or constraints.
- Consider fixtures and hardware such as hinges or catches.
- Examine possible themes.
- Examine existing solutions and examples.
- Which safety features does the design need to include?

Measure any items that will be relevant to your design

Information sources

Several sources should be used in your investigation. Sources include, but are not limited to:
- the internet
- magazines
- shop catalogues
- the library
- furniture, hardware, and gift shops.

Photos can be used in your folio to illustrate your research and design inspiration.

Planning a jewellery box

Working in pairs, make a list of the different features of the jewellery box that must be researched. Compare your list with the class.

Important
You must show all of the evidence of your research in your folio.

Step 3: Design Ideas and solutions

A successful investigation will provide you with plenty of inspirational images to trigger some good design ideas. Aim for at least three different possible ideas from which you can develop one final design solution. Your final design may be one of the ideas or possibly a combination of ideas. Sketch your ideas out clearly and add some labels with extra information. The sketches should include basic overall measurements as well as listing the materials to be used. Also include comments about the good and bad points of each idea.

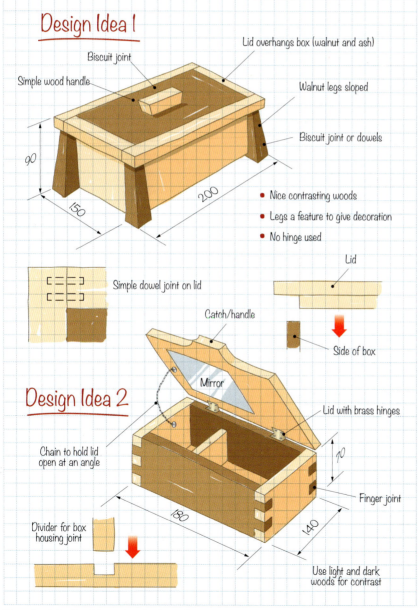

Sketch of design Ideas for the jewellery box

✔ Include at least 3 ideas.
✔ Include notes and descriptions with your sketches.
✔ Explain your choices.
✔ Describe materials, decorations, and features of the item.
✔ Show the overall dimensions.

Step 4: Working drawings and prototypes

You must produce a working drawing or detailed sketch of your final design. This drawing usually includes an elevation plan and end view (orthographic views) with the main dimensions (measurements) clearly visible. The drawings are used to make the artefact so measurements are essential in order to prepare the materials. Sketches of the joints and details such as decorations and other important parts of the piece should also be done separately. Often these details are done on separate sheets to a larger scale so they give greater detail.

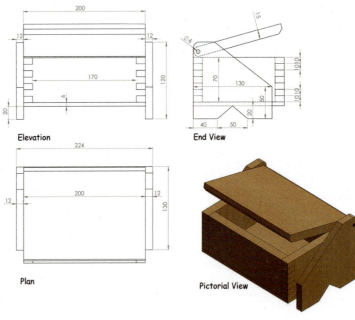

Working drawing of jewellery box

✔ Include elevation, plan, and end view.
✔ Pictorial sketches or drawings can enhance your presentation.
✔ Sketches of joints, details, or features should be included.
✔ A cutting list of your individual pieces mustbe included.
✔ A plan of work might be included.
✔ Most people will do a drawing of the piece, but well-presented sketches with measurements are acceptable.
✔ A CAD (computer-aided design) drawing could also be included.

Prototypes/models

Prototypes or scale models are made of the final idea. A scale model is an exact copy of an artefact, made in a size smaller or larger than the final piece. It will help you visualise and test the piece, which will then help you to create the final artefact. It may also gain you marks. Models need not be very detailed

Scale models or prototypes will help you to make the final piece

to effectively show you how the artefact will function.
Models can also be made using CAD (computer-aided design)
software. Changes are easily made and final drawings
produced. You may identify improvements that can be made
when examining the model and **incorporate** them into your
final drawings.

Cutting List

A cutting list outlines all of the required parts of the artefact
from the drawings. Each part is listed together with the
material, number required, length, width, and thickness.
A complete cutting list will also detail screws, panel pins,
hinges, and other materials required for the completion of
the piece.

Item	Qty	Length	Width	Thickness	Material
Sides Long	2	200	70	12	Red deal
Sides short	2	150	70	12	Red deal
Legs	2	120	130	12	Red deal
Top	1	200	150	15	Red deal
Base	1	300	150	4	Ply/hardboard
Dowel	2	30	6mm dia		
Screws	4	3.5 X 25mm countersunk			

Cutting list. Parts for the jewellery box.

Step 5: Manufacturing

Once you've completed the working drawings and cutting list,
the materials can be prepared. You should start to work on
the pieces and record the main points of the process in your
folio. Recording how the main elements of work or significant
processes were done (i.e. laminating or carving) will assist you
later on when you review and evaluate your work.

1 Mark out lengths of each piece.
2 Mark out the details of the joints.
3 Work and process the joints.
4 Mark and process decorations.
5 Assemble and finish the final piece.

Step 6: Evaluation

When the work is complete, you will review what you have done with a critical eye. However, the easiest way to do this is to assess your work as you progress by keeping notes in a project copy or folder. If you document the ups and downs of making your artefact as they arise, you won't have to rely on your memory at the end of the project.

All the best craftspeople evaluate their work to try to improve it. Evaluation is a way to explore the elements of your work so that you can improve and create better designs in future. Examine the design and execution for the good and bad points and to identify where you could improve or learn from what you have achieved. Effectively evaluate any item by using the three headings below.

The design

Review and examine the final design for its good and bad points. Describe what worked well and what did not.

The making

Describe what you learned from completing the work. Describe problems you encountered and how you solved them. What would you change if you were to repeat the project?

The completed artefact

How well does the finished piece meet the elements in the original brief? What were your impressions about the finished piece? Describe possible improvements you might make. Always include some sketches to aid your explanations.

- It turned out well but the thin trench for the ply was difficult to remove.
- The wood split as I was chiselling it out.

- I like the colour and it went on easily.
- It was difficult to get the legs on the piece.
- A small piece broke off the side because it was very small.

Self-evaluation Checklist

In your copy, answer the questions below and explain your answers.
- ○ How well did your item satisfy the brief?
- ○ Discuss how all points of the analysis were covered.
- ○ Were the materials and finishes suitable and appropriate? Explain how.
- ○ Comment on the attractiveness of the design.
- ○ Were you happy with the joints that you used?
- ○ Are you content with the overall quality of your work and with how you communicated the relevant information through your folio?
- ○ Outline anything new you learned about designing or the process of creating an artefact.
- ○ If you could go back and change anything, what would it be?

Case study: Lamp Project

The brief

Design and make a small decorative lamp suitable for use on a small side table. It should incorporate a musical theme.

Analysis

- This table lamp will be used as an accent light in the living room of a house.
- Since the table is small, I think the base of the lamp should be 150mm in diameter at the bottom and stand 400mm tall.
- A shade will be needed for the lightbulb. I'll also need to line the bottom with something non-slip, such as felt.
- The base of the lamp needs to be smaller at the top than the bottom if I use a traditional shade.
- I'll need to wire the lamp with a plug, a flex, a switch, a bulb holder, and a shade holder.
- For the theme of music, I can go with something literal, such as a note motif, or maybe something abstract, such as sound waves.
- The lamp must be correctly wired, secure, and stable.

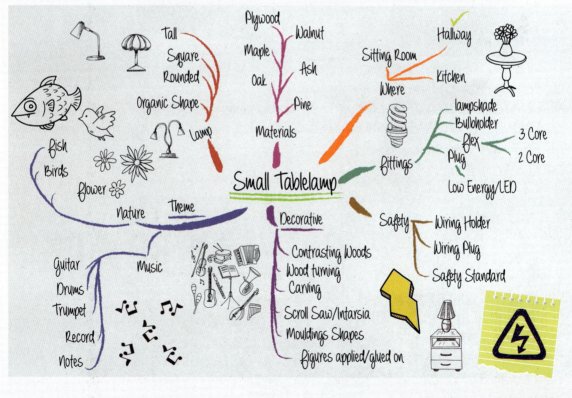

Investigation

Existing lamps

I researched different types of table lamps and found that there were some non traditional styles that were really interesting. Some were traditional and simple with clean lines, but I also liked the organic styles that used natural wood. A couple of them use vintage bulbs and no shade, while others use the shade as an integral part of the design. I noticed that nearly all of the lamps have a heavy or wide base.

I also looked at music symbols and motifs and found these examples. I am considering whether to decorate the lamp with these patterns or else use them in the shape of my lamp.

Design Ideas and Solutions

Lamp Ideas   Development

300
400

• Solid base
• Not too high
• Simple shape

• Circular style
• Taller looking
• Turned stem
• Hardwood light & dark

Lamp base is built up with hardwood pieces

Very basic construction but nice idea

Music idea

400

Base curved and built up in 2 colours hardwood Basic construction – too simple

Bulbholder

Similar to above but based on parabola

Music note carved/ decorative

Musical note on a base for stability

Bulbholder

Ash base

Mortise tenon joint

Walnut

Looks different but a little too unusual

30
20
300

Working Drawings

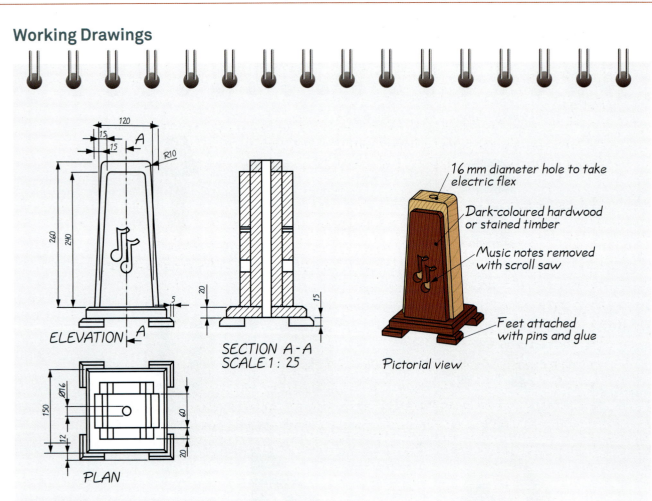

ELEVATION

SECTION A-A
SCALE 1 : 25

PLAN

16 mm diameter hole to take electric flex

Dark-coloured hardwood or stained timber

Music notes removed with scroll saw

Feet attached with pins and glue

Pictorial view

My final design is influenced by the shape of a monument I saw in the park. I decided to use contrasting wood and a cut-out in the shape of musical notes so the light wood would show through. To achieve this, I'll use a scroll saw. The base of the lamp will be lifted with feet that have bevelled edges.

Cutting List

Item	Qty	Length	Width	Thickness	Material
Main stem	1	260	120	60	Ash
Sides	2	240	90	20	Walnut
Legs	4	40	40	15	Walnut
Base	1	150	150	20	Walnut

Evaluation

Design

I really like how the lamp came out, but if I could alter the design I'd probably make the feet from the lighter coloured ash wood. I felt that the side pieces were too thick. I would make them from 12mm wood if I was to repeat the project.

Making the lamp

It was difficult to cut out the music notes on the sides. They were very small and it would have been easier if they were bigger. There wasn't as much room to work with as I expected. The feet were difficult to attach evenly. I had to remove a couple of them and re-attach. I ended up making a guide out of scrap wood to help me fit them rather than trying to measure them with the ruler.

The finished product

The lamp came out really well, especially with the <u>energy efficient</u> lightbulb, which gives off a warm, soft light. The varnish finish brings out the wood grain and the contrasting wood achieved the look I was hoping for. However, I can see that the front piece is slightly off-centre, so I'll have to be more careful measuring in future.

CHAPTER QUESTIONS

1 List the stages of the design process in the correct order.

2 You have been asked to design a decorative mirror for a narrow hallway. Briefly outline three aspects of the design you should investigate.

3 Explain what a prototype is and how it is useful in the design process.

4 Explain the meaning of the following terms used in design:
   (a) analysis
   (b) investigation
   (c) design ideas
   (e) evaluation.

5 Write a brief analysis for the following artefacts:
   (a) a desk tidy for a young person's room
   (b) a money box to encourage saving.

6 Outline three sources of information that would be useful when doing an investigation and describe why they are useful.

7 In your own words, explain what working drawings are and what sort of information they should include.

 PowerPoint Summary   Weblinks

Section
4

PROJECTS

31 Project 1: Letter stand

Design and make a decorative stand to hold a small number of letters in a tidy manner.

Analysis

What do we know?

- It must hold envelopes.
- It should hold envelopes of different sizes.
- Should look attractive.
- It could stand on a surface.
- It could hang on a wall.

Skills I can use:
- marking out & measurement skills
- sawing
- sanding and surface preparation.

Investigation

Envelopes

- Find the sizes of common envelopes.
- How many envelopes can/should be stored?
- Do a survey and discuss.
- Agree a practical amount and the sizes you need to accommodate.

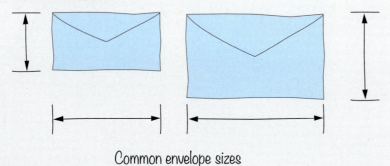

Common envelope sizes

Existing solutions

I found some examples of envelope stands.

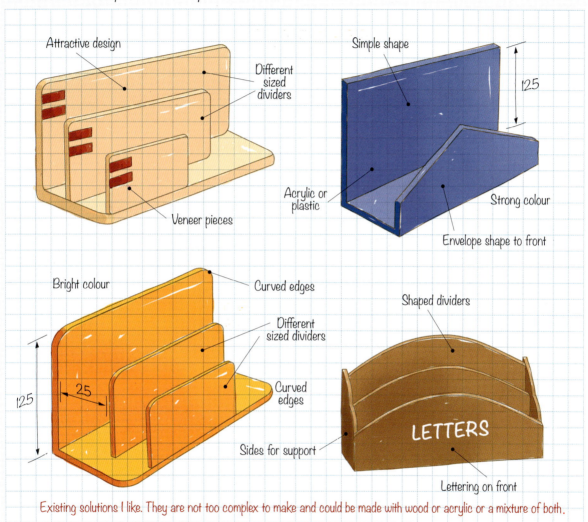

Attractive design

Different sized dividers

Veneer pieces

Simple shape

125

Acrylic or plastic

Strong colour

Envelope shape to front

Bright colour

Curved edges

Different sized dividers

Curved edges

125

25

Sides for support

Shaped dividers

LETTERS

Lettering on front

Existing solutions I like. They are not too complex to make and could be made with wood or acrylic or a mixture of both.

307

Ideas

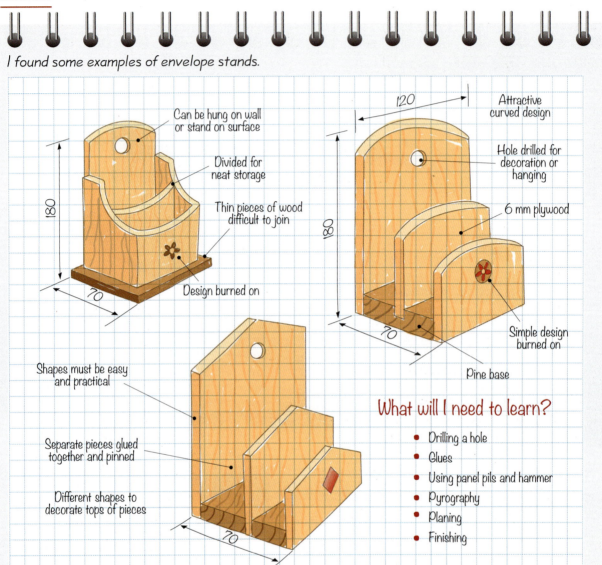

I found some examples of envelope stands.

Can be hung on wall or stand on surface

Divided for neat storage

Thin pieces of wood difficult to join

180

70

Design burned on

120

Attractive curved design

Hole drilled for decoration or hanging

6 mm plywood

180

70

Simple design burned on

Pine base

Shapes must be easy and practical

Separate pieces glued together and pinned

Different shapes to decorate tops of pieces

70

What will I need to learn?

- Drilling a hole
- Glues
- Using panel pils and hammer
- Pyrography
- Planing
- Finishing

Final Design

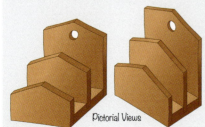

Pictorial Views

The two separate sections will hold different envelopes in a tidy way.
The design will rest easily on a flat surface.
The hole in the back will also enable the piece to be hung up on the wall if needed.

Working Drawing

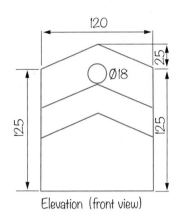

Elevation (front view)

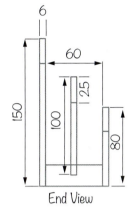

End View

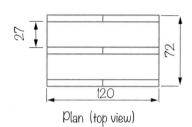

Plan (top view)

Evaluation

What I learned

Design

- The design I chose was the most streamlined, which meant that I needed to be very accurate in my work so that it wouldn't appear lopsided and so the lines would be clean and straight.

Making

- I learned about marking out and drilling a hole accurately.
- I learned about the pillar drill and how to use a drill safely.
- I found that I was more confident about getting a smooth finish on my work.

Finished piece

- I realised I need to be more accurate when marking out and cutting.
- I learned not to use too much glue and to clean the excess when finished.

32 Project 2: Model car

Design and make an attractive model car which will travel along the ground freely.

Analysis

What do we know?

- It should resemble a car in appearance.
- It should have wheels that move freely.
- It must look attractive and well proportioned.
- It should be safe in use.

Skills I can use :
- measuring and marking out
- sawing
- sanding and finish
- assembly
- organising and managing time
- drilling
- paring
- finishing techniques.

Investigation

Wheels

- I must find suitable wheels of the right size and shape.
- I found suppliers of wooden wheels on the internet.
- Different sizes are available. One type is 23mm in diameter.
- I found that the wooden wheels could be fixed to a dowel with glue. The dowel spins freely like an axle through a hole drilled in the body of the car.

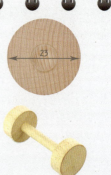

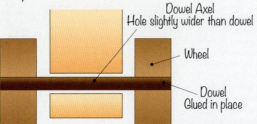

Dowel Axel
Hole slightly wider than dowel

Wheel

Dowel
Glued in place

Finish
The finish could be varnish or paint could be added to give extra colour.

Existing solutions

I found some examples of model cars when I searched. There were lots of examples some were beautiful but very complex.

Spoiler and cab

Plain shapes and nice colours

Curved design with smooth edges

Seat cut-out, guards over wheels
Might be too difficult?

Ideas

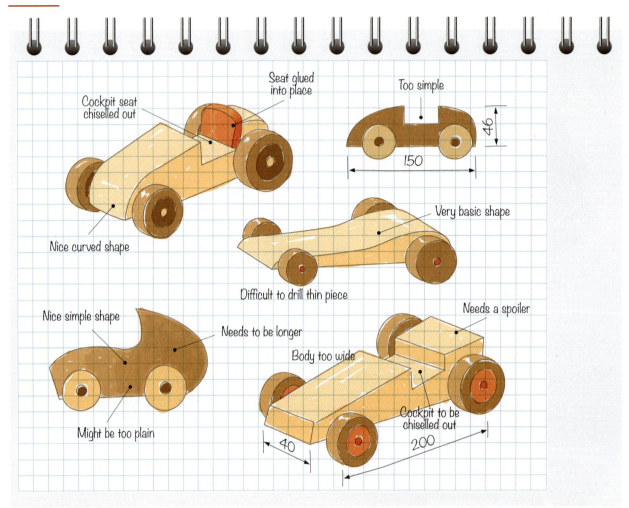

Cockpit seat chiselled out

Seat glued into place

Too simple

46

150

Nice curved shape

Very basic shape

Difficult to drill thin piece

Nice simple shape

Needs to be longer

Body too wide

Needs a spoiler

Might be too plain

Cockpit to be chiselled out

40

200

Final Design

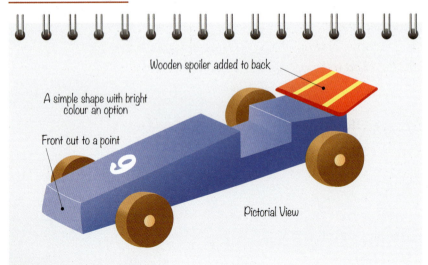

Wooden spoiler added to back

A simple shape with bright colour an option

Front cut to a point

Pictorial View

Working Drawing

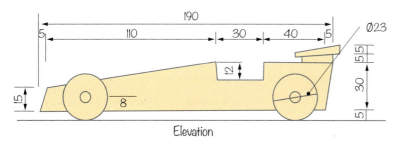

Elevation

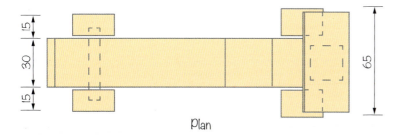

plan

Evaluation

What I learned

Design

- The design was simple and effective. The sloped shape added to the appearance. The spoiler made the piece much nicer. The wheels were difficult to get right. Plastic wheels would look much nicer.

Making

- I learned to improve my sawing and chiselling skills. I was careful to keep the bottom of the trench clean and smooth. Drilling the holes accurately was difficult. Attaching the spoiler was tricky; I had to be patient and my friend helped me.

Finished piece

- There are too many small pieces on this car so it is a model not a toy. It turned out well and I finished it better than the last project I did so I know I am improving.

33 Project 3: Desk organiser

Design and make a compact artefact for your desk to organise writing and study accessories in a neat and attractive way.

Analysis

What do we know?

- It must organise desk items in an orderly way.
- The main study accessories should fit inside it.
- It must look neat and attractive.
- The items should be easily accessed.
- The artefact needs to be compact on the desk.

Skills I can use:
- thinking critically
- managing and organisation
- simple jointing
- assembly and finish.

Investigation

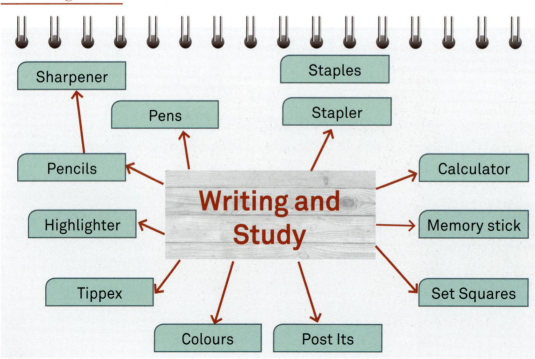

Sharpener

Pens

Staples

Stapler

Pencils

Calculator

Highlighter

Memory stick

Writing and Study

Tippex

Set Squares

Colours

Post Its

I recorded the sizes and drew sketches showing the sizes.

Existing solutions

Nice shapes and contrasting colours.

Small drawers for staples, pencil, pointer and clips.

Box like shapes and drawers to hold cables and small items.

I notice that very few are on legs or feet.

Separate sections to store different items neatly.

315

Ideas

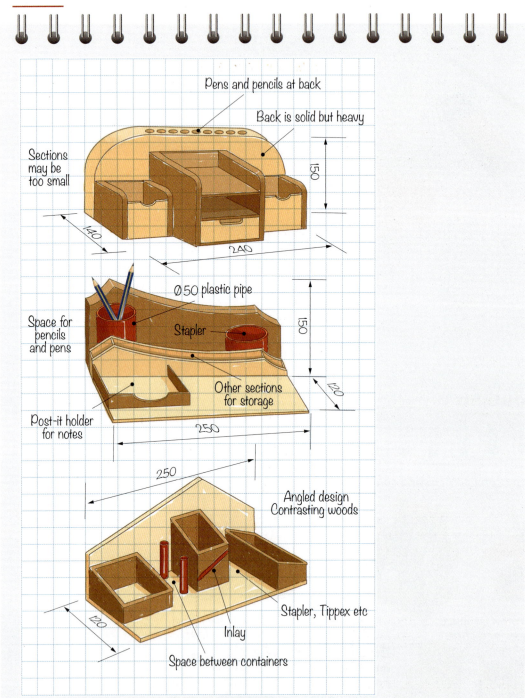

Pens and pencils at back

Back is solid but heavy

Sections may be too small

150

140

240

Ø50 plastic pipe

Space for pencils and pens

Stapler

150

Other sections for storage

120

Post-it holder for notes

250

250

Angled design Contrasting woods

Stapler, Tippex etc

Inlay

Space between containers

120

Final Design

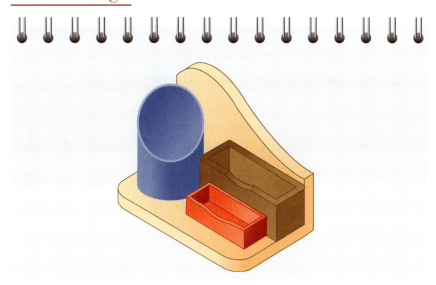

Working Drawing

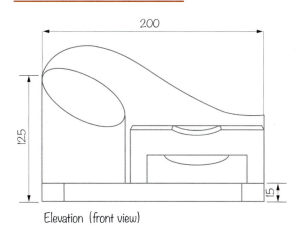

Elevation (front view)

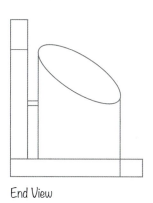

End View

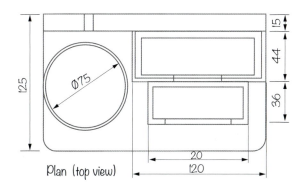

Plan (top view)

317

Evaluation

What I learned

Design

- The design was effective. The different woods gave a nice contrast and the coloured acrylic was bright and attractive. The curved pieces at the front allowed better access to the containers. A small drawer might have been a good addition.

Making

- I used screws to connect the base and back. These were easy to do, but they do not look well. I have not worked with acrylic before and I found it difficult to smooth and polish the edges properly. Assembling the parts before putting on the varnish was a mistake. Applying the finish was more difficult as a result.

Finished piece

- The finished piece looks well and is attractive. I could have been more precise when I was applying the finish and I am not happy with the result. Some marks have remained on the acrylic. The base of the piece should have felt stuck on it to stop it scratching the desktop.

34 Project 4: Money box

Design and make a small decorative container to store coins and encourage saving.

Analysis

What do we know?

- *This will be a container for coins/money.*
- *It must look attractive.*
- *It should contain a small amount, so be not too large.*
- *It should be secure (lock or secret opening).*
- *Money should easily be accessed.*

Skills I can use:
- *research skills*
- *planning*
- *accuracy when making simple joints*
- *assembly and finishing.*

Investigation

Areas to investigate

- *Coins: How many?/What size? How big is the coin slot?*
- *Methods of storing money.*
- *How big should the container be?*

Finishes I might use
- *research skills*
- *Varnish – it is clear and will enhance and protect the wood.*
- *Danish oil*

I must investigate further a way to make the box secure and to allow access to the contents.
- *Add a lock*
- *Some hidden access*

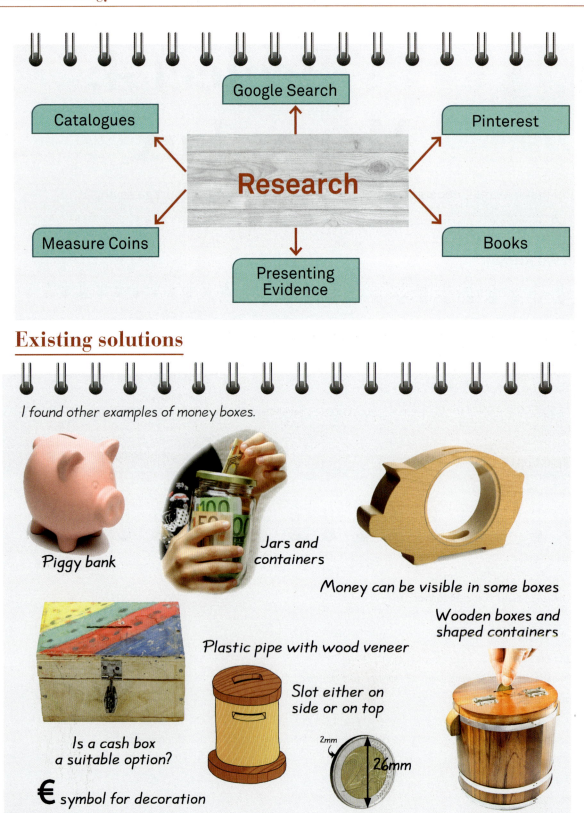

Google Search

Catalogues

Pinterest

Research

Measure Coins

Books

Presenting Evidence

Existing solutions

I found other examples of money boxes.

Piggy bank

Jars and containers

Money can be visible in some boxes

Wooden boxes and shaped containers

Plastic pipe with wood veneer

Slot either on side or on top

Is a cash box a suitable option?

€ symbol for decoration

2mm

26mm

Ideas

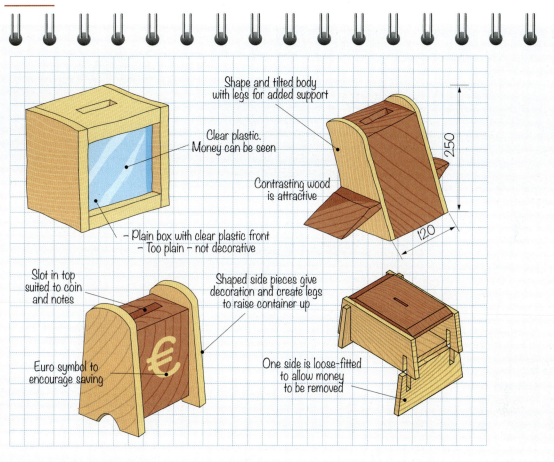

Shape and tilted body with legs for added support

Clear plastic. Money can be seen

Contrasting wood is attractive

– Plain box with clear plastic front
– Too plain – not decorative

250

120

Slot in top suited to coin and notes

Shaped side pieces give decoration and create legs to raise container up

Euro symbol to encourage saving

One side is loose-fitted to allow money to be removed

Final Design

Working Drawing

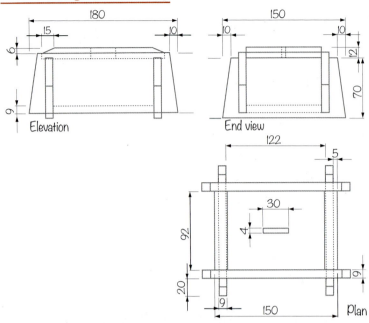

Evaluation

What I learned

Design

- I found it difficult to get ideas that were decorative. I measured coins and decided on a slot 30mm X 4mm. The Euro symbol added to the design. I found there were few examples of existing money boxes.

Making

- The joints used were simple, but it was important that they are accurately done. The wood was thin to make the box lightweight and conserve wood.
- The base was hard to glue into position.

Finished piece

- The sliding side for getting to the money was a good idea, but the joint must fit accurately and firmly. I thought that the contrasting woods look well together. Ash would have been a better wood for the sides because it is harder than pine and should be more durable.

35 Project 5: Decorative artefact

Design and make a decorative artefact with a theme of Aquatic Activities. The piece should include a range of handcraft skills.

Analysis

What do we know?

- *A decorative piece must look attractive and beautiful.*
- *It must be well made and finished.*
- *It must reflect an aquatic activity theme.*
- *The piece should be small to be displayed in a cabinet or mantelpiece.*
- *It should be easily cleaned.*
- *It must include a range of handcraft skills.*

Skills I can use:
- *Some research skills: internet, surveys, interviews.*
- *Possible handcraft skills:*
  - *carving*
  - *turning*
  - *joints*
  - *scroll saw work.*

Investigation

Areas to investigate

- *Suitable sizes, materials, finishes*
- *Different aquatic sports*
- *Handcraft Skills*

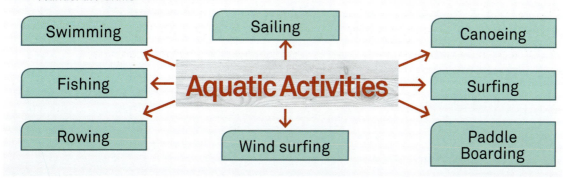

323

Existing solutions

I located simple images and logos that suggest water activities. These logos could be created in wood or cut out or carved into wood using a number of skills.

Logos I like:

Simple shapes easily produced

Variety of activities

These suggest movement

Ideas

I enjoy sailing and focussed on this sport.

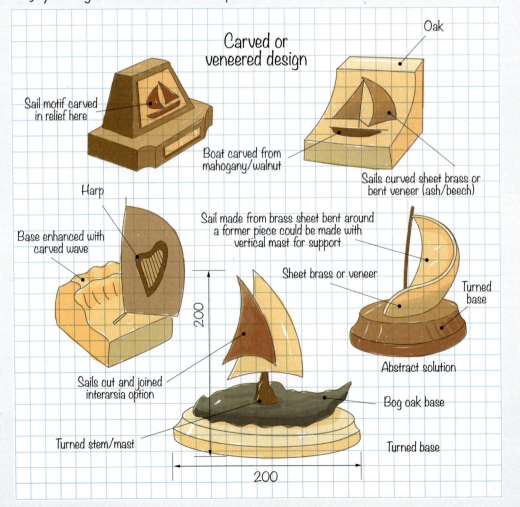

Carved or veneered design

Oak

Sail motif carved in relief here

Boat carved from mahogany/walnut

Sails curved sheet brass or bent veneer (ash/beech)

Harp

Base enhanced with carved wave

Sail made from brass sheet bent around a former piece could be made with vertical mast for support

Sheet brass or veneer

Turned base

Abstract solution

Sails cut and joined interarsia option

Bog oak base

200

200

Turned stem/mast

Turned base

324

Final Design

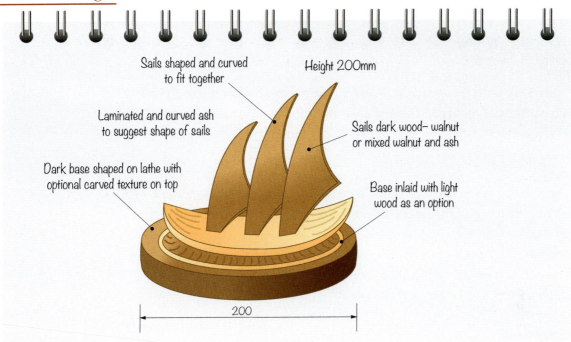

Sails shaped and curved to fit together

Height 200mm

Laminated and curved ash to suggest shape of sails

Sails dark wood– walnut or mixed walnut and ash

Dark base shaped on lathe with optional carved texture on top

Base inlaid with light wood as an option

200

Working Drawing

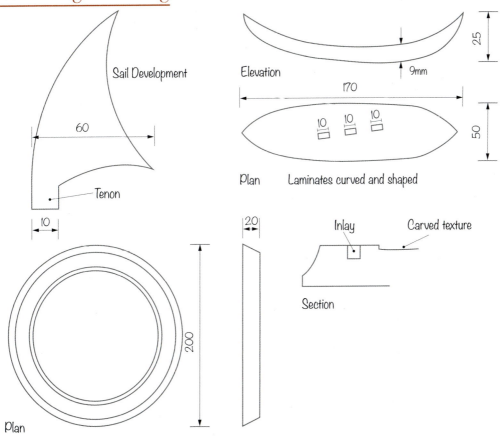

Sail Development

60

Tenon

10

Elevation

25

9mm

170

Plan   Laminates curved and shaped

50

10 10 10

20

Inlay

Carved texture

Section

Plan

200

Evaluation

What I learned

Design

- I am happy with the design. It includes jointing and other handcraft skills. It has challenged my woodworking abilities and it is finished to a high quality. The sail shapes were difficult to join to the base.

Making

- The mortise joints were difficult to complete because they were cutting across the grain of the wood. The laminates look well but took time to set up and produce well.
- I had to cut a deeper mortise than expected to make the sails stable.
- The carved texture on the base was nice but it was hard to get the surface even.

Finished piece

- The finished piece is attractive and I think it is well done. I found it hard to complete a working drawing and had to make some changes during the manufacture. I learned to be prepared to check details and adapt and change accordingly.

36 Project 6: Wall mirror

Design and make a simple attractive mirror suitable for hanging on a wall. The mirror should include decorative features that appeal to you.

Analysis

What do we know?

- *The artefact must include a mirror. Where can I get one?*
- *The finished piece must have some decorative features.*
- *The piece must hang on a wall or vertical surface. How is this done?*
- *It should be of a suitable size – not too big (I must investigate this).*
- *How might a proper solid frame be made?*
- *How will it be finished?*

Skills I can use:
- *possible joints: halving, mortise, bridle, dowel*
- *nails/pins/screws*
- *using a smoothing plane*
- *using a sander.*

New skills:
- *making a square frame*
- *attaching fittings*

Investigation

Mirrors

- *Suitable sizes*
- *Decorative features*
- *Materials and finishes*
- *Research possible joints and frames*

The piece will be used in a small room such as a small bathroom or on the back of a cupboard door.

Not too big. An A4 size (300 mm X 200 mm) mirror is suitable.

327

Existing solutions

There are a large variety of shapes available.
Some are too complex to make easily.

Some with simple joints or with mirror glued
to a shaped plain back piece.

Simple rectangle or circular shapes

Mirrors can have organic shapes or have simple or useful additions as features.

Fitting a mirror into a frame

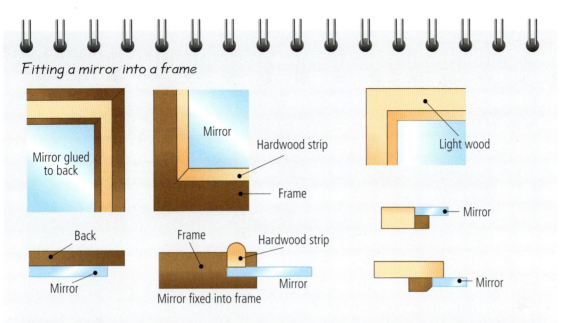

I researched ways to put the mirror into the wooden frame and also different fittings that I could use to hang the mirror on the wall.
Evidence of my research is shown below.

Hanging on a wall

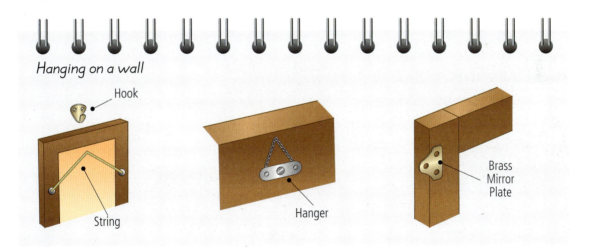

Ideas

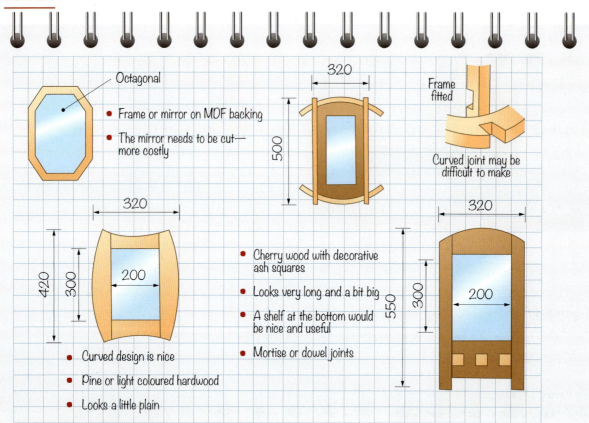

Octagonal

- Frame or mirror on MDF backing
- The mirror needs to be cut— more costly

320
500

Frame fitted

Curved joint may be difficult to make

320
420
300
200

- Curved design is nice
- Pine or light coloured hardwood
- Looks a little plain

- Cherry wood with decorative ash squares
- Looks very long and a bit big
- A shelf at the bottom would be nice and useful
- Mortise or dowel joints

320
550
300
200

Working Drawing

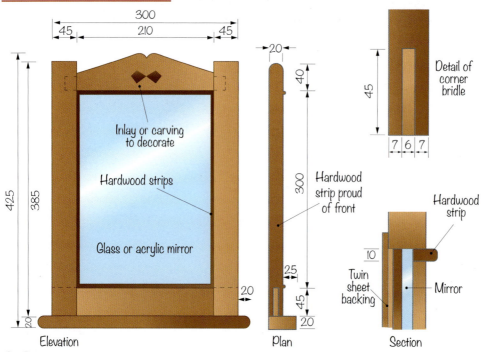

300
45 210 45
425
385
20

Inlay or carving to decorate

Hardwood strips

Glass or acrylic mirror

Elevation

20
40
300
25
45
20

Hardwood strip proud of front

Plan

45
7 6 7

Detail of corner bridle

Hardwood strip
10
Twin sheet backing
Mirror

Section

Evaluation

What I learned

Design

- The design is simple but looks well with the rounded edges and decoration on the top rail. The thin shelf could be made a little wider with hooks for hanging jewellery on. I based the size on a 300 X 200 mirror, which is quite small. I would make it larger if doing another mirror.

Making

- Making the frame was difficult. Keeping the lengths of the opposite pieces equal so the frame is square is essential. It was good practice for future projects where many pieces are involved. I had to be aware how work on one piece affects other elements of the project.
- Using different joints was a challenge which worked well. It is hard to estimate how much time will be needed for each stage and they usually take longer than expected.

Finished piece

- Although I had to use a little bit of filler on two joints, I feel the finished piece looks well. I put the mirror in after varnishing, so as not to mess up the glass. It is a small project, but it has pride of place in a neat area of the kitchen. The shelf could be wider, which would make it more useful.

Index

Image Credits